THE POLITICAL ECONOMY
OF FOREIGN INVESTMENT IN MEXICO

The Political Economy of Foreign Investment in Mexico

Nationalism, Liberalism, and Constraints on Choice

VAN R. WHITING, JR.

THE JOHNS HOPKINS UNIVERSITY PRESS
BALTIMORE AND LONDON

Written under the auspices of the Harvard University
Center for International Affairs
A revised version of parts of Chapter 8 appeared in the *Columbia Journal
of World Business* (Summer 1991).

Chapter 7 is a revised version of "The International Food Processing
Industry," published in Richard N. Newfarmer, ed., *Profits, Progress and Pov-
erty: Case Studies of International Industries in Latin America*
(Notre Dame: University of Notre Dame Press, 1985).

The Johns Hopkins University Press
701 West 40th Street
Baltimore, Maryland 21211-2190
The Johns Hopkins Press Ltd., London

The paper used in this book meets the minimum requirements
of the American National Standard for Information Sciences—
Permanence of Paper for Printed Library Materials, ANSI Z39.48-1984.

Library of Congress Cataloging-in-Publication Data

Whiting, Van R.
    The political economy of foreign investment in Mexico :
nationalism, liberalism, and constraints on choice / Van R. Whiting, Jr.
        p.   cm.
    Includes bibliographical references and index.
    ISBN 0-8018-4227-1
    1. Investments, Foreign—Government policy—Mexico.   2. Industry
and state—Mexico.   I. Title.
    HG5162.W48   1992
    332.6'73'0972—dc20 ·   91-17669

for CHRISTINE

Contents

vii

Figures and Tables

Figures

Tables

Preface and Acknowledgments

THE POLITICAL PREFERENCES of the Mexican policymaking elite toward foreign investment have shifted over time. In the 1970s, the slogan was *"mejor socios que dueños."* Loosely translated, this means "better partners than owners." Mexicans would become partners, not employees *(socios, no empleados)* through forced joint ventures required by the state. By the late 1980s the attitude had become much more accommodating; the slogan was *"mejor socios que prestamistas,"* or "better partners than moneylenders." Mexico entered the 1970s as a leader of the nationalist Third World, but by the 1990s was one of the leaders in a global shift toward economic liberalism. It is the rise and fall of economic nationalism that concerns me here.

Many debts have been accumulated in writing this book. Institutionally, I have benefited from associations with El Colegio de México; with the Center for International Affairs at Harvard, where I was an associate as a graduate student and later as a visiting scholar; and with the Center for U.S.-Mexican Studies at the University of California, San Diego. Financial support came from a Fulbright Fellowship, the Social Science Research Council, and a Wriston Fellowship from Brown University. Colleagues who have commented on the whole or on parts of this book include Doug Chalmers, David Collier, Karl Deutsch, Jorge Domínguez, Gary Gereffi, Louis Wolf Goodman, Joe Grieco, Steph Haggard, Terry Hopmann, Peter Katzenstein, Blair Krueger, Jr., Paul J. Krustapentus, Kevin Middlebrook, Pat Murphy, Eric Nordlinger, Ken Oye, Ken Sharpe, Tom Skidmore, Gabriel Székely, and several anonymous reviewers.

In Mexico, more than a hundred informants contributed to the study. They include scholars, a president, ministerial *secretarios,* and office *secretarias.* Most of the interviews were confidential, and even then, in a regime where knowledge is acknowledged as power, information was carefully guarded. Two people were especially helpful: the late Miguel Wionczek, an economist and an unreconstructed nationalist to the end, and Jaime Alvarez Soberanis, a legal scholar and public official, former director of both the Foreign Investment Registry and the Technology Transfer Registry.

Many of my students at Berkeley and at Brown, especially those in my courses on international political economy, offered their comments and spurred me to make major modifications. A number of student assistants helped; among them Anne Lutz, J. B. Shank, and Michael Stone deserve special mention. Katherine Hagedorn edited and typed the manuscript and saw it through a labored production process. The translations of Spanish sources (published and unpublished) are mine unless otherwise noted. Henry Tom has been most encouraging at the Johns Hopkins University Press.

My parents have been generous in their support and in their faith. My wife, Christine, has borne the brunt of my preoccupation with this project with every kind of encouragement and with remarkable patience. For me, there is no *mejor socia.*

Part One

The Role of the State in Foreign Investment

SINCE THE TIME of the Mexican Revolution and the Constitution of 1917, Mexico has been engaged in a curious and contradictory quest to build a developed economy using both the market power of private enterprise and the political power of the state. For sixty-odd years nationalism was the predominant development ideology, and an interventionist, nationalist state grew in power and importance. The statist trend accelerated throughout the 1970s. Following the debt crisis of 1982, President Miguel de la Madrid (1982–88) and his successor Carlos Salinas de Gortari declared a fundamental shift in direction toward economic liberalism. This marked the end of an era of growing economic nationalism.

The successes of the nationalist state, and its failures, demand explanation. One version of the story is this: (1) an irresponsible political elite, insecure in its position in the world, recklessly indebted the country and (2) now has been forced by international banks and creditor nations to change direction. But neither part of this version captures the complexity of Mexico's nationalist project. Foreign direct investment provided the most direct challenge for state policy in the nationalist period. The story of nationalist choices and structural constraints in foreign investment policy is the story of one vision of development in an internationalized world economy and its replacement with an alternative vision. In this book I endeavor to explicate the logic of nationalist policy and explore the structural constraints that frustrated that policy.

The question of state policy, highlighted in earlier studies of modernization, was relatively neglected by most of the authors working within the dependency school. An active state policy would not be predicted by the structural analysis of *dependentistas*. The centrality of state action as an object of analysis and scholarly study forces us to face squarely the question of choice. It also points to a set of constraints on choice, explicitly political and institutional.[1] This formulation of the relationship between state policy and structure follows the work of Herbert Simon on rationality and extends his notion of bounded rationality. The analysis of choice within constraint provides for the integration of the systematic analysis of leadership and policy formation that was prominent in the modernization literature with the analysis of structure that two decades of dependency scholarship developed.

The integration of choice with structural determination requires a reexamination of positivist views of scientific explanation. The development of state policy involves the use of power, which is, in Bertrand Russell's definition, the production of intended effects.[2] Choices of policymakers are inherently indeterminate; moreover, because they

3

are intentional, they are necessarily future oriented. It is difficult to reconcile an emphasis on choice with the search for absolute determination. Likewise, constraints shape choices but do not uniquely determine outcomes. Chapter 1 is thus an overview of scholarly debates among three schools of thought (modernization, dependency, and state), with a brief discussion of the status of choice and constraint in scientific explanations.

State strength entails the historical development of several aspects of the collectivity that constitute potential power. In order for a regime to survive within the state, it must be resilient; the Mexican regime is resilient. Mexico is a strong state but not necessarily an autonomous one domestically or internationally. If even a strong state is prevented from developing and successfully implementing policy in the issue areas that it defines as important, then this would be a telling critique of the statist argument.

This formulation contrasts with that of scholars who conflate the concepts of strength and autonomy. Historically, Mexico has developed a strong state; I identify aspects of state strength that accurately characterize Mexico. Mexico is strong in spite of an objective situation of economic dependence (narrowly defined) on the United States. But such strength does not ensure autonomy, either from actors in the international system or from actors within society. A strong state provides the best test of limits on autonomous action.

In short, an abundant literature from international relations seeks to explain outcomes by reference to international economic structures and international regimes, which limit the choices of state actors and operate as constraints on the state. These constraints, which in the Mexican case worked against state intervention, help to explain the failure of the nationalist project. Yet the political choices of state policymakers were clearly an important part of the explanation of Mexican development policy. In order to understand choice we must study the constraints that bound the choices. In order to understand structural and institutional determinants, we must understand that those partial determinants act not as causal forces with necessary outcomes but rather as conditioning factors or constraints on choice.

As constraints change, political visions of possible futures, which (following Hirschman) we may call "metapreferences," will change as well.[3] As internationalization of the world economy has increased, the nationalist vision, a metapreference for nationalist policies, has been replaced by a more liberal vision.

Political choices involve who gets what, when, and how, in Lasswell's classic formulation. Development is best understood as an increase in the power of the collectivity to satisfy its needs and wants. The dual focus on choice and constraint points us not only at choices that will be effective in achieving goals in the realm of distribution and exchange but also at choices that themselves transform the constraints of structure. In the case of transnational enterprises and the nation-state, the issues are not just the distribution of economic surplus but, more important, the integration of a national political and economic order with an international order based on knowledge, wealth, and the power of markets.

One

State Policy and the Question of Choice

But 'tis the very point in question, whether every thing must have a cause or not; and therefore, according to all just reasoning, it ought never to be taken for granted.

DAVID HUME
A Treatise of Human Nature, pt. 2, sec. 3, bk. 1

POLITICAL CHOICES may reveal the essence of greatness, when men and women imagine the possible and choose to make it real. But choices also constitute the minutiae of everyday political life, so circumscribed by the constraints of structure (and the power and choices of others) that freedom seems an illusion. This book is about political choices, political structures, and the relationship between structure and choice in the explanation of policy. Its principal argument is that internationalization has transformed structural constraints, making possible a shift from nationalism to liberalism.

Among the countries of the developing world, the young industrial countries have made remarkable advances in industrialization during the last fifty years. Railroads and highways, airports and seaports link the people with national and international markets; power grids provide energy for industry as well as for consumers; television and radio, telephones and fax machines, computers and communications satellites all make possible the rapid exchange of information required by industrial society; automobiles, steel, chemicals, processed food, and a variety of machines are all produced in the industrial plants of these countries. The effects of industrialization are everywhere evident.

Two institutional actors have shaped this momentous transformation of these emerging industrial countries: foreign investors (foreign enterprises or foreign corporations) and the state. In this book

I study the policies of one new industrial state to regulate and control the structure and behavior of foreign investors.

For years, the dependency school provided the dominant perspective on foreign involvement in Latin American development. Replacing the systemic approach of earlier modernization theory with "historical-structural" analysis, dependency writers tended to emphasize the disproportionate power of foreign firms, their alliances with powerful national actors, their flexibility, and their freedom of action. Based on dependency analysis, one would not have expected aggressive action by an interventionist state against the freedom of private foreign investors.

The study of the state thus provided an alternative perspective to dependency by emphasizing the choices of policymakers and requiring analysis of the autonomy of the state. Statist theory developed to explain the interventionist state. This book examines one of the most interventionist states in the nationalist period. My analysis is informed, however, by the knowledge that just as nationalism was a response to dependency, international liberalism emerged in Mexico as a response to the failures of nationalism and statism.

State Policy: Constraints on the Prince?

Sitting in the waiting room of the undersecretary of industry in Mexico, I found myself in conversation with a consultant to the government, also awaiting his long-delayed appointment. The consultant and the undersecretary would confer on policies toward foreign investment in Mexico; the undersecretary would later make his recommendations directly to the president of the Republic. Looking back on that encounter, I realized that these were the advisers to the Prince; the president of Mexico was as close to a modern-day prince (and his party, the Institutional Revolutionary Party, as close to Gramsci's Modern Prince) as leaders of stable governments come to be. Together, officeholders and advisers in state institutions shared the responsibility for devising and implementing policies that affected the development of Mexico. Which policy options were considered and discarded, and which were pushed forward? Once agreed upon as official policy, which were implemented, which revised, and which ignored? How can we conceptualize and begin to explain the opportunities for action and the limits on power, even in so presidential and centralized a system as Mexico's? Clearly not even the most powerful sovereign— or sovereign state—is totally free or completely bound.[1] What choices are made, what paths are taken, what limits are accepted? What are the constraints on choice?

The basic argument that I will make may be summarized in a phrase: Choice transforms structure, and structure constrains choice. This encapsulates three propositions that I apply to the case of Mexico's policies on foreign investment:

1. State policy, involving the metapreferences and strategic choices of policymakers, can transform the structure underlying national development. In Mexico, the state has been active and interventionist, with policies that have included expropriation, regulation, and promotion.
2. Structural factors constitute constraints that shape the opportunities and the limits of choice. International industrial structure and global issue/regime structure provide partial explanations for policy choices.
3. The explanation of policy cannot be limited to the search for efficient causes. Structural constraints are important parts of the explanation. So too are choices of policymakers. Neither structures nor choices operate as efficient causes of policy outcomes, but together they provide a sufficient explanation.

Although some may argue that choice may be subsumed under causal analysis, I argue that the analysis of choice within constraints cannot be seen as a positivist exercise in causal explanation.

Simplifying and anticipating the arguments to come, let me give the following example. Suppose we are interested in a particular policy that has important consequences; it is this policy we want to explain. One kind of argument might explain this policy with reference to presidential leadership: the president made a decision to support it, communicated that decision, and the policy was adopted. This argument is based on choice, though it takes a causal form: the policy was adopted because the president made a decision and took certain actions. But as soon as we push beyond this narrow form of explanation, we must consider noncausal elements. Suppose we ask: why did the president support this policy rather than others? This too may be answered in a causal fashion: he did so because of the way he was educated. But we might posit a very different kind of explanation, one that refers not to the past but to the future: the president chose this policy because he wanted to improve the balance-of-payments deficit. This explanation refers to the president's goal; it is future oriented; it is teleological (though not in a functionalist way). It is intuitive, since we all base our actions on our goals, at least at times. And it helps to explain the choice of policy.

But even this is not satisfying. A more complete answer is likely to take the following form: the president chose this policy because he wanted to improve the balance-of-payments deficit, given (*a*) the necessity for certain technologies available only from foreign firms, (*b*) the probable reactions of the U.S. government, (*c*) the position of national business on this issue, and (*d*) the status of relations between two key ministries and the president's own worries about the record his administration would leave. Given all these factors, the president preferred this policy over others. We do not want to say that conditions *a*, *b*, *c*, and *d* caused the president to act in a certain way. Nonetheless, they are part of the explanation of the policy; they were constraints on the choice of the president.

Following Jon Elster's distinctions between causal, functional, and intentional explanations, and consistent with Mario Bunge's work on causality and Von Wright's on explanation and understanding, I view political (collective) choices (understood as rational, intentional, goal-directed action) as major elements of social scientific explanations.[2] These political choices are made in an environment shaped by structural conditions that limit and define options; these conditions help explain outcomes in probabilistic fashion but do not constitute efficient causes. For those who find graphic presentations useful, figure 1 presents these relationships.

We are thus concerned with political power, understood as the ability to produce intended effects. And we are concerned with ra-

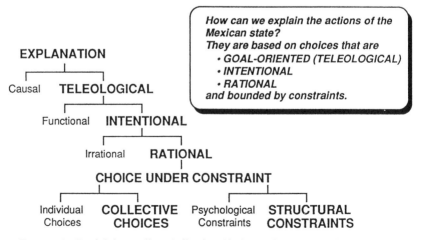

FIGURE 1. Explaining Policy: Collective Choice under Structural Constraints

tional action in the dual sense that Herbert Simon has indicated: "rationality denotes a style of behavior (A) that is proportionate to the achievement of given goals, (B) within the limits imposed by given conditions and constraints."[3]

The Received Wisdom

Those concerned with explaining development and development policy work within one of several approaches or schools of thought. Modernization, dependency, and statism, respectively, dominated a decade or more of development theory. To these we must add international liberalism (see fig. 2). These approaches provide the foundations for the analysis of choice under constraint.

In the pages that follow, I consider the received wisdom in the field of development,[4] looking first at modernization and dependency and then turning to the successor schools, statism and international liberalism. I then link these to a discussion of choice, determinism, and explanation.

Modernization

The study of modernization included analysis of choice and determination: both values and leadership, on the one hand, and social structure, on the other.[5] Its distinctive method, especially during its heyday after World War II, was a "systems approach" to development.

The antecedents of modernization go back to the turn of the century. At the end of the nineteenth century the rapid growth of urban society and industrial production was conducive to a variety of stage theories of development. These theories accepted the fundamental

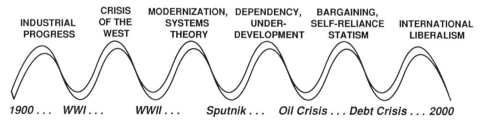

FIGURE 2. Evolution of Approaches to Development

identification of development and progress and often explicitly recognized the organic metaphor that development implied. Ferdinand Tönnies's conceptions of community and society (*Gemeinschaft* and *Geselschaft*) exemplify early work that indicated the movement from a traditional to a modern society. If Marx doubted the survival of capitalism, it was because he was optimistic about the socialist society that class conflict was to produce. The common element of such dissimilar theories was a view of society changing by stages, usually based on a typology of the stages involved.[6]

The cataclysm of World War I brought the emphasis on progressive change by stages to an abrupt halt. Contemporary accounts brought awareness of the horrors of "modern" warfare to those not there to experience them. The Roaring Twenties, the Crash of 1929, the ensuing Great Depression, and the rise of fascism in Europe all pointed away from theories of progress to cyclical theories about the future that development might bring. Rather than an analogy of species evolution, Oswald Spengler used a cyclical analogy in his two-volume work *The Decline of the West* (actually begun before World War I). In this widely read treatise, Western society is described as emerging from spring into summer, passing through fall maturity, and entering a winter. His work became an exemplar of studies that featured cyclical rise and decline.

Paradoxically, World War II signaled a shift in the opposite direction, as modernization studies began to compare the newly independent nations with the United States. The United States emerged nearly unscathed from the conflict, with its industrial base greatly strengthened and its relative position in the world improved at the expense of Japan and the European countries that had borne the brunt of the destruction.

By combining the powerful new tools of systems theory and behavioral social science, theories of modernization were developed that used the historical and current patterns of life in the United States as an implicit or explicit model of what development could achieve. The wave of newly independent countries joining the rank of nation-states provided the raw material for a major expansion of comparative studies of development. By the 1960s, modernization studies were in full swing, using a systems approach to organize and analyze the diversity of beliefs, cultures, regimes, and patterns and levels of development among the new states.[7]

Stage theories and cycle theories left a rich heritage of concepts and typologies relevant to development. But modernization was the first school to attempt to develop a distinctive methodology for the analysis of development. Utilizing the general scientific advances in cybernetics made accessible by Norbert Weiner and the advances in many disciplines generated by systems theory,[8] the modernization theorists abandoned the traditional political focus on the state and on political institutions in order to build more "systematic" theories of political behavior. Drawing on the anthropologists such as Lévi-Strauss who studied the common structures and functions of societies and on sociologists such as Talcott Parsons,[9] a postwar generation of political scientists applied systems theory to politics. In so doing, they moved away from the state. Although sociology has maintained a concern with state and society,[10] for years the foremost analysts in political science in the United States eschewed the concept of the state altogether. In a work that influenced an entire generation, David Easton attacked the preoccupation with the state and went to the extreme of denying it any usefulness at all.[11] In its stead he posed the question, How are values authoritatively allocated for a society?[12] Gabriel Almond, who shared the critique of the state and claimed that an alternative approach constituted "a major step forward in the nature of political science as science," also adopted the political system as a concept to replace the state.[13]

The modernization theorists applied the systems approach to explain either political participation (usually democracy or its absence) or political stability (usually revolution or its absence).[14] Borrowing concepts from economics, some conceptualized the political system as a system for aggregating demand (political inputs) and allocating values or utility (political outputs). Some took a somewhat different approach, using an organic system analogy and introducing the concept of steering capacity to explain the ability of the system to accommodate choice and to direct change.[15] Others used more psychological approaches within the general systems framework. But despite their differences, the distinctive contribution of the school was the disciplined effort to analyze political arrangements for participation, control, decision making, and change as varieties of systems for linking the structures and functions common to modern society.

Dependency

By 1960 events were already beginning to lead to a reevaluation of existing theories, initially within Latin America itself. The launching of *Sputnik* in 1957 raised an indisputable challenge to the hegemony of the American way. The triumph of the Cuban Revolution in 1959 and its subsequent embrace of socialism suggested alternative routes to development and, at least in Latin America, led to an examination of the costs of development in societies closely tied to the United States.

Studies such as Cardoso and Faletto's book *Dependency and Development in Latin America* argued that some development was possible under the international domination of capitalism but that "dependent development" had high costs.[16] Dependency analysis came into its own in the United States in the 1970s, through a gradual dissemination of the ideas of the dependency approach from south to north. By the time of the 1979 appearance of the long-delayed English translation of Cardoso and Faletto's *Dependency and Development,* and the almost simultaneous publication of Peter Evans's study of Brazil, *Dependent Development,* the dependency approach had moved into a position of seeming predominance in the North American study of development.[17]

Stage theories, cycle theories, and systems theories tended implicitly or explicitly to take the nation-state for granted as the unit of analysis, and although exogenous variables at times played a role in explaining change, the international system was not built into the analysis.[18] Dependency theory, drawing on a different disciplinary and intellectual tradition, kept the emphasis on structure but used a historical method of analysis.[19] The *dependentistas* also put foreign investment at the center of the analysis, with foreign enterprises as the major link between the structure of the international economy and the structure of Latin American society.

Structural dependency analysis provided a contrast both with reformist, liberal interpretations of political economy and with the analysis and prescriptions of the revolutionary Left. Cardoso and Faletto's book *Dependency and Development in Latin America* has come to be the standard sourcebook from Latin America on dependency. The book was written while the authors were in Santiago, Chile, participating in debates and seminars with some of the leading intellectuals of the region. Though the authors were hosted by the Economic Commission for Latin America (ECLA, also known by its Spanish acronym CEPAL),[20] they did not accept the prevailing "cepalina" doctrine of import substitution as the preferred policy for development. Whatever the merits of Raul Prebisch's thesis on the declining terms of trade,[21] Cardoso and Faletto foresaw the structural costs of reliance on foreign investment to replace the importation of manufactured goods.[22] In this sense, theirs was a critique from the left of CEPAL doctrine, which itself was already critical of the status quo. On the other hand, Cardoso and Faletto were also challenging the revolutionary left, epitomized at the time by the French romantic Regis Debray. Debray supported the internationalism of Ernesto "Ché" Guevara, the brilliant erstwhile Argentine doctor who joined Fidel Castro to fight the Cuban Revolution and then tried unsuccessfully to carry armed guerrilla struggle to the rest of the continent.[23] Cardoso and Faletto also engaged the debate against those who argued that only underdevelopment could result from contact of the Latin American periphery with the economies of the center.[24] Thus, their critiques were a moderate response to revolutionaries who urged action toward the logical consequences of Gunder Frank's argument as suggested in his book's title *Underdevelopment or Revolution?* For Cardoso's native Brazil as well as for Mexico and other Latin American countries growing at historically high rates, dependency could allow for development within dependency, or "associated dependent development" in Cardoso's phrase,[25] while still limiting the potential of the country.

Whether comparative surveys of broad scope or more detailed country studies, dependency studies utilized a historical approach to identify the basic economic and class structures of the societies of the regions. The approach tended to produce more criticism than solutions, more generalities than specifics.[26] This was its weakness as well as its strength. As a critical, yet deterministic perspective, dependency paid little attention to historical counterfactuals or to possible futures.

Gary Gereffi terms this inattention to alternatives the "value asymmetry" of dependency: "dependency studies document with the greatest detail the condition they reject."[27] The historical method enabled dependency theorists to identify broad trends but not to generate falsifiable propositions. Gereffi argues that this is because dependency studies are designed, not to test particular characteristics of "dependence,"[28] but rather to elucidate "significant areas of social reality (in the fashion of Weberian ideal types) . . . [A]t the structural level of sociohistorical configurations, where the idea of situations of dependency is located, the question of falsifiability is not relevant."[29] For their part, Cardoso and Faletto argued (in the 1976 preface to the English edition of their book) that for them the historical structural method was based on the dialectical analysis ("which found its highest expression in Marx") of the interaction of social movements with "relatively stable global structures."[30]

Transnational enterprises were central to these global structures. The dependency school analyzed national development in the context of changes in the advanced countries, especially the increase in foreign investment, first in export-oriented agricultural and mining sectors but increasingly in manufacturing for the domestic market. Three points were emphasized by the *dependentistas*:

1. Crucial processes and decisions are controlled outside dependent countries.

2. Foreign investment affects the class structure and political alliances in dependent countries in a way that makes continued activity by foreign corporations possible and likely.
3. Although an active state may increase benefits to host countries, those benefits are likely to accrue to economic and technocratic elites; development with equity (as contrasted with "dependent development") is likely to occur only under socialism.[31]

These distinguishing features of dependency analysis—concern with external control, class alliances within capitalism, and the emphasis on social action toward a noncapitalist alternative—gave attention to state policy to the extent that it played a role in shifting class alliances. These characteristics reflected the weaknesses as well as the strengths of dependency analysis: a critical but nonfalsifiable perspective, an emphasis on the economic over the political, an emphasis on the external over the internal, and a relative neglect of policy.

In sum, Cardoso and Faletto developed dependency theory in Latin America as a radical structural critique of import substitution as a development model, as well as a moderate response to leftist revolutionaries. As such, a major contribution was to draw attention to the role of foreign enterprise in Latin America and to the class linkages in national systems of domination. But their theoretical and methodological orientation led them to seek "verification" in the "capacity of social movements to implement what are perceived as structural possibilities."[32] Though recognizing an expanded role of the state and advocating political action within the limits of structures, they were not primarily concerned with explaining state action.[33]

The State as Agent of Change

By the late 1970s, doubts were beginning to set in about dependency analysis, not least among some of its founders. In a theoretical and philosophical overview of development written in 1979, Fernando Henrique Cardoso posed, as a self-criticism, one of the key problems with the dependency paradigm: "Perhaps, the Achilles heel of the theories of dependency can be summarized in the following question: By means of what historical agent will it be possible to overcome dependency?"[34] The possible answers are many, including the working class, the national bourgeoisie, regional and international organizations, the state, or the market. I am arguing that this is precisely the question, and that the answer, in Mexico and in much of the developing world, has been the state.[35] The action of the OPEC states in 1973, 1974, and 1979, together with the defeat of the United States in Vietnam, confirmed that the United States was not invincible and suggested that countries could improve their situation, at least temporarily, by joining together and pooling their efforts, even when natural resources rather than industrial goods were the basis of their strength. A renewed emphasis on state action to overcome the obstacles to development became apparent in the calls for negotiated change and for strategies of "self-reliance." This flexing of muscles was often rhetorical, but renewed emphasis on policies of state intervention at the national level and calls for a "new international economic order" at the international level both pointed to a statist response to conditions of real or perceived dependency. Bargaining by the state characterized these policy choices and state actions.

In the United States, Raymond Vernon had already pointed the way with his identification of the "obsolescing bargain" to describe the increasing power of nations that were producers of petroleum and raw materials.[36] More and more scholarship examined the role of state policy. Studies went in two directions: some considered the state as a social-engineering organization, and others considered the state as the bargaining agent in the national interest. In the latter sense, the statist approach began where dependency left off, with the foreign enterprise. A major strength of dependency analysis was to make foreign investment and foreign enterprise the focus of their studies of the "ties that bind" the periphery to the center, correcting a shortcoming of most of the modernization studies in the United States.[37]

The early literature on foreign investors in the United States had addressed the question of why firms expanded abroad. Some studies carefully analyzed factors internal to the firm.[38] Much of the best of this literature came out of the Multinational Enterprise Project at the Harvard Business School. A two-volume history discussed the emergence and maturing of the foreign enterprise.[39] As Europeans worried about the "American challenge,"[40] Raymond Vernon raised the more general question of the challenge to sovereignty of the state posed by the rise of large international corporations.[41] Vernon's path-breaking study (and the larger research effort he headed) began to address the complexities of the impact of foreign investors in host countries. But he emphasized the ambiguity of evidence on economic losses due to foreign investment and attributed most of the complaints that he called "the dependencia syndrome" to "clashing elites, clashing ideologies, and clashing cultures."[42]

However, Vernon also stated, at least for raw materials industries, the kernel of what would come to be known as the obsolescing-bargain thesis (on which more below). Referring in 1971 to the major oil-producing nations, Vernon gave us a master-stroke of understatement: "In the course of time, the demands by the local bureaucrats on the foreign investors tend to increase and the protection afforded to the investors has tended to decline."[43]

Most of the Latin American dependency literature seemed part of a different discourse from the North American literature on foreign investment, with the former analyzing and criticizing the impact without recommending state policies and the latter dismissing both policy and critique as "psychological" or "sociological."[44] But some Mexican authors combined critique and policy analysis. Already by 1955 Pablo González Casanova had raised the issues of dependency and foreign direct investments in policy terms: "The absence of a policy for the control of foreign investments (while still permitting certain sectors to continue provisionally to maintain and even increase their profits) will subject Mexico in a short time to the most 'disloyal competition' of capital, goods, and services, such as will limit our capacity for independent as well as dependent development."[45] Miguel Wionczek's studies of the electric power and sulphur industries in Mexico emphasized the exercise of state power; they were published under the title *El nacionalismo mexicano y la inversión extranjera* (Mexican nationalism and foreign investment).[46]

Theodore Moran provided a bridge between the Latin American *dependentistas* and the Harvard Business School studies of Vernon and others. In his study of copper in Chile, he elaborated on the bargaining between host countries and foreign investors, explaining the economic rationale and the political process of evolving national policy toward foreign investors.[47] His study of the "balance of bargaining power" provided an analytical framework for understanding state actions, and his conceptions of the "learning curve" provided an explanation, if not of the exact timing, then at least of the potential for success or failure of state efforts to regulate and eventually to replace foreign enterprises in natural resource industries: "Successful ventures, however, provide an incentive for the host country to develop skills and expertise appropriate to the industry. Beginning with elementary attempts to tighten the bargaining process, the country starts to move up a learning curve that leads from monitoring industry behavior to replicating complicated corporate functions."[48]

Moran, like Wionczek and González Casanova, thus provided the linkage between an analysis of the impact of foreign investment on national political and economic development and an analysis of the bargaining that results when states use the instruments of public policy to change those impacts.

Moran extracted a succinct set of propositions implicit in dependency analysis about the impact of foreign enterprises on host countries.[49] According to Moran, the first proposition is that the benefits of foreign investment are "poorly" (or "unfairly" or "unequally") distributed between the foreign investor and the host, or the country pays "too high" a price for what it gets. The second proposition is that "foreign corporations create distortions within the local economy" by squeezing out local business, introducing inappropriate products or technologies, and concentrating income. Third, foreign investors pervert or subvert host country political processes (1) by co-opting the local elites and/or (2) by using their influence in their home countries to bring pressure to keep host governments "in line" and/or (3) by structuring the international system to respond to their needs to the detriment of host authorities.

Dependentista work did include a number of these perceived impacts.[50] But as Cardoso and Faletto argue, their historical structural method is not designed to test, measure, or negotiate isolated aspects of dependency. It was Moran's contribution to arrange the effects on development in a neat list of issues that could be debated, tested, and negotiated. Moran and Vernon, unlike the dependency authors, shifted the focus to state actions designed to change those effects.

The "statist" paradigm that emerged in the 1970s was as heterogeneous as any of its predecessors. Nevertheless, several elements were common to the statist approach:

1. It renewed emphasis on political variables, in contrast with dependency's relative emphasis on economic variables. The statist paradigm gives state officials a positive role. Sovereign political action and state legitimacy are central to the process of development.
2. The capacity for initiation of action and change exists within the developing countries themselves. This was a momentous change, although it started with only a shift in emphasis. The dependency concept implied the existence of its opposite, namely, autonomy. But the values and especially the initiation of action that affected development were seen as originating elsewhere. Though the limitations analyzed by the dependency perspective are still understood, the fact that action is possible is in itself important. The analysis of "situations of dependence" was suggestive of the passivity that comes with reflection and criticism rather than of action arising from the power of the state. The statist approach suggested the possibility of initiative and action.
3. The international system may be a source of support and allies as well as of limitations and enemies. The United States was not invincible, and the Third World was growing stronger. Reflected in

regional integration efforts that had their roots in the 1960s, a more active use of international organizations for information, learning, and support developed, captured in that UN catchphrase TCDC—technical cooperation among developing countries.

Together, state politics, national initiative, and Third World co-operation constituted a statist paradigm of development that went beyond dependency. Dependency corrected the tendency within mod-ernization to neglect both economic factors and the international arena, but it gave little emphasis to policy and choice. In emphasizing the necessity to ground analysis in history, the dependency school was also searching for structure: as Cardoso and Faletto argued in *Depen-dency and Development*, "the analysis of social life is fruitful only if it starts from the presupposition that there are relatively stable global structures."[51] The more sophisticated dependency analysts did not take these structures as unchanging, however, and acknowledged that "social structures can be, and in fact are, continuously transformed by social movements."[52] To the extent that the state was considered by dependency authors (and this was not common until later works), the tendency was still to emphasize structural aspects of the state's relationship to international and national classes; these structural con-nections, with all their contradictions, still did not highlight policy choice.[53] Nor did they emphasize the transformative effects of changes in market structures.

In the analysis of state policy, I do not examine the impact of policy per se. Rather, I am asking why the nationalist state intervened in the economy, particularly when that state intervention challenged the interests of large international corporations, and why that interven-tion failed to achieve its goals.

The Analysis of Constraints
and the Shift to Liberalism

When I set out to study the relation between foreign investors and the Mexican state, the two-actor bargaining model represented an advance over earlier literature by providing a framework for the analysis of the type of bargaining that went on during expropriation procedures, increasingly common (especially in natural resources) in the late 1960s and early 1970s in Latin America and elsewhere. In such a situation, two "actors" (or, actually, their representatives) may sit down face-to-face at a bargaining table under conditions that approximate a zero-sum game. The issue of the compensation price in an expropriation is most clearly such a case.

In the regulation of manufacturing the situation may be similar at times to expropriation proceedings but is frequently more complex. State regulation affects not just the terms of entry and exit but the political and economic conditions of everyday firm operations. The entire package of resources of foreign firms may be affected: capital equity ownership, patented and unpatented technology, know-how, goodwill attached to the company name or trademark, access to foreign markets, and supplies of inputs from the parent company or a related affiliate. Changing national rules may affect one or more of these; but the firm may be able to take compensatory action in another part of the enterprise or in another subsidiary of the global firm. Such action may frustrate the state policy, as when payments reduced by regulation of technology transfer are taken out through transfer pricing (the pricing of inputs or materials from the parent company). But regulations may permit both sides to gain or to reduce negative impacts: if the home country allows foreign tax credits, the host country can increase taxes up to home country levels with little negative effect. If the host government encourages or forces increased exports, the effect may be negative on some third country, but both the host country and the firm may gain. The complexity of normal relations and their regulation make a strict zero-sum situation less likely than in the case of bargaining over price.

These differences between regulation and expropriation and between manufacturing and extractive industries could be handled within the framework of a two-actor bargaining model. A more fundamental critique questions the assumptions of the model of two autonomous actors facing each other across a table, with their range of options determined by economic factors alone. Even in a situation in which representatives of the state and of a global firm actually sit down together to engage in bargaining, many other actors not present may have a decisive influence on the outcome. Also, political norms and economic structures may be as important as actors in influencing the outcome.

The constraints on the autonomy and capacity of the state define the parameters within which bargaining may take place; those limits may be broad, or they may be very narrow indeed.[54] Our task here is to explain nationalist regulatory policy—one form of state intervention in the economy—not an international regime change. Domestic variables thus must take on more importance, as Keohane and Nye recognize in their own retrospective review.[55] To explain state regulatory policy and its failures, two sets of constraints are considered: structural constraints derived from the global organization of industry and constraints derived from the logic of the regime itself.

At the systems level, the world economy or international economic system is the most general and most permanent constraint on state policy. Historically, the international economy has been important in the patterns of resource utilization, export commodity specialization, and the degree of development of developed countries with respect to the less-developed countries. The sovereignty of states is the second component at the systems level. Although supranational aggregations and international groupings exist, states are still the basic units of political organization in the world and are likely to remain so for the foreseeable future. The state system of administration and rule concerns the ways in which political power is articulated, power holders are recruited, succession of power is carried out, and decisions among competing and conflicting interests are formulated and implemented. These constraints on state action reflect contiguous and interacting systems that find concrete expression at the organizational level.

Within the international economic system, both commodity markets and industries have a particular structure. In the case of industries, the degree of oligopoly (few producing firms) or competitiveness reflects the size and number of firms, the barriers to new entry such as economies of scale or exclusive access to technology or marketing, and the degree of explicit or implicit cooperation or collusion among the leading firms in an industry. In highly concentrated industries, the market structure may become formalized in an organization, such as a cartel. Concentration has favored nationalist policy responses. As global competition has increased, industrial structure favors liberalism.

At the level of regime structure, several factors mark the failure of statism and nationalism and the emergence of liberalism. In *Structural Conflict* Krasner argued from a statist perspective that the north is liberal and the south is nationalist.[56] The perspective is self-consciously state-centric. Third World nationalism emerged, he argued, in response to (1) state sovereignty, (2) declining U.S. hegemony, and (3) Third World consensus. In contrast, in this study I find that (1) liberalism emerges in the south even as nationalism grows in the north; (2) many of the functions of global firms are beyond the reach of the state, sovereignty notwithstanding; (3) nationalism was strong during periods of U.S. strength, whereas the economic growth of Japanese and European competitors has favored the emergence of liberalism; and (4) though liberals are currently in the ascendancy, there is no consensus: nationalists and liberals hold competing visions in the south and in the north.

The study of constraints on state action allows an escape from the polarized concepts of voluntarism (executive discretion) and determinism. The polar positions are reflected also in the Marxist debate regarding instrumentalism versus relative autonomy of the state—though the center of that debate is shifted considerably to the left. Clearly, by focusing on constraints, the voluntarist position is rejected. Two factors keep the analysis of constraints from being static and deterministic. First, there are feedbacks among the different levels of analysis that make the analysis dynamic and capable of change: feedback from national to international, from political to economic. Second, any particular decision will take place at a given historical moment, and the constraints at that point in time leave a greater or lesser leeway or decision-making "space." The ability to judge the appropriate and favorable conjunction of circumstances marks the great executive or political leader. At a given historical moment or conjuncture, latitude for action may widen for an individual or a state—especially a strong state.

Two

Mexico: Dependence and State Strength

METHODOLOGICALLY, a good test of hypotheses about constraints on state action should meet two conditions. First, the constraints should not be incongruent with state preferences.[1] Although the point is discussed in more detail later, let me assert that nationalist policy toward foreign investment is congruent with conditions that favor global liberalism.[2] Second, a "best test'" would consist of a case in which the state has (1) a historically strong institutional capacity, understood as strength and resilience; (2) access to resources relevant to the issue; and (3) demonstrated metapreferences—or second-order preferences—for nationalist policy. These factors would become important variables to explain Mexico's nationalist bargaining. Mexico had the economic and political strength to challenge the multinationals.[3] By selecting a case that maximizes these important elements of potential power, the effect of constraints on state autonomy can be isolated.

Although Mexico has a clear bilateral dependence on the United States, it is relatively strong in basic resource endowment and development infrastructure. Foreign trade is not very important, in comparative terms, and foreign investment is not quantitatively important in most sectors. Historically, the state is strong. A strong state has not only economic resources but, more important, political resources at its disposal. In a strong state, resilience (the ability to perdure and adapt) is concomitant to strength. Both socioeconomic analysis and political analysis suggest that Mexico is a strong state and has the potential to bargain successfully with foreign investors. Therefore, Mexico's choices need not be determined by conditions of dependency. The first task is to show the limits of Mexico's dependency and thus demonstrate Mexico's economic capacity to make endogenously determined choices. The second task of the chapter is to show state strength and regime resilience.

24

Dependence and Strength

Dependency theory emphasizes the structural disproportions in strength and in patterns of interaction between developing and developed countries. But by almost any indicator, except trade dependence narrowly defined, Mexico is among the most developed of the developing countries.

Caporaso has distinguished "dependency" (a structural condition of limited autonomy) from "dependence," which he defines as "a highly asymmetric form of interdependence."[4] At the risk of simplifying a complex situation, only two aspects of "dependence" will be considered here: trade with one country and reliance on one export. Two crude indicators offer some measure of this type of dependence of one country on others: the share of exports going to the major receiving country and the share of the leading commodity among all exports. If exports tend to go to one country, the external sector of the economy is dependent on the demand for those exports in the recipient country. If one commodity predominates among all exports, the external sector of the economy is dependent on the worldwide demand for that commodity.

If we may call these two kinds of trade relations country dependence and commodity dependence, it is clear that Mexico traditionally exhibited high country dependence. Mexico's location and extensive border with the United States have meant that a majority of foreign trade (both imports and exports) has been with the United States. Historically, between two thirds and three fourths of Mexico's trade has been with the United States. The asymmetry is evident when we consider that only a small portion of the world trade of the United States is associated with Mexico. This asymmetry holds, in spite of the fact that Mexico is now a major supplier of oil, a major purchaser of grain, and the fourth largest single trading partner of the United States.

A small quantitative indicator can be used to show the extent of the asymmetry. If we create an index of trade dependence between two countries A and B, with a range from 0 to 1, such that a score near 1 means that A is highly dependent on B and a score near 0 would be very little dependence (0.50 would be perfect interdependence), then Mexico's trade dependence on the United States has been about 0.93 whereas the trade dependence of the United States on Mexico has been 0.07.[5]

Another indicator can be used to make the same point. If we compare the gross national product (GNP) per capita of contiguous countries, Mexico and the United States show one of the greatest disparities in the world. The per capita GNP ratio for the Soviet Union and Afghanistan is about 10 to 1; for Israel and Egypt, it is about 8 to 1; for the United States and Mexico, it is about 9 to 1. In this company, the relationship looks remarkably healthy and amicable.

Commodity dependence, the reliance on one or a few basic commodities, has traditionally been low in Mexico. Mexico has a diversity of natural resources and exportable products; Mexican exports have included petroleum, silver, cotton, livestock, sulphur, coffee, tomatoes, and, more recently, manufactured goods. As an indication of Mexico's diverse commodity resource base, Mexico ranks among the top ten world producers in many agricultural and mining commodities: in agriculture, steroid hormones, coffee, corn, cotton, tomatoes, and poultry; in mining, silver, strontium, graphite, fluorite, sulphur, lead, mercury, zinc, and, of course, petroleum. In addition to the diversity of exported primary products, Mexico has until recently relied less on primary products than other Latin American countries. In 1965, approximately 84 percent of Mexico's merchandise exports were accounted for by fuels, minerals, metals, and other primary commodities.[6] Though this figure is high, it is lower than the primary commodity dependence of other countries in 1965. For example, the percentages of merchandise exports accounted for by primary commodities in Brazil, Argentina, Chile, and Uruguay were 92, 94, 96, and 95 percent respectively. Thus, Mexico was not dependent on only one or a few primary commodity exports and was less dependent on primary commodities in general than other Latin American countries. This changed briefly during the oil boom, but Mexico once again has a diversified export base. By 1986 fully one third of exports were manufactured goods.[7]

The petroleum discoveries of the 1970s have made Mexico a leading oil producer; by the mid-1980s Mexico ranked fourth in world oil production. As table 2.1 shows, Mexico is a major global producer of oil. Although oil has made Mexico more vulnerable to fluctuations in its export income and certainly contributed to the massive increases of debt, especially in 1980 through 1982, the availability of oil is on balance a strength of the Mexican economy, both as a source of revenue and as a strategic export to the United States.

Thus far, we have used fairly standard measures of trade dependence: commodity dependence and country dependence. According to these measures, Mexico is highly dependent on the United States as a trading partner and has recently become dependent on oil exports. This portrayal of Mexico as highly trade dependent is misleading, however, because the importance of trade to Mexico's economy is relatively low in comparison to other countries of similar size.

TABLE 2.1 Mexico's Growth as an Oil Producer: Global Oil Production, 1973–1983 (in Billions of Barrels)

Year	World Total	OPEC	U.S.	USSR	Mexico
1973	21.2	11.3	4.0	3.1	0.2
1975	20.2	9.9	3.6	3.6	0.3
1977	22.6	11.4	3.6	4.0	0.4
1979	24.0	11.3	3.7	4.3	0.5
1981	21.6	8.2	3.7	4.5	0.8
1983	20.6	6.3	3.7	4.5	1.0

Source: La economía mexicana en cifras (Mexico: NAFINSA, 1986), cuadro 15.4, p. 356.

The relative importance of trade to an economy is often forgotten in evaluating trade dependence. In comparison with the trade shares of eleven of the world's largest countries, Mexico's trade share of GNP was in the same realm as that of the United States, the Soviet Union, China, and India (between 0.10 and 0.19). Japan, Brazil, and Bangladesh had trade shares between 0.20 and 0.29 of their GNP, and Nigeria, Indonesia, and Pakistan had trade shares of 0.30 and higher.[8] Smaller countries were much more dependent on trade.

Mexico has many strengths that offset its dependence on its neighbors and provide a resource potential for strong bargaining with foreign investors. Working in its favor are the size of its economy, its work force, and its well-developed infrastructure and solid industrial base.

Industrial Strength in Comparative Perspective

Mexico does not approach the production levels of developed countries, with only about one quarter of the total production of West Germany, a country of lesser population.[9] Compared with other developing countries, Mexico has a large economy, larger than almost all national economies in Asia, Africa, and Latin America.

Among developing countries, Mexico is one of the "big eight" in terms of population and one of the "big four" in terms of gross domestic product (GDP). (See table 2.2.) Mexico is among the most developed of the big eight that figure on both lists (China, India, Indonesia, Brazil, Poland, Nigeria, South Korea, and Mexico).

The population of Mexico in 1985 was estimated to be about 80 million. It is the eleventh largest country in the world, whether measured by population or by GDP. This large population, combined with

TABLE 2.2   Potential Resources: Mexico as a Middle Power

25 Largest Countries (1985 Populations in Millions of People)		25 Largest Countries (1985 total GDP, in Millions of Dollars)	
1. China	1,040.3	1. United States	3,946,600
2. India	765.1	2. Japan	1,327,900
3. Soviet Union	277.4	3. Soviet Union	644,824
4. United States	239.3	4. West Germany	624,970
5. Indonesia	162.2	5. France	510,320
6. Brazil[a]	135.6	6. United Kingdom	454,300
7. Japan	120.8	7. Italy	358,670
8. Bangladesh	100.6	8. Canada	346,030
9. Nigeria	99.7	9. China	265,530
10. Pakistan	96.2	10. Brazil[a]	188,250
11. Mexico	**78.8**	**11. Mexico**	**177,360**
12. Vietnam	61.7	12. India	175,710
13. West Germany	61.0	13. Spain	164,250
14. Italy	57.1	14. Australia	162,490
15. United Kingdom	56.5	15. Netherlands	124,970
16. France	55.2	16. Sweden	100,250
17. Philippines	54.7	17. Saudi Arabia	95,050
18. Thailand	51.7	18. Switzerland	92,690
19. Turkey	50.2	19. Indonesia	86,470
20. Egypt	48.5	20. South Korea	86,180
21. Iran	44.6	21. Belgium	79,080
22. Ethiopia	42.3	22. Nigeria	75,300
23. South Korea	41.1	23. East Germany[b]	72,816
24. Spain	38.6	24. Poland	70,439
25. Poland	37.2	25. South Africa	67,710

Source: World Bank, *World Development Report, 1987* (New York: Oxford University Press, 1987), pp. 202–3, 206–7, unless otherwise noted.
[a]Data not for 1985.
[b]Data are derived from United Nations, *Statistical Yearbook, 1983/84,* pp. 96, 99, 297.

the highly industrialized nature of the economy, provides a large internal market. In contrast to small states that have no alternative to trade, large countries can develop large-scale industry on the basis of the domestic market. Size matters, and Mexico's size favored nationalism.

Dividing the GNP by total population gives a measure of the goods and services available on the average for consumption by each person.[10] Mexico, with a GNP per capita of about U.S. $2,000, lagged behind a few smaller countries in Latin America and Asia but was well ahead of most other Third World countries, including most of the big eight.

Other statistics besides GDP and GNP per capita also demonstrate the highly developed nature of Mexico's economy. Industrial production accounted for 40 percent of Mexico's GDP in 1984; services accounted for 52 percent. Agricultural production accounted for only 9 percent. This contrasts with most other developing countries. The World Bank divides developing economies into three categories: lower income, lower-middle income, and upper-middle income. Most developing countries are lower and lower-middle income. In lower-income economies, agriculture accounts for 36 percent of GDP on average; for lower-middle income countries, this figure is 22 percent. The percentage of production accounted for by industry in Mexico even eclipses many developed-country economies, which are increasingly based on services more than industry.

The manufacturing sector in Mexico is highly developed. Manufacturing accounts for 24 percent of the GDP. In terms of value-added, Mexico has a larger manufacturing sector than any other developing country except Brazil and China. Manufacturing and industrial production in Mexico are no longer relegated to light industry, such as simple assembly of consumer goods. Mexico also has highly developed capital, intermediate, and consumer durable goods sectors. Machinery, transport equipment, and chemicals account for one quarter of total manufacturing value-added. To use another measure, Mexico is among the top six developing countries in terms of capital goods value-added and gross output; in 1979 Mexico satisfied over half of its own internal consumption (apparent consumption) with domestic manufacturing.[11] In 1980, Mexico ranked somewhere between twelfth and fifteenth worldwide in production of passenger cars, production of cement, railroad cargo, total energy consumption, and steel consumption.

The development of infrastructure has also been impressive during this century. State action in the provision of infrastructure is necessary to enable the penetration of modern means of communication throughout the country and to make possible the participation of rural inhabitants in the national economy. Railroads were built in the last century linking major centers of commerce and production; railroad passenger service (measured in passenger-miles) tripled in the last fifty years. Roads increased seven times in the 1930s, doubled from 1940 to 1950 and again from 1950 to 1960, grew more slowly in the 1960s, and then more than tripled in the 1970s. In recent years, electric energy has been made available for the first time to many people, with electric energy production growing from about 2 billion kilowatt-hours in the late 1930s to 8.5 billion in 1960 to 43 billion in 1975 to almost 67 billion in 1980. Most of the growth in electric service has been provided by the state, especially after the acquisition of the American Foreign Power Company in 1960.[12]

Most of the construction of infrastructure has been the work of the state. The growth process, however, was part of a public-private partnership. Not only does infrastructure serve the private sector and build the conditions for promoting national capitalism, but national firms also benefit from state contracts. Ingenieros Civiles Asociados (ICA), one of the leading industrial groups, became what it is today largely through state construction contracts. On the other hand, much infrastructure is directly controlled by the state. More than 90 percent of electric power production is now provided by public enterprise.[13]

The industrialization of the Mexican economy has been accompanied by social changes: urbanization, changes in the structure of the work force, and increased communications. At the time of the Mexican Revolution, most Mexicans made their living from tilling the land. Since that time the demographic pattern of the country has changed significantly, so that a majority of Mexicans now live in cities or towns and work in industry or services rather than agriculture. In 1980, two thirds of the population lived in towns and cities of over 2,500 persons, a reversal of the situation fifty years ago. Literacy is one of the prime requirements for participation in an industrial society; in 1981, 82.7 percent of Mexico's population was literate. In India, by contrast, only 36 percent of the population was literate in 1981.[14]

Communications are essential to modern business. Mexico falls short of developed countries in terms of telephones, radio receivers, and television receivers per inhabitant, but this equipment is far more scarce in other less-developed countries.

In sum, despite dependence on the United States as its major trade partner, Mexico shows strength on the measures that matter for foreign investors: size of population and GDP, representing a large internal market; an urbanized, literate work force; a rich and diverse resource endowment; and a developed industrial infrastructure.

Dependence and Foreign Investment

So far, we have seen that Mexico is highly dependent on the United States as a trade partner but is not very dependent on trade compared with other developing countries and that Mexico is dependent on oil but is not very dependent on primary commodity exports compared with other countries. Is Mexico dependent on foreign investment? The answer is complex and will emerge through the analysis of the coming chapters. At this point, some basic data will show that by 1970, when Mexico began to formalize and extend its regulatory policies,

TABLE 2.3   Stock of Foreign Direct Investment (FDI) as Percentage of
GDP (in Millions of U.S. Dollars)

Year	GDP	FDI	FDI[a]	FDI/GDP (%)
1910	1,242	1,451	4,986	117
1926	1,974	1,700	3,327	86
1940	1,481	449	1,023	30
1946	5,538	575	862	10
1950	4,747	566	706	12
1958	10,286	1,170	1,170	11
1960	12,471	1,081	1,046	9
1966	22,157	1,938	1,701	9
1970	33,496	2,822	2,087	8
1975	79,064	5,017	2,699	6
1980	186,332	8,459	3,205	5
1981	238,964	10,160	3,517	4

Source: David P. Glass, "The Politics of Economic Dependence: The Case of Mexico" (Ph.D. diss.,
University of California, Berkeley, 1984).

[a] 1958 dollars.

foreign investment was high in absolute terms but low by many standards.

In absolute terms, Mexico continues to be one of the largest hosts
for foreign investment among developing countries. (Brazil is the
other leader in dollar value of investments.) Mexico's stock of foreign
investment has increased steadily since 1940 and rapidly since 1960.
As global investment has grown, however, Mexico's share has shrunk
as the world economy has become increasingly internationalized. Domestically, the stock of foreign investment has shrunk steadily as a
share of GDP (see table 2.3).[15]

In terms of all investment in the Mexican economy, beginning in
1960, flows of foreign investment were between 2 and 3 percent of
gross fixed investment, with state and private investment making up
the balance (see table 2.4).

Finally, in comparative terms Mexico ranked fifty-ninth in its ratio
of direct foreign investment to GNP in a sample of 114 countries;
it ranked in the middle of a subset of seven developed countries.
By these measures, despite its premier rank as the developing country "host with the most" foreign investment, Mexico was in fact
fairly typical in its dependence on direct foreign investment (see table
2.5).

TABLE 2.4   Flows of Foreign Investment as Percentage of Gross Fixed
Investment

Period	Total	Public	Private	Foreign
1902–3	100	5	50	45
1939–50	100	40	54	6
1950–59	100	39	51	10
1960–69	100	40	57	3
1970–79	100	40	58	2
1980	100	43	54	3
1981	100	44	53	3

Source: David P. Glass, "The Politics of Economic Dependence: The Case of Mexico" (Ph.D. diss.,
University of California, Berkeley, 1984).

TABLE 2.5   Dependence on Foreign Investment (FI)

Country	Percentage of Stock of FI/GNP (1978)	Rank in Sample of 114 Countries[a]
Japan	0.30	2
United States	1.97	22
Italy	3.07	34
West Germany	5.21	52
Mexico	6.61	59
United Kingdom	10.78	77
Netherlands	12.14	82
Canada	24.14	99

Source: David P. Glass, "The Politics of Economic Dependence: The Case of Mexico" (Ph.D. diss.,
University of California, Berkeley, 1984).

[a]This sample includes 107 developing countries and 7 developed countries.

Dependence and Inequality

Mexico's population growth has been extremely rapid over the past
twenty-five years. In 1980, Mexico had 20 million more people than
it did in 1970.[16] This population growth puts a tremendous strain on
the economic resources of the country. The Mexican economy, however, shows a high rate of growth. The growth of GNP was over 6
percent per year during the 1960s, and although growth was more
variable during the 1970s, average growth for 1965–80 was 6.5 percent. The debt crisis brought growth to a halt, with only 0.4 percent
growth on average for 1980–86. When this economic growth is corrected for population growth, however, by subtracting the percentage

of growth necessary to keep per capita production at the same level, then per capita economic growth has been much less. Income distribution figures show that the average per capita growth rates do not signify corresponding increases in the incomes of the poorest members of the population; in fact, they may not increase at all.

The strain on the Mexican economy resulting from a high rate of population growth is well illustrated by the age structure of the population. In 1980, 45.4 percent of the population was under fifteen years old.[17] Thus a large percentage of the population is dependent on the income of working adults. The economically active sector comprised only 35.6 percent of total population in 1980 (and this includes the unemployed who are seeking employment).[18] As the young people mature, there will be an increasing demand for jobs. Unless family patterns change dramatically, these young people will also have large families and thus continue the process.

"Mexico is the land of inequality," said Alexander von Humboldt. In the 1970s, the bottom 40 percent of the population was poorer in relative terms than in the 1950s, with a dramatic loss by the poorest 20 percent.[19] The share of the top 10 percent has remained almost constant, earning about 40 percent of the national income (although within that elite, the top 5 percent has seen its share of Mexico's national income drop from about 30 percent to about 26 percent). The middle class—the top 40 percent—gained the most from Mexico's growth. The inadequacies of the surveys should suggest caution in drawing conclusions based on any one of them, especially when they reflect dramatic shifts in income distribution in periods as short as two years (such as from 1975 to 1977).[20] Nevertheless, the general trends are clear.

What effect has foreign investment had on the distribution of income? Let us leave aside the question of the distributive effects of changes in consumption patterns attributable to the efforts of foreign enterprises (which could be considerable). On the basis of wages and salaries paid to workers and employees of foreign firms in Mexico, it seems that foreign enterprises encourage the trend observed in the aggregate data on income distribution: an increase in the income of the upper 30 or 40 percent of the population. A study prepared for the International Labour Office (ILO) of the United Nations in 1976 sheds light on this, with data supplied by the government at the firm level.[21] With data on 232,885 workers in 254 Mexican subsidiaries of foreign enterprises, the average annual per capita income was U.S. $4,414.80. A large majority, 72.8 percent of the individual workers, had annual incomes over U.S. $2,200. By comparison, 52.6 percent of all urban families (not individuals) had incomes under U.S. $2,000 at about the same time. Most workers for foreign enterprises are clearly in the upper deciles of Mexican income distribution.

The ILO study also looked at data for 20,280 workers in 30 national companies with similar characteristics, as a control group. The per capita income of the workers was quite similar: U.S. $4,324.50 per worker, on average.

There were significant differences in the distributions of income within the firms, however; and there were differences in the intrafirm distributions of income between national and foreign-owned firms (see table 2.6). Despite the similar per capita incomes, the foreign subsidiaries had more workers at both extremes: above U.S. $4,400 per year, and below U.S. $750 per year. About one quarter of the workers of the foreign-owned firms were in the upper income level, compared with about one fifth of the workers in national firms. Over a quarter (27.2 percent) of the workers of the foreign firms were in the bottom category, compared with 8.8 percent of the national firm workers. Manufacturing enterprises were close to the averages for all foreign subsidiaries; the few mining firms had more workers in the upper-income bracket (52.9 percent) and fewer in the lower (9.7 percent). Commerce showed the opposite trend, with 19.5 percent of workers in the upper bracket and 35.8 percent in the lower.

In sum, workers in large firms, national or foreign, earn higher average wages than most Mexicans. But disaggregating, foreign firms have more highly paid elites and more low-paid workers than comparable national firms.[22] The authors of the ILO study only speculate on the causes of the distributional difference, suggesting that foreign firms use a more complex and differentiated technology, requiring both highly skilled and unskilled labor. The national firms, in contrast, probably use more semiskilled labor. The study clearly demonstrates that, even ignoring consumption, foreign firms contribute to a more unequal distribution of income than large national firms.

The degree of inequality within a state and the extent of dependence on another state affect a state's potential to bargain from a position of strength with foreign investors. But, absolute welfare gains outweigh relative inequalities in distribution. First, disparities in the distribution of growth notwithstanding, major gains have been made in basic welfare indicators affecting the poorest, thanks in large part to state policies. Over a generation, from 1965 to 1985, life expectancy rose by eleven years for women and by seven years for men. Infant mortality per 1,000 live births fell from 82 to 48 in the same period. In 1985, 66 percent of the population lived in urban areas, up from 55 percent in 1965; 16 percent of the appropriate age-group in 1985 was enrolled in higher education compared with 4 percent in 1965;

TABLE 2.6   Income Distribution in 30 National and 254 International Firms, 1973 (in Percentages and U.S. Dollars)

National Firms[a]							
$750–$2,200/worker		$2,201–$4,400/worker		Over $4,400/worker		Total %	
Workers	Income	Workers	Income	Workers	Income	Workers	Income
8.8	3.9	69.7	53.9	21.5	42.2	100.0	100.0

International Firms[b]							
$750–$2,200/worker		$2,201–$4,400/worker		Over $4,400/worker		Total %	
Workers	Income	Workers	Income	Workers	Income	Workers	Income
27.2	11.9	44.9	35.5	27.9	52.6	100.0	100.0

Source: Victor M. Bernal Sahagún, *El impacto de las empresas multinacionales en el empleo y los ingresos* (1976), pp. 126–33.
[a]Workers: $n = 20,280$. Income = $87,700,000. Per capita income = $4,324.
[b]Workers: $n = 232,885$. Income = $1,028,100,000. Per capita income = $4,415.

55 percent made it to secondary school, compared with 17 percent in 1965. Daily calorie supply was up 20 percent, on average, over the period.[23] Of course, averages can be misleading. But these figures reflect the welfare of the poorest more than per capita income figures, as Morris David Morris argued in defense of his "physical quality of life index." The crisis of the 1980s notwithstanding, the lot of most Mexicans has improved over the course of one generation. Second, to the extent that inequality has increased and to the extent that foreign investment has contributed to unequal income distribution, the potential power of the state should increase. Inequality, especially in a country with rhetorical tradition of revolutionary justice, provides ideological support for state control of foreign investment, despite the real absolute improvements from growth.

Characteristics of a Strong State

Recent scholarship generally categorizes Mexico as an authoritarian polity; with somewhat less agreement, it is sometimes considered an example of "bureaucratic authoritarianism" as well. Linz includes authoritarian regimes in a typology that also includes democratic and totalitarian regimes. His definition of authoritarian regimes provides

clear conceptual boundaries with democratic polities: [authoritarian regimes are] political systems with limited, not responsible, political pluralism, without elaborate and guiding ideology, but with distinctive mentalities, without extensive nor intensive political mobilization, except at some points in their development, and in which a leader or occasionally a small group exercises power within formally ill-defined limits but actually quite predictable ones.[24]

Linz terms Mexico "the most debated case." Indeed, the primary argument for classifying Mexico as an authoritarian political system with limited pluralism is the difficulty with which opposition parties compete effectively with the Institutional Revolutionary Party (PRI) at the national level. In his comparison of bureaucratic authoritarianism in several other Latin American countries, Robert Kaufman adds several other indicators that could apply to Mexico: use of the state apparatus to control organized labor and a technocratic policy elite with linkages to international capital.[25]

Mexico nonetheless contrasts markedly with most other authoritarian regimes in Latin America. A military coup is by most accounts highly unlikely (though scholarly prediction is scant reassurance in this field). Moreover, there is little probability of irregular succession by other means, such as assassination, forced exile, or even special elections under nonconstitutional rules; the claims of political challengers such as Cuauhtémoc Cárdenas are for increased access and influence, not for a fundamental change of the constitutional order. Mexico enjoys a regularized succession of presidents. Though it is tempting to call this a "serial monarchy," there are in fact substantial institutional limits on the powers of the president. The greatest constraint is the political heritage of the Mexican Revolution: effective suffrage; no reelection. However cynical one may be about *sufragio efectivo*, the norm of no reelection is respected. In fact as well as in law, the Mexican president steps down at the end of his term, giving full power to his successor.

Political freedoms of speech and assembly are relatively unencumbered, compared with many other Latin American regimes. Organized groups are able to participate actively in politics, and increasingly this participation has taken electoral form. Mobilization and cooptation through the dominant party and through other state-sponsored organizations is still much more common than overt repression. The leadership is centralized but is also institutionally routinized, and regular turnover is ensured. In short, although not a U.S.-style multiparty democracy, it is highly atypical as an authoritarian regime.

Faced with conditions that in other countries have produced political crisis and regime change, Mexico has been able to maintain its political system more or less intact. My argument is that the Mexican regime is embedded in a historically strong state and that the regime itself has developed resilience by balancing corporatist and pluralist linkages between state and society.[26]

Definition of the State

The modernization theorists abandoned the concept of the state, and dependency theorists largely ignored it. But as Charles Tilly argued, most political analysts "sneaked back to the state" as their basic unit of analysis.[27] Though the shift is no longer surreptitious, there is little agreement over the meaning or even the definition of "the state." Perhaps the most common shorthand is to use "the state" to refer to the institutions and offices from which authoritative decisions emanate or to refer to "institutional domination." This institutional aspect is a necessary component of the state. But "the state" has a more fundamental meaning.[28]

The state is a political community, with compulsory membership, in a formally defined territory. That community is bound together by a relationship of authority and obedience. Authority is exercised collectively by those in positions to make binding rules; obedience is demanded from every member of the community. The political community that is the state includes not just the officeholders but also the citizens, not just the rulers but also the ruled.[29]

This compulsory community is also a political unit in an international system composed of sovereign states. In this sense the state is a historically limited concept, as Almond, Powell, and Easton argued in their critiques.[30] The state emerged as a historically specific form of social and political organization out of the fragmentation of feudal Europe and the evolution of political sovereignty from the earlier subjugation of kings and kingdoms to papal authority. Machiavelli, acknowledged as the first modern political scientist, devoted his energies to advising rulers during the first period of state formation. Most of the new states of Latin America became part of the world state system during the later stage of its formation. Upon independence, the new states assumed the primary mark of statehood: recognition as territorial units in the international system.

Historical Patterns of State Strength

Stephen Krasner uses a definition of state strength that is less concerned with historical strength and ability than with policy-making autonomy. He identifies three graduated measures of state strength: the ability to resist private pressure, the ability to change private behavior, and the ability to change the social structure. But these measures entail both strength and autonomy. The two concepts are quite different. We can see this with an example from everyday usage: a bulldog may be quite strong, but as long as he obeys my commands he is not autonomous. Krasner's conception of strength presumes autonomy. Nordlinger posits three types of autonomous states: one that acts against societal preferences (type I), one that changes societal preferences (type II), and one that simply agrees with societal preferences (type III).[31] These conceptions of state strength are too limited.[32] Both conceptions of state strength unnecessarily limit the focus to state-private interactions. Strength must also be considered vis-à-vis external actors (sovereignty), regional or local powers (centralization), functional overload (differentiation), and temporal instability (institutionalization). A state that is strong on these grounds may or may not be autonomous vis-à-vis the private sector, so I use *strength* for this set of characteristics rather than *autonomy*. With these qualifications, let me discuss the several historical processes characteristic of strong states.

The Consolidation of Sovereignty. Sovereignty entails the achievement of exclusive jurisdiction over a territory, the external definition of the "arena of politics." As the international state system developed, sovereignty was recognized as an authority above which there was no higher law, first as monarchical sovereignty, then extended to popular sovereignty. The first step was achieved relatively rapidly in Mexico, as in the rest of Latin America: recognition as an independent unit in the international system. But the preservation of this independence, the maintenance of an international "monopoly of legitimate violence" was more difficult to achieve, especially for some states. Mexico suffered the loss of Texas and California following war with the United States. Then, the United States failed to enforce the Monroe Doctrine, allowing imposition of the Austrian prince Maximilian by Napoleon. In the present century, Mexico suffered invasion by the United States during the Mexican Revolution (at Veracruz in 1914 and again in the north when Pershing's troops fruitlessly chased Pancho Villa). But territorial sovereignty has not been threatened since then. In most economic and diplomatic conflicts between Mexico and the United States, the military superiority of the United States is no longer a relevant variable. Indeed, it works to the advantage of Mexico to the extent that an expensive military apparatus has not been necessary.

The Centralization of Power and Dominance. Whereas sovereignty may be understood with reference to external forces, the process of centralization takes place within the state. It involves first of all the concentration of sufficient military power under the central control of the state to dominate armed competition from internal challengers and regional bosses (*caudillos*), as well as to provide for the external defense (control of borders) required by sovereignty. Centralization also involves the ability of the state to pass and enforce laws and in general to safeguard life and property within its bounds. Where sovereignty is not fully consolidated, it is often more important to safeguard the lives and property of foreigners than of citizens, in order to avoid foreign intervention.

The law of the state was increasingly centralized as it achieved independence not only from competing foreign and domestic political jurisdictions but also from civil authority, most notably the Roman Catholic church, which in many states initially exercised quasi-legal social functions. The state attack on the jurisdiction of the church, begun with the liberal reforms of Benito Juárez in the mid-nineteenth century, ended only with the defeat of the Cristero rebellion at the end of the 1920s.

A necessary corollary was the power of the state to collect taxes to pay the military and administrative expenses it incurred. This usually implied increasing state regulation of trade and commerce, even when there was no consistent policy of state intervention in the economy. Internal power was consolidated militarily in Mexico in the nineteenth century with the conquest of the fiercely independent Yaqui Indians in the north and the Maya in the south (the latter in the so-called Caste War of the Yucatán beginning in 1847). Porfirio Díaz furthered centralization with the help of the *rurales* (rural police) and encouraged the expansion of capitalist industry and commerce by both nationals and foreigners. The revolution marked the last major challenge to centralization, and with the exception of the Cristero rebellion, no significant threat to centralization has emerged since. Though the nineteenth-century liberals favored federalism, Mexico is only nominally a federal system; the state is in fact highly centralized.

The Institutionalization of Authority. For our purposes, the institutionalization of authority involves what Weber terms "legal-rational" authority: the provision for the orderly change of government and for succession of leadership within the state. Huntington has defined institutionalization in general as "the process by which organizations and procedures acquire value and stability.[33] For institutionalization of authority in a state, control must be able to be transferred in a peaceful and orderly fashion. Authority is then institutionalized in the state rather than merely being vested in a particular individual or ruling group.[34] A country ruled by a strong individual leader may well experience a crisis of authority stemming from the aspirations of others: Francisco I. Madero's revolutionary challenge to the Díaz dictatorship was "Effective Suffrage, No Reelection." But even when stability of succession is achieved by means of institutionalization, it is not necessarily permanent. The permanence of institutionalized processes of succession depends on the degree of consensus in society as to the legitimacy of the process.[35]

The 1917 constitutional limits on property and subsequent land reforms weakened the traditional rural elite that provided the basis for conservative reaction in other countries. In Mexico the incorporation of workers and peasants in state-sanctioned corporatist organizations enabled the state to continue to exercise control over them. The key step to the institutionalization of authority was the founding in 1929 of the National Revolutionary Party (PRN) by Plutarco Elias Calles, in the wake of the assassination of Alvaro Obregón. In 1938, Lázaro Cárdenas reorganized the party into the PRM (Party of the Mexican Revolution), bringing the military into the system along with workers and peasants. The PRI was formed in 1946. With peasants included in the party through the National Peasants Confederation (CNC), the authority of the revolution was institutionalized.

The Mexican system is institutionalized in fact as well as name. Roger Hansen has challenged the notion of the institutionalized revolution and suggested that important aspects of "praetorianism" and incipient instability persist.[36] Hansen emphasized the cultural characteristics of a mestizo elite and suggested a tendency toward personalist rule. "Calles, not Cárdenas, most closely approximates the model behavior of the mestizo revolutionary and his heirs."[37] This overstates the case. First, whatever importance the mestizo racial composition of the elite had under Porfirio Díaz, racial stereotypes are not helpful in understanding modern Mexican power politics.[38] Mestizos rule Mexico, but since they have done so for generations, this tells us little. Second, although it is true, as Hansen argues, that economic and political elites have common interests in the model of capitalist development that Mexico has followed since World War II, this hardly makes Mexico "praetorian" any more than the "swinging door" between business and government in the United States makes the United States praetorian. Others have suggested that state preferences themselves undermine institutionalization.[39] But as I argue below, the control of the state is balanced by pluralism, however limited; and the result is strength, not weakness.

The crucial difference between Calles and Cárdenas was their behavior out of office: Calles controlled the weak presidents that followed him, during his period of indirect rule, the so-called *maximato* (1928–34). Cárdenas, and every president after Cárdenas, allowed power to pass to the successor. The action of outgoing presidents supporting the system, rather than building personal power bases, is the best indication of the institutionalization of the revolution. In spite of recurring predictions of a "mini-maximato" (the extended influence of an outgoing president), such has not occurred. Luís Echeverría, after appointing his boyhood friend José López Portillo to office, meekly accepted his posting as ambassador, first to Unesco in Paris, then to Australia, New Zealand, and the Fiji Islands. That the system itself favors elites as a whole is a structural characteristic; both economic and political elites benefit.[40]

The Differentiation of Organization. Differentiation of organization involves the ability of the state to develop organizations to suit its needs as it expands its functions in the society. Liberal reforms separating church and state led the state to develop the bureaucratic capacity to perform more or less efficiently such social functions as education and the registration of births, deaths, marriages, and burials that had formerly been carried out exclusively by the church. Economic expansion and foreign trade under Díaz led to the development of specialized bureaucracies for taxation and tariffs and to some regulation of commerce and industry. Financial needs of a growing economy required an expanded state role in monetary matters; the Bank of Mexico was founded under President Plutarcho Elias Calles in 1925. As the economy became more complex, the state became involved in the provision of infrastructure consisting of too large a scale and too diverse a benefit for the private entrepreneur to undertake, such as roads, dams, and large-scale irrigation projects.[41] At a later stage, the state moved into the control of basic industries necessary for development, such as oil and electricity. Major efforts that led to what are now the largest state-owned enterprises, PEMEX (Petroleos Mexicanos) and the Federal Electricity Commission (CFE), were undertaken during the last year of the extended indirect rule of Calles in 1933, as Miguel Wionczek has pointed out.[42] This was a full year before the "interventionist" president, Lázaro Cárdenas, took office; differentiation was not the result of any single president's policies.

As both the work force and industry became more complex, the state was increasingly called upon to expand education and health care services. The basic labor law was passed in 1931. Reforms of outmoded structures of land tenure were demanded and implemented, with major distribution of land to the *ejidos* (village communities) coming under Cárdenas. The differentiation of state functions both followed and led economic growth. When economic development required investments in human capital, infrastructure, or natural resources, and when the private sector was unable or unwilling to respond, further involvement of the state became necessary for growth. In Bennett and Sharpe's phrase, state intervention had a "last resort" character; but the last resort was sought often.[43]

Of all the processes that we are discussing, the differentiation of state organizations and functions is perhaps the most permanent. It is difficult for the state to retreat from responsibility for a function once it has been assumed. Indeed, as Huntington pointed out, the organizations themselves often outlive the function for which they were created.[44] Weber indicated that the "bureaucratic machine" has a permanent character with regard to control as well as function: "The once-existing apparatus . . . is easily made to work for anybody who knows how to gain control over it. A rationally ordered system of officials continues to function smoothly after the enemy has occupied the area: he merely needs to change the top officials."[45] Although expansion of state functions has proceeded faster under some administrations (Cárdenas, Echeverría) than under others, the trend toward expanded functions continued from the 1920s to the 1980s.

As state functions expanded, differentiated organizations were created. Understandably, the state employees who work in these organizations argue that the state should continue and even expand the functions that provide their jobs. This leads some to argue that there is a "separate state interest" that explains the expansion of state functions.[46] This interpretation is either uninteresting or wrong. If all it tells us is that state workers want to protect their jobs (or even expand their existing responsibilities), this is relatively unimportant; it does not explain the relation of forces in society that oppose or favor the expansion of the state. If other groups oppose, why do state workers prevail? Why do the interests of other groups coincide with those of state employees, and how did this come about? If, on the other hand, a state interest in the continuation and expansion of existing functions is projected backward as an explanation of the political decision to adopt those functions in the first place, then it is wrong. The existence of a general tendency within the state toward self-preservation and of state workers who are in favor of preserving their jobs explains neither important decisions—why the state takes on new functions— nor nondecisions—why the state has not taken on other functions.[47] It is more plausible to argue, as does James Malloy, that certain state functions tend to expand in the developing countries just as they have in the developed: partly in response to demand and partly as instruments of legitimation and control.[48]

A Resilient Regime

Although Mexico has had remarkable continuity in its political institutions, the country has seen significant political changes, even in its
postrevolutionary history. For example, the "ruling party" that was
formed more than a decade after the 1917 Constitution has been
reorganized and renamed twice so far (1938 and 1946). The conservative National Action Party (PAN) and, on the liberal side, a new
schism led by Cuauhtémoc Cárdenas, son of Mexico's most popular
president, took advantage of state-initiated reforms and ended the
PRI's electoral monopoly. Government-sponsored organizations no
longer hold a representational monopoly on interest groups. The mix
of participation and control has changed over time. Given its ability
to respond and adapt, resilience rather than stability captures the
political strength of the Mexican regime.

The concept of resilience is drawn from systems theory to describe
a system that can persist and absorb shocks. Resilience allows shocks
to disrupt but not destroy the system. The concept was described in
the 1970s by an ecologist who later headed the International Institute
of Applied Systems Analysis, C. S. Hollings. In studying systemic
survival capacity, Hollings found that the conceptual difference between resilience and stability was crucial.

> It is useful to distinguish two kinds of behavior. One can be termed
> stability, which represents the ability of a system to return to an
> equilibrium state after a temporary disturbance; the more rapidly
> it returns and the less it fluctuates the more stable it would be. But
> there is another property, termed resilience, that is a measure of
> the persistence of systems and of their ability to absorb change and
> disturbance and still maintain the same relationships between pop-
> ulations or state variables.[49]

In contrast to stability, resilience does not depend upon an equilibrium
as a point of reference. Indeed, as Hollings pointed out, resilience
may produce movable equilibria. The system at time $t + 1$ would not
have the same equilibrium as at time t, but the basic relationships
within the system would survive. In this conception a very resilient
system may endure great fluctuations; that is, it may show low stability.
Indeed, the perturbations that upset a stable equilibrium may in fact
increase the resilience of a system.

Relating resilience to political change, the regime best able to perdure may not be the stable state system with few challenges and few
changes. Such a system, stable in the short run, might harden in the

face of great stress, even to the breaking point. More likely to survive is the resilient system, able to change and evolve, responding to challenges and crises along the way. When stability is threatened, resilience prevents the decline of the system into chaos.

Resilience appropriately describes the Mexican political system. Although the concept itself has seldom been analyzed in political terms, it has frequently been applied as a descriptive term to the Mexican regime. Wayne Cornelius argued against pessimists who doubted the ability of Mexico's political institutions to cope with the crisis of 1982: "Such skepticism was grounded in a misperception of the De La Madrid group as well as significant underestimation of the resilience of traditional political control mechanisms and relationships between the Mexican state and its key support groups." Henry Schmidt, writing on Mexico's foreign debt problems, came to a similar conclusion: "In confronting its crisis of 1982–83 the Mexican government demonstrated the resilience and pragmatism with which, deviation from the Revolution notwithstanding, it has guided the nation for more than half a century." Even Steven Sanderson, with a much more somber assessment of the fiscal crisis in the wake of a failed oil boom (in which patronage politics replaced an exhausted traditional populism), felt obliged to specify an important caveat: "One must remember that the old constraints—still in force—are political unpredictability and amazing party resilience in the face of crisis." During the Salinas administration, his political recovery in office posed a sharp contrast to his campaign weakness. Without agreeing exactly what resilience is, scholars have argued that Mexico has it.[50] The events of 1982–88 notwithstanding, the Mexican regime is still resilient.

Following Cardoso, we may consider the political regime to include not only the rules regulating the formal institutions of government (parties, the legislature, the judiciary, and the executive) but also "the political nature of the ties between citizens and rulers."[51] In Mexico, although the formal institutions of the political regime are important and well established (and indeed would merit a separate extended analysis), I argue that resilience results from more complex linkages between the rulers and the ruled, between citizen and government.

The most important linkages are political participation and political control. First, the regime is able to effectively exercise control over society. Even though that control is not absolute, it is pervasive, multidimensional, and sophisticated. Second, the regime includes pluralist mechanisms for participation and communication between citizens and the political leadership. The conflicting characterizations of the Mexican regime as both authoritarian and pluralist reflect the coexistence of control with significant and increasing levels of participation. Indeed, as the financial resources for cooptation decline, the regime has turned to political liberalization as the basis for renewed regime legitimacy at the cost of party dominance.[52]

Control

Control of the masses is a central characteristic of political control in Mexico's regime. Most conventional analyses place the PRI at the center of the political system of control, with the three bases of the PRI exemplified by its formal political components: the national confederations for peasants, for labor, and for the remaining popular mass organizations.[53] This places an unnecessarily narrow focus on the political institutions of a one-party-dominant system. In contrast, and drawing on the work of David Ronfeldt,[54] I argue that there are three bases of control available to the regime. The first consists of corporatist functional organizations for interest representation, the second is a one-party-dominant competitive electoral machine, and the third is an army loyal to civilian political control and available for the maintenance of political order.

The first element of this tripartite system approximates the corporatist model described by Philippe Schmitter. This model suggests that interests are represented through a series of functionally differentiated, hierarchically ordered organizations created or sanctioned by the state. In exchange for the supposed exclusivity of representation, the state obtains influence over the leadership of the organizations. The National Peasants Confederation (CNC) has been a classic example, as has the massive labor organization, the Confederation of Mexican Workers (CTM). Each of these organizations was designed to be the exclusive agent of interest representation for specific functional units in society, namely, peasants and workers. It is part tribute to the effectiveness of these organizations that labor and peasants have been so quiescent in the aftermath of the 1982 economic crisis. Octogenarian labor leader Fidel Velásquez for generations has spoken for labor and through the CTM exercised a consistently moderating influence on labor demands.

Corporate interest groups are no longer linked to the state solely or even primarily through the party. "Independent" unions in city and country have reduced the power of the PRI unions. Although some of the new automobile plants specializing in exports have shown a preference for the CTM, the independent unions have helped buttress the legitimacy of the regime precisely by demonstrating their ability to compete with the PRI. Indeed, we may be witnessing a shift from state corporatism to societal corporatism, in Schmitter's terms.

Though peasant and labor interests are most clearly controlled and coopted through corporatist organizations, business and government likewise have their functionally specific organizations. Although not formally part of the PRI's party network, every business has its officially sanctioned industry organization; these associations are in turn aggregated at the national level into the national chambers of industry (CONCAMIN) and of commerce (CONCANACO). With the rapid growth of government and of state-owned enterprises over the last several decades, government workers have become an important functional group in their own right. One of the largest unions is now the union of state workers. Thus, the regime relies upon a comprehensive system of state-initiated or state-managed organizations for every functional group in society in order to provide it with channels of control.

The second base of the regime's control is the electoral system. The PRI takes full advantage of both the revolutionary heritage that it claims and the state resources at its disposal. The flag of the nation and the flag of the party echo one another faithfully. During elections the PRI used government vehicles throughout the country preparing its candidacies. The ideological, organizational, and resource advantages of the PRI have been substantial enough to ensure dominance. And indeed the PRI does win nearly every election of national importance, though recently by smaller margins, especially since the 1977 reforms broadening the terms of party competition. Table 2.7 gives the results of recent elections.

It would be a mistake to view the survival of the party in purely authoritarian terms. As Ruth and David Collier have pointed out, corporatism relies upon the carrot as well as the stick (in their terms, upon inducements as well as constraints).[55] In recent years, increased political participation has become an important inducement, and the political leadership has imposed reforms that aid the regime at the expense of the old-style dominant party.

The party in power traditionally used its resources to distribute real benefits to the masses. In the peasant *ejidos* (which occupy half of the national farmland), in the profit-sharing provision of the Constitution of 1917 finally put into practice, in the fund for popular housing (INFONAVIT), and in the social security system, the health system, and the education system, the PRI used its leverage to political advantage; but the benefits were real for those who received them. Consider some basic statistics. Life expectancy increased from less than fifty years in 1950 to sixty-six years by 1980. Coverage under some form of state-sponsored social security included less than a million people in 1950; thirty years later, that number was over 26 million.

TABLE 2.7   Results of Congressional and Presidential Elections in Mexico

Year	PRI (%)	PAN (%)	Largest Left Party (%)	Null Votes (%)	No. of Parties	Abstention Rate[b]	Actual Votes
			Presidential Elections[a]				
1964	87.82	11.05	(PPS) 0.68	—	5	30.66	9,422,560
1970	83.32	13.85	(PPS) 0.86	1.27	4	35.11	14,052,079
1976	86.89	—	(PPS) 3.65	5.23	4	31.31	17,606,772
1982	68.43	15.68	(PSUM) 3.48	4.47	9	25.16	23,592,886
			Midterm Congressional Elections[a]				
1961	90.23	7.59	(PPS) 0.96	—	5	31.67	6,836,365
1967	83.32	12.41	(PPS) 2.79	—	4	37.65	9,864,089
1973	69.66	14.70	(PPS) 3.55	9.95	4	39.68	15,009,984
1979	69.74	10.79	(PSUM) 4.86	5.85	7	50.67	13,782,568
1985	64.99	15.45	(PSUM) 3.24	4.62	9	50.54	17,830,529

Official Results of the 1988 Presidential Election		
Candidates	Votes	Percentage
Carlos Salinas de Gortari	9,687,926	50.74
Cuauhtémoc Cárdenas Solórzano	5,929,585	31.06
Manuel J. Clouthier del Rincón	3,208,584	16.81
Gumersindo Magaña Negrete	190,891	1.00
Rosario Ibarra de Piedra	74,857	0.39
Total	19,091,843	100.0

Sources: For 1964–85: Federal Electoral Commission (Mexico), published in *Uno más uno*, 28 July 1985. For 1988: *Las elecciones de 1988: Crónica del sexenio 1982–1988* (México: Presidencia de la República, 1988), p. 263.
Note: PRI, Institutional Revolutionary Party; PAN, National Action Party; PPS, Popular Socialist Party; PSUM, Unified Mexican Socialist Party.
[a]Votes for top three parties.
[b]As percentage of registered voters.

Students enrolled at the National University and the National Polytechnic Institute, barely 38,000 in 1950, numbered almost 400,000 thirty years later. Income distribution figures reflect the shift to the new middle class created in large part by the state.[56]

The military, little studied in Mexico until recently, is the third base of control. Cooptation is not the only resource of the political regime; repression is available and is used.[57] The role of the army is crucial for understanding the authoritarian aspect of the Mexican regime. But perhaps the most important point about the Mexican army is not that it is occasionally used for repression and control. Rather, it is that these occasions are rare; moreover, they take place in a context of civilian dominance of the military institution.

According to the bureaucratic authoritarian thesis, the Mexican army may have substantial incentives to change. Indeed, it is only in the last fifteen to twenty years that the Mexican military has begun the process of modernization that took place in other military establishments in Latin America in earlier decades. Combined with this institutional modernization, there have been numerous challenges to the military: sporadic guerrilla threats in the city and the countryside in the 1970s; a new mandate for countrywide surveillance and control under drug eradication programs; the necessity to protect the new oil and gas facilities; and external security, an unusual problem for Mexico, entailing the protection of its southern border from immigrants, refugees, and combatants in the civil strife in Central America. Moreover, the economic crisis of the 1980s and the growing power of the technocrats in the state apparatus provided the classic incentives for a "coup coalition," in O'Donnell's phrase. Thus, it is all the more impressive that the Mexican military accepts the necessity of modernization while subordinating its political authority to the civilian structure. The army serves as both an enforcement and an information arm of the state, extending throughout the provinces and the countryside. As Ronfeldt indicated, this is important for continuing state control.[58] In spite of the crises, the army has fulfilled this role without seeking to increase its political power as an institution; the tradition of civilian dominance is secure.

Participation

In a resilient regime, a leading ideology generates voluntary compliance and regime loyalty from the mass of the population. In other words, most people share beliefs that lead them to voluntarily obey the laws without espousing a change in regime, even if they oppose particular policies. They are "system loyal" in Juan Linz's phrase;[59] they grant legitimacy to the regime. Such voluntary compliance depends in large part on opportunities for participation. Institutionalized voting participation, usually taking place through political parties, is the most obvious way in which opportunities for participation are extended to the masses.[60]

In Mexico, high levels of participation and a highly institutionalized regime classify Mexico as a civic participant regime, in Huntington's typology.[61] But the function of the major party in Mexico, the PRI, has not been "to organize participation, to aggregate interests, to serve as the link between social forces and the government."[62] Rather, the PRI has been an instrument for political socialization to the ideology of the Mexican Revolution, a vehicle for patronage, and an instrument for controlling the participation of workers and peasants. Extended eligibility (to women, youths, and illiterates) helps increase the legitimacy of the party in these functions, but it also helps legitimize the regime by bringing new voters to competing parties.

Several hypotheses suggest that possibilities for social mobility or the provision of state benefits in an urban, differentiated policy may lower the incentive to vote.[63] It has even been suggested that high voting rates, especially when they occur suddenly, are signs of instability, reflecting widespread dissatisfaction with government policies.[64] To the extent that this hypothesis holds true, low rates of turnout supported increased party pluralism in Mexico.

Under the electoral reform, several new parties were legally recognized and now compete for national offices.[65] An expanded House of Deputies now includes seats reserved for opposition parties. This does not change the role of parties as instruments of legitimation rather than interest aggregators; but it does imply that regime loyalty is no longer identical with party loyalty.[66]

Foreign economic policy does not depend on electoral politics. No party—not even the PRI—is important for most policy. The president, various bureaucracies, business organizations, labor confederations, peasant groups, politicians, and *técnicos* all influence policy, but their influence is not exercised electorally. Roderic Camp, the author of a study on the role of economists, has said that "there is no evidence . . . other than impressionistic observations by various authors, that PRI has a major role in the decision-making process in Mexico."[67] Hansen concluded that "the PRI is better conceptualized as an apparatus through which the Revolutionary Coalition controls Mexican politics than as a mechanism for representing and implementing the demands of its component interest groups."[68] This control, allowing but limiting participation, helps explain the ability of the state to adopt first nationalist and later liberal policies.

Conclusion

A strong state, combined with a resilient regime and a relatively high degree of development, provides the best test case for a theory of choice under constraints. A state elite with nationalist policy preferences would have maximum opportunity to confront successfully the constraints of structure and to transform their metapreferences into policies. This chapter has shown that Mexico satisfies the conditions of potential power in terms of state and regime characteristics. Part II will show that in Mexico the state has acted on its metapreferences for nationalist policies in a systematic way.

Part Two

Nationalism versus Liberalism

THE STATE IN Mexico in the nationalist period demonstrated a long-term pattern of state intervention in the economy. Dependency and Marxist interpretations of development tend to emphasize the determining influence of private market forces on development, but Mexico had not in fact developed an unrestricted free market economy. Rather, the state had been quite active in the process of economic development and change. State intervention helped to shape the economy in Mexico since the revolution, especially by stimulating the sectoral transformation of the economy from a commodity export economy to an industrializing economy based on import substitution.

Mexico's sectoral differentiation of policy requires modification of the "obsolescing bargain" argument that the state gains bargaining power over time in all sectors vis-à-vis foreign investors. Moreover, state intervention in Mexico showed long-term continuities that do not reflect the personal preferences of individual leaders. This fact counters the overemphasis on presidential power and especially qualifies the "pendulum" hypothesis of Mexican policy-making.

State intervention in general and regulation of foreign investors in particular tended to increase over time. Policymakers chose new policy instruments as new problems were identified. As the economy grew, state policy tended to become more differentiated. Policy instruments and the choices that they reflected imposed alternatives to market solutions in response to collective goals identified within the state. This pattern of state action was not one of irrational nationalism; nor did it reflect passive submission to the preferences of foreign investors.

Although Mexico is strong by Third World standards, it is nonetheless not a "core" state. The realist approach to international behavior emphasizes the power of other states and the constraints that power imposes; a modified realist perspective looks not only at the action of other states but also at the principles, norms, rules, and procedures that make up international regimes in particular issue areas. International regimes are intervening variables between the power and interests of states and political outcomes. They serve as powerful constraints on the action of states in the developing world. Perhaps what is most remarkable is not the eventual liberalization of Mexico's political economy but the strength and endurance of its nationalist metapreference in the midst of a global liberal regime. Part Two shows the evolution of the nationalist policy regime and its eventual failure, not only by liberal standards but in terms of the very nationalist goals the policy was meant to achieve.

Three

The Nationalist Tradition

State Power and Market Power

As Mexico has come to rank among the most industrialized of the developing countries, the state has been an active promoter of that growth.[1] State industrialization policies have variously entailed the export of primary commodities, with the development of associated infrastructure; the substitution of imports by local manufacture and assembly of products destined for the domestic market; and the promotion of exports to the world market, especially manufactured exports (sometimes termed nontraditional exports). These patterns represent three stages of industrial development, each emphasizing different sectors of the economy. They constitute the historical sequence of development in Mexico.

Mexico's policies constituted a coherent program of industrial development. I call this the nationalist vision or metapreference. It was not a socialist vision; it by no means implied a preference for all means of production to be owned by the state. The main tenets of this nationalist metapreference for local ownership were (1) exclusive state ownership of strategic or basic industries, especially those based on raw materials or physical infrastructure; (2) national ownership of all industries in which the domestic private sector could produce efficiently; and (3) foreign ownership to complement nationally owned industries and to produce what state and domestic private firms could not. Behind this nationalist metapreference lies the assumption that the nationality of ownership matters for industrial outcomes. Direct ownership by the state is a related, but separate, issue from the nationalist preference for local (state or private) ownership.

A few words about my terms. As I use them, *nationalism* refers to an ideology. A *metapreference* (or *second-order volition*) refers to a preferred possible future. A *policy* refers to a preferred possible future and a class or set of actions designed to make that future happen; policy is thus a second-order decision, a decision about a class of

55

decisions. (I may also use *policy* to refer to a specific example or subset of this larger class.) A *decision* refers to the choice of a particular policy (as part of a larger, general policy) or the application of a policy to a particular case.

If a metapreference produces no action, we may doubt that it exists, or we may give it another name, such as a dream or a fond wish. A metapreference becomes significant when it becomes the basis for action. We are concerned with collective actions. A successfully implemented policy is, absent coercion, prima facie evidence for a collective metapreference on the part of those who designed and implemented the policy. In the sections and chapters that follow, successful nationalist policies will be taken as evidence of a nationalist metapreference. I also argue that failed proposals for policies can be evidence of a metapreference for a possible future.[2]

The alternative to nationalism was the international liberal metapreference for free, or freer, markets. Global firms and hegemonic states profess the superiority of untrammeled access to markets—to barter, license, invest, sell, export, import, or disinvest at will. I assume the existence, but not the dominance, of a liberal international metapreference for privately owned firms and unregulated markets for trade and investment.

Economic nationalism is expressed in practice as state policies, which, in turn, reflect metapreferences and collective choices arrived at and implemented over time. Long-term continuities characterize state power used for nationalist policies in Mexico. The historical use of state power in Mexico provided a countervailing force to both foreign investors and their home governments.[3]

The dependency arguments about foreign enterprise have taken several forms, all asserting the preponderance of power of firms over the state. The first asserts simply that foreign investors get what they want from the state. This is similar in form to the more general instrumental Marxist approach to power: the state has no autonomy from dominant classes in society. The state responds to the wishes of capital and especially to foreign capital. This perspective is fairly easy to refute. State policies have often caused shifts in the patterns of investment. In contrast to the simple dependency thesis, state actions for several decades helped shape the composition and direction of foreign investment in ways that did not coincide with the preference of the foreign investors themselves. In other words, the historical counterfactual, market conditions without state intervention, would have been closer to the preferences of the foreign firms. Although the nationalist program was ultimately reversed in the 1980s, nationalism inspired the dominant development program for several decades. This outcome was clearly counter to any hypothesis of foreign dominance.

The more complex dependency argument, like the structural Marxist approach to state-society relations, holds that even when the state acts against the interests of particular firms, it necessarily acts in the long-term interests of capital. In its general form this argument is hardly a hypothesis at all, since nothing short of a revolution or a catastrophic crisis would falsify it. Although the state may have some autonomy from individual capitalists, particular enterprises, and even certain industries, there is little or no structural autonomy of the state from the leading capitalist classes.[4] Yet we should not assume that all forms of state intervention in the economy are subordinated to the interests of a dominant class that is itself partly domestic and partly foreign. Although foreign investors have played a leading role during most phases of Mexican industrialization, state policymakers have intervened frequently to expropriate or regulate them.

The state intervened in Mexico in the process of economic development all along the way, and much of that intervention was against the interests of foreign capital.[5] How can we explain this pattern of state intervention? Analysts of the bargaining (or statist) school suggest an answer. Expressed at its most general level in the works of Raymond Vernon,[6] the argument suggests that the behavior of the state is explained primarily by characteristics of the international marketplace. Firms make decisions to invest abroad under conditions of competitive advantage. Over time, that advantage is lost, creating an opportunity for nationalistic policymakers to take action against the foreigners. The original "bargain" between the firms and the state becomes obsolete, and the state prevails. In looking in more detail at the economic patterns of foreign investment and the state policies that helped to shape its direction, we shall see that sometimes economic history supported the pattern that Vernon called the obsolescing bargain, while in other sectors a more complex pattern has emerged. Krasner argued that perceived vulnerability causes nationalist responses, even at the cost of inefficiency. But nationalism was prevalent during the decades of most rapid growth in Mexico. The policies were responses to real economic problems, not to perceived psychological threats.

Before turning in the balance of this chapter to the demonstration of Mexico's interventionism from the turn of the century to the 1970s, let me consider more formally the notion of state intervention.

State Intervention

By state intervention in the economy I refer to decisions made by the state rather than by private individuals or enterprises. These include decisions determining the accumulation of capital, the techniques of production, the product mix, and the distribution of goods and services.

A "mixed economy" with high levels of state intervention differs from the pure model of competitive capitalism. In a competitive market economy, private firms, interacting (according to the model) through the market, accumulate capital and decide what to produce, how to produce it, and how the products are distributed. Firms interact with each other in an impersonal market over which none has control; the critical decisions are those of sovereign individual consumers. The interaction of supply and demand is understood as a "self-steering system." In this system the role of the state is only to guarantee the conditions for private enterprise by guaranteeing social order. The state also extracts resources from the economy through taxation in order to maintain its own operations, but not to accumulate capital for production.

At the other extreme, in a state "command" economy, the accumulation of capital and the decisions of production and distribution are conducted by the state itself.[7] In the pure model of state control there is neither need nor opportunity for private production and capital accumulation. But most of the developing countries of the world are self-styled mixed economies in which the state is active but not exclusive. In any system, the state ensures the conditions for economic advance by guaranteeing the obedience and compliance of the citizens and thus by maintaining the social order. Legitimation of the existing system is a constant goal of states (though success or failure is another matter). We are concerned here with the direct participation of the state in the economy, since this is the variable element.

Three specific forms of state intervention can be distinguished: ownership, regulation, and promotion. Ownership refers to direct state control of productive assets. Regulation is the mechanism by which the state introduces nonmarket criteria into the productive process by means of its legal authority. (Note that this does not necessarily represent a distortion of a competitive market, since the market may not be perfectly competitive. Regulation may thus be a corrective to distortions of the market due to monopoly or oligopoly.) Promotion involves the selective use of incentives—financial assistance or fiscal or regulatory relief—to influence the behavior of private enterprises. Economic planning may utilize any of these three forms, since planning consists of second-order decisions (decisions about decisions): how the state and private actors should behave in making their investment, production, and distributional choices; specifically, how to use ownership, regulation, and promotion to achieve state goals.

State Intervention in Mexico before the Revolution

Foreign enterprise has been important to Mexico since the end of the nineteenth century, and Mexico has represented an important market and source of raw materials for foreign enterprises. In the last century, under the modernizing influence of Porfirio Díaz and his positivist *científicos*, foreign investment was invited to make investments that Mexican enterprise was not ready or able to undertake: building railroads more than anything else, but with important mining ventures as well in gold, silver, copper, lead, and oil. Men such as Daniel Guggenheim in mining; Sir Weetman Dickinson Pearson (Lord Cowdray) in railroads, engineering, and oil; and Edward L. Doheny in oil were important investors who cultivated the good graces of Díaz. Foreigners, often at the invitation of the government, helped introduce modern methods of mineral extraction, transportation, and communications, integrating a previously backward, rural country and connecting it with the Western world. In so doing, foreigners became owners of large parts of Mexico's wealth.

In the nineteenth century, foreign investment in Mexico came from Britain, France, and Germany as well as from the United States, but by the turn of the century, as the United States embarked upon its imperialist adventures in the Caribbean, investment by the United States had begun to predominate. Expansion of U.S. firms across the border was part of the first movement of American investment abroad, at a time when mergers and acquisitions among firms were accelerating at home. Mexico was a logical first choice for firms wishing to step into the international arena. Table 3.1 shows the early importance of Mexico as a share of all U.S. investment. In 1897, 31.5 percent of all worldwide foreign investment by U.S. firms was in Mexico; Mexican investment represented nearly two thirds of all U.S. investment in Latin America at the time.

Foreign investment thus had gotten a strong start under Porfirio Díaz. At the end of the so-called Porfiriato, the Mexican economy was based on exports of primary products, with communications and other infrastructure designed to serve the needs of the export companies or the small elite of importing consumers. René Villarreal summarized the role of foreign enterprise at the start of the revolution: "By 1911 the main economic activities of the country were controlled

TABLE 3.1   Value of U.S. Investment in Mexico, Latin America, and the
World, 1897–1970 (in Millions of Current U.S. Dollars)

Year	World	Total for Latin America	Latin America as % of World	Mexico	Mexico as % of Latin America	Mexico as % of World
1897	635	308	48.5	200	64.9	31.5
1908	1,638	754	46.0	416	55.2	25.4
1914	2,652	1,281	48.3	587	45.8	22.1
1919	3,880	1,988	51.2	644	32.4	16.6
1929	7,553	3,706	49.0	709	19.1	9.4
1940	7,000	2,771	39.6	357	12.9	5.1
1946	7,200	3,100	43.0	316	10.2	4.4
1950	11,790	4,590	38.9	415	9.0	3.5
1955	19,313	6,608	34.2	607	9.2	3.1
1960	32,778	8,387	25.6	795	9.5	2.4
1965	49,328	9,391	19.0	1,182	12.6	2.4
1970	78,178	12,252	15.7	1,786	14.6	2.3

Sources: For 1897–1914: Wilkins, The Emergence of Multinational Enterprise (1970), p. 110. For 1919–
50: Wilkins, The Maturing of Multinational Enterprise (1974), pp. 55, 283, 330. For 1946 and 1950
for Mexico: Newfarmer and Mueller, Multinational Corporations in Brazil and Mexico (1975), p. 51.
For 1955–70: Robinson and Smith, The Impact of Foreign Private Investment on the Mexican Economy
(1976), p. 188.

by foreigners. The participation of foreign capital in mining was
97.7 percent, in petroleum 100 percent, in electricity 87.2 percent, in
railroads 61.8 percent, in banking 76.7 percent, and in industry 85
percent."[8]

Capitalist production and foreign investment survived the revolution without serious damage.[9] The revolution destroyed property
on many of the large haciendas, whether owned by Mexicans or foreigners, and a number of foreigners lost or gave up their agricultural
holdings. But other enterprises with foreign investment continued to
maintain production throughout the revolution. Mining suffered a
large decline; but petroleum production, almost entirely in foreign
hands, actually increased, to the extent that by 1920 Mexico was the
world's leading oil exporter. Villarreal evaluated the period from the
Porfiriato to the Depression thus: "During this period the organization
of the economic system was characterized by a model of outward-
looking growth, in which the state played a passive role and the economy worked under the free interaction of the market forces, which
were linked directly to the international market."[10]

Redefining the Role of the State

The revolution expanded the role of the state in the economy. The Constitution of 1917 provided the parameters not only for foreign investment regulation specifically but also for state intervention in the economy more generally. Though the impact of the revolution upon the structure of the economy was not radical to the extent that it did not replace capitalism, the Mexican Revolution established the ideological and political grounding for a fundamentally different role of the state.

Underlying the interventionist tradition in Mexico is the distinctly non-Anglo-American conception of the social function of private property embedded in the Mexican Constitution:

> Art. 27.—Ownership [*propriedad*] of all lands and waters contained within the boundaries of the national territory is vested originally in the nation. The nation has had, and has, the right to convey title thereof to individual persons, so establishing private property . . . The nation shall have at all times the right to impose on private property such modalities as the public interest dictates, and the right to regulate the use and exploitation of all natural resources susceptible to appropriation, in order to preserve and to effect an equitable distribution of the public wealth.

The same article of the constitution goes on to specify the property rights that have served as the basis for Mexico's extensive agrarian reform and that have given the state dominion over subsoil and mineral rights.[11] (Because of its importance, article 27 is excerpted at length in appendix 1.) National control of subsoil rights laid the legal basis for the expropriation of the foreign oil companies in 1938, and more generally for state control of basic industries.

But as important as the scope granted to state intervention are the limits placed upon it. The regulation of private property may be undertaken only for the public interest. Expropriation must be with compensation and is aimed primarily at "appropriable" natural resources.[12] The rationale for state intervention is not an equitable distribution of wealth per se but an equitable distribution of the public wealth.

Foreign ownership of subsoil rights was an issue of international contention. During and after the revolution, the United States was wary of Mexican economic intervention that violated North American and Anglo-Saxon norms of protection of private property. The secretary of the interior of the United States under Woodrow Wilson,

Franklin K. Lane, spoke of the right of Americans to the resources of other countries, with specific reference to Mexico and Russia:

> "The world is mine" is not the mere dramatic utterance of an escaped convict or of an over-mastering leader of men . . . What a people hold, they hold as trustees for the world . . . It is good American practice. The Monroe Doctrine is an expression of it . . . That is why we are talking of backward peoples and recognizing for them another law than that of self-determination, a limited law of self-determination, a leading-string law.[13]

The "leading string" to Mexico was closely tied to banks and oil companies in the United States. Conflicts with Mexico over debt payments and over the application of article 27 led to the postponement of recognition of Mexico's government by the United States until 1923. Nevertheless, through the 1920s U.S. economic activity in Mexico expanded in most areas rather than contracted.[14] Robert Freeman Smith concluded that "whatever success U.S. economic interests enjoyed in Mexico was based more on the activities of certain less ideological [American] business groups than on 'skillful' diplomacy or official meddling."[15] Despite U.S. government objections, U.S. business came to an accommodation with Mexican nationalism.

A new set of ideas was evolving, with a more prominent, central role for the state. Mexico remained open to foreign capital, but the revolution had raised aspirations for the reassertion of national control over natural resources. Land reform hesitatingly was begun, and the institutional groundwork for national control of water, electric power, and oil was initiated under the presidency of Plutarco Elías Calles (1924–28) and his subsequent period of powerful influence over the presidency, the so-called maximato (1928–34).[16] During his presidency, Calles had overseen the establishment of both the Bank of Mexico and the National Bank of Agrarian Credit, and had passed the Law on Patents, Inventions, and Trademarks protecting industrial property.[17] Many of the interventionist policies attributed to the avowedly interventionist administration of Lázaro Cárdenas (1934–40) in fact were the continuation and deepening of policies initiated by Calles.[18]

With the convergence of international economic conditions and domestic politics in the 1930s and 1940s, a second period of development, based on import substitution industrialization (hereafter referred to as ISI), began. Mexico's economy was tied to that of its major trading partner, the United States; when the U.S. economy grew, so did the Mexican; and when it crashed during the Depression, the neighboring economy came down as well.[19] As a result of the decline in production and trade, Mexico began to produce some of the consumer goods that had previously been imported. The growth model based on primary exports was no longer feasible as export prices dropped and foreign exchange was depleted. Land reform and the 1938 nationalization of the foreign oil companies also disrupted export production. The unavailability of imported consumer goods continued during World War II as the United States converted its industrial capacity to war production. In part, ISI was an unintended consequence of the Depression, the war, and domestic expropriations, but by the end of the 1940s, ISI was nurtured by state actions such as import barriers and devaluations.[20]

Public ownership of land and other natural resources is not the only area where the Mexican state has differed from the assumptions of a free market. The relationship between labor and capital was likewise mediated by the state in Mexico. This position was often reiterated by Cárdenas: "According to the principles that govern our legal system [*nuestro derecho*], the public power is the mediator in the conflicts that emerge daily in worker-management relations [*en las relaciones obrero-patronales*]."[21] Thus, the proper role of the state was to mediate and intervene in favor of the weaker party (labor) in labor-management conflicts. Cárdenas sponsored organizations for workers and peasants, after splitting them apart to avoid the formation of a power separate from the state.[22] The bases were laid for the corporatist control of social groups in Mexico—if those groups were workers or peasants.

The theme of state protection of the weaker party in economic endeavors recurs frequently in Mexican political economy. When employers complained of Cárdenas's partisanship on the side of workers in union struggles, he challenged the businessmen to give their enterprises to the state if they were tired of the social struggle. State intervention, however, benefited business as well. Mexican business was considered the weaker party in the economic struggle when national capital faced foreign capital. In the 1930s and 1940s this took the form of tariff protection for nascent national enterprises, but the principle would later be applied to foreign enterprises that leaped those tariff barriers to establish local subsidiaries in manufacturing industries.

In short, by the start of World War II, Mexico had survived a revolution, established a national constitution and a dominant national political party, controlled labor and the peasantry, and continued the process of industrial modernization that had begun with the Porfiriato. In contrast to that prerevolutionary period, the leaders of the postrevolutionary era were committed to state intervention in the economy. The state would intervene to protect the social function of agrarian land and ownership of natural resources, to protect labor from the worst abuses of management, and to protect national capital from foreign competition. Mexico's experience recalls the assessment of Karl Polanyi in *The Great Transformation*: "the market system will no longer be self-regulating, even in principle, since it will not comprise land, labor, and money."[23] The state in Mexico regulated and limited the private economy in land, labor, and capital. Mexico was an early example and continued to be a prime example of a mixed economy with an interventionist state.

Postwar Growth of Transnational Enterprise to 1970

Mexico's preeminent position as the prime host of U.S. investment eroded after the turn of the century, declining to one quarter of U.S. worldwide investment by the outbreak of the revolution in 1910, less than 10 percent by the start of the Depression, and under 2 percent since 1960. This has been a declining share of a rapidly growing pie. The United States has invested massively in Europe and other developed countries, but Mexico has remained the leading investment location among developing countries, with the sole exception of Brazil. The accumulated value of U.S. foreign investment in Mexico went from 200 million dollars in 1897 to over 1.7 billion dollars in 1970, and investment from the United States still surpasses that from any other country, though that dominance is slipping (see tables 3.1 and 3.2). State policies both stimulated and regulated this growth of foreign investment.

Since the turn of the century, the composition of foreign investment has shifted away from extractive and toward manufacturing industries, and those changes have followed state actions: either expropriations (forced sales) or purchases (amicable sales) of foreign investments. In 1903 José Limantour, the *científico* minister of finance, began to purchase foreign-owned railways, and by 1908 the government controlled majority shares of the major lines through the newly formed National Railways of Mexico.[24] During the revolution, mining declined but petroleum grew, until Cárdenas took the oil share of foreign investment down to almost nothing. In the post-1940 period, manufacturing accounted for nearly all the growth. The amicable purchase of the two major utility companies in 1960 and the forced Mexicanization (majority Mexican ownership) of foreign enterprise in sulphur mining in 1967 completed the series of large nationali-

TABLE 3.2   Selected Data on Foreign Investment in Mexico, 1939–1976
(in Millions of Current U.S. Dollars)

Year	Long-Term Capital Inflow (net)	Total Foreign Investment	New Foreign Investment	Reinvested Profits	Acquisitions of Foreign Companies	Remittance on Foreign Investment
1939	39.5	—	41.7	—	—	14.8
1940	2.5	—	7.2	—	—	25.3
1941	11.6	—	16.8	—	—	32.7
1942	18.2	—	26.9	—	—	41.1
1943	−4.7	—	9.3	—	—	33.0
1944	28.5	—	42.7	—	—	27.3
1945	7.6	—	3.3	—	—	28.9
1946	35.9	—	24.3	—	—	44.2
1947	51.6	—	42.5	—	—	55.2
1948	17.2	—	26.5	—	—	56.9
1949	17.6	—	10.7	—	—	30.8
1950	51.2	72.4	53.9	18.5	—	47.5
1951	48.9	120.6	70.7	49.9	—	51.7
1952	47.5	68.2	31.2	37.0	—	70.6
1953	49.4	41.8	38.3	3.5	—	79.4
1954	98.7	93.2	80.4	12.8	—	62.5
1955	116.8	105.4	92.9	12.5	—	67.1
1956	120.6	126.3	97.2	29.1	—	91.0
1957	162.8	131.5	102.5	29.0	—	88.3
1958	166.4	100.3	74.2	26.1	—	96.5
1959	125.5	81.1	65.0	16.1	—	112.5
1960	109.5	−38.0	67.9	10.6	−116.5	131.0
1961	260.3	119.3	94.1	25.2	—	122.9
1962	224.7	126.5	90.3	36.2	—	123.1
1963	265.4	117.4	81.4	36.0	—	149.6
1964	462.3	161.9	111.7	50.2	—	185.9
1965	111.0	213.9	152.6	61.3	—	174.8
1966	213.2	182.8	109.1	73.7	—	203.7
1967	346.0	129.5	88.6	105.3	−64.4	216.1
1968	379.0	227.0	116.8	110.2	—	265.7
1969	692.9	297.4	195.7	119.7	−18.0	315.8
1970	503.9	322.8	200.7	122.1	—	357.5
1971	669.1	306.7	196.1	110.6	—	383.0
1972	753.5	300.8	190.0	120.8	−10.0	451.5
1973	1,676.1	456.3	286.9	191.6	−22.2	528.4
1974	2,730.8	678.1	362.1	318.1	−2.1	633.7
1975	4,318.0	748.8	372.4	412.3	−35.9	632.6
1976	4,654.9	588.7	231.3	369.4	−12.0	742.0

Source: Calculations by the author on the basis of confidential data from the Bank of Mexico, CEPAL (Economic Commission for Latin America), and the World Bank.

TABLE 3.3A U.S. Investment in Mexico by Sector, 1897–1978 (in Percentages)

Year	Total[a]	%	Manufacturing	Mining	Petroleum	Railroads	Utilities	Other
1897	200	100	—	34.0	0.5	55.5	3.0	7.0
1908	416	100	2.4	56.2	12.0	13.7	5.3	10.4
1914	587	100	1.7	51.4	14.5	18.7	5.6	8.1
1919	644	100	1.2	34.5	31.0	19.1	4.9	9.3
1929	709	100	0.8	35.0	29.0	11.6	12.7	10.9
1940	357	100	2.8	47.0	11.8	32.5[b]		5.9
1946	316	100	21.0	35.0	2.0	35.0		6.0
1950	415	100	32.0	29.0	3.0	26.0		10.0
1960	795	100	49.0	16.0	4.0	15.0		16.0
1966	1,248	100	64.0	9.0	3.0	2.0		21.0
1970	1,786	100	67.0	9.0	2.0		22.0[c]	
1972	2,025	100	69.0	6.0	2.0		23.0	
1978	3,712	100	74.0	3.0	1.0		22.0	

Sources: For 1897–1940: Wilkins, *The Emergence of Multinational Enterprise* (1970), p. 110; and idem, *The Maturing of Multinational Enterprise* (1974), pp. 55, 182. For 1946–66: Newfarmer and Mueller, *Multinational Corporations in Brazil and Mexico* (1975), p. 51. For 1970–78: *Survey of Current Business*, various numbers.

[a]Total in millions of current U.S. dollars.
[b]Railroads and Utilities combined after 1940.
[c]Railroads, Utilities, and other combined after 1970.

TABLE 3.3B   Investment in Mexico by Sector, 1980–1990

Year	Total[a]	%	Industry	Services	Commercial Trade	Mining	Agriculture and Fishing
1980	8,459	100.0	77.5	8.5	8.9	5.0	0.10
1983	11,470	100.0	78.0	11.2	8.6	2.2	0.05
1987	20,927	100.0	75.0	17.2	6.0	1.7	0.10
1990	30,309	100.0	62.3	29.0	6.8	1.6	0.30

Source: Dirección General de Inversiones Extranjeras y Transferencia de Tecnología.
[a]Total in millions of current U.S. dollars.

zations that ended the dominance of extractive industries in foreign investment in Mexico.[25] As tables 3.3A and 3.3B show, the growth in absolute magnitude of U.S. foreign investment in Mexico was clearly due to the expansion of manufacturing industries. By 1970 over two thirds of all U.S. investment was in manufacturing, rising to three quarters by the mid-1970s.

Investment from the United States clearly predominated in the postwar period. The U.S. share of all foreign investment declined only slightly for manufacturing as a whole from 1957 to 1970, from 84.5 percent to 78.5 percent. The U.S. share declined modestly in chemicals and electrical machinery and more sharply in tobacco and transportation equipment; it increased in food products, especially in beverages. In none of these sectors, however, was the U.S. share less than 70 percent.

As total foreign investment in manufacturing industries grew from one third to two thirds of all foreign investment between 1950 and 1970, that manufacturing investment grew in value from U.S. $148 million in 1950 to U.S. $2,083 million in 1970. As table 3.4 shows, four industries have accounted for most of manufacturing investments in that period: chemicals, food and beverages, transportation equipment (including automobiles), and electrical machinery. Tobacco declined in relative importance; electrical machinery showed the greatest increase over the period.[26] Investments in Mexico in food products showed a slight decline relative to other manufacturing, with the sharpest decline in share between 1950 and 1955; beverages grew more steadily between 1950 and 1970. Manufacturing investment was greatest in those industries for which the growing Mexican population represented an important present and future market: consumer goods, nondurable and durable.

Since 1939, moderately reliable statistics exist for total foreign investment in Mexico, and since 1950, reinvested profits and outflows due to national acquisitions of shares in existing companies (nation-

TABLE 3.4 Mexico: Share of All Foreign Investment in Selected Manufacturing Industries, 1950–1970 (in Percentages)

	1950	1955	1960	1965	1970
Food, beverages, tobacco	25.7	20.1	13.4	14.3	14.1
Food	11.7	7.8	7.2	7.3	7.1
Beverages	1.7	2.6	3.3	2.6	4.2
Tobacco	12.3	9.7	2.9	4.4	2.8
Chemicals	26.2	27.3	35.4	30.0	29.7
Electrical machinery	4.9	9.3	8.7	7.6	10.3
Transportation equipment	12.8	9.6	6.1	13.0	10.2
Other manufacturing	30.4	33.7	36.4	35.1	35.7
Total manufacturing	100.0	100.0	100.0	100.0	100.0
Value (in millions of Current U.S. dollars)	147.9	331.5	602.2	2,206.4	2,083.1

Source: Sepúlveda and Chumacero, La inversión extranjera en México (1973), appendix.

alizations and Mexicanization) have been available as well. Table 3.2 gives a complete series on new investment, reinvested profits, acquisitions, and total direct investment.[27] The figures show that foreign investment was the major source of long-term foreign capital, from the start of the series in 1939, through the mid-1960s. For most of that period, due to the drawn-out conflicts over the petroleum expropriations, Mexico had been out of financial markets that were not mediated by foreign investors.

Foreign investment had come to play a major role in the manufacturing sector, a role disproportionate to its numbers. In 1965 (the date of the last industrial census prior to the new regulations of the early 1970s), firms with foreign participation accounted for less than 1 percent of all manufacturing firms but accounted for 16.9 percent of the industrial work force, 32.2 percent of the value of production, and 35.4 percent of invested capital. Firms with majority foreign ownership, only 0.58 percent of all firms, accounted for 10.2 percent of all industrial employment and 20.0 percent of both production and investment.[28] Even this does not reflect the importance of foreign-owned enterprises in the manufacturing sector, for majority foreign-owned firms accounted for 52 percent of the assets of the 300 largest manufacturing firms in Mexico by 1972 (see table 3.5). In chemicals, electrical machinery, and transportation equipment, between three fifths and four fifths of the assets of the largest firms were in majority foreign-owned enterprises. In the diverse food products sector, only one quarter of the assets were in foreign subsidiaries, but as we shall see later, foreign firms dominated particular product markets (such as canned milk and instant coffee), leaving others (such as tortillas, beer, and fresh milk) to national firms.

The largest firms accounted for a disproportionate share of the value of production. In a study of Mexican industry based on the 1965 census, Ricardo Cinta found that over half of the industrial production of 938 firms was concentrated in the largest 110 firms. Foreign-owned firms accounted for almost half of the production of those 110 firms; their share of production of all 938 firms was 26.7 percent.

In the period from World War II until the late 1960s, though foreign investment was a small part of total investment in the economy, its role in manufacturing was much greater.[29] As foreign investment moved out of extractive industries and utilities and increasingly into manufacturing in the decades following the war, foreign-owned firms accounted for important shares of capital and production, concentrated in large firms, in the most important and dynamic sectors of Mexican manufacturing industry. This was not

TABLE 3.5   Participation of Majority Foreign-Owned Firms in Mexico in
1972, by Sector and Ownership of Assets, in the Largest 300
Manufacturing Firms

| | Percentage of Assets | | | | | |
| | Majority foreign-owned | | | Mexican | | |
Sector (N)	U.S.	Other	Total Foreign	Private	State	Total Sample
Food (50)	20	6	26	67	7	100
Chemicals (48)	54	14	68	12	20	100
Electrical Machinery (25)	35	25	60	24	16	100
Transportation (18)	70	9	79	8	13	100
Total						
Manufacturing (300)	36	16	52	32	16	100

Source: Newfarmer and Mueller, Multinational Corporations in Brazil and Mexico (1975), p. 55.

accidental; it reflected not only the international push and domestic
pull of economic factors but also state policy.

Postwar Foreign Investment Policies:
Mexicanization and Regulation

The era from World War II to the late 1960s forms a coherent period
with respect to foreign investment in policy terms as well as economic
terms.[30] In manufacturing, the period as a whole was characterized
by state efforts to continue and deepen the process of import substitution, thus extending local production into new areas and encouraging the growth of local enterprise. Foreign investment was restricted in traditional areas but was encouraged and even welcomed
to the extent that it participated in the local production of manufactured goods that had previously been imported. As the preceding
section demonstrated, foreign enterprise responded energetically to
these new opportunities.

Mexicanization and Regulation in the 1940s

The Depression and World War II provided an opportunity for local
industry to get started in the production of consumer goods while

Mexico's major trading partner and investor, the United States, was occupied with more pressing concerns at home. But while these concerns and the 1938 expropriation of oil resulted in a sharp decline in the value of U.S. investments, other foreign investors displaced by the war were interested in investment opportunities in Mexico. Concerned about the possibility that these foreigners rather than Mexican entrepreneurs would benefit from the growth to come, President Manuel Avila Camacho (1940–46) took advantage of his extraordinary wartime powers to issue an Emergency Decree in 1944 that would serve as the major formal statement of official policy on foreign investment for more than two decades. Wright described the Emergency Decree of June 29, 1944, as follows: "It was feared that this [flight of capital from Europe] would be used to displace existing Mexican investments and to monopolize sectors of the economy and that a large-scale inflow of capital having no permanent ties to the economic and social interests of the country and its subsequent withdrawal to its country of origin after the war would result in severe damage to the Mexican economy."[31] Though the extraordinary powers of the president were lifted in 1945, the revoking decree provided executive orders relating to state intervention in the economy that would be retained with the force of law.

On the basis of this Emergency Decree and in the absence of other industry-specific legislation, the Ministry of Foreign Relations was given the authority to approve, deny, or condition the acquisition of existing companies, the formation of new companies, the purchase of any type of real estate, and concessions on mines, water, and combustible materials. Most important, the ministry was empowered to impose the requirements that in any firm, a majority of the directors must be Mexicans and that a majority of the capital must be owned by Mexicans. This nationalist condition, which was optional and was applied by the ministry on a case-by-case basis, has come to be known as Mexicanization. The perceived vulnerability of the economy resulting from foreign war thus provided a unique opportunity for the expansion of state policy.

In 1945, the Ministry of Foreign Relations issued an interim list of industries in which Mexicanization would be required; these were transportation and communication industries (domestic air and ground transport, radio broadcasting and motion pictures, and publishing and advertising), fishing and fisheries, and the production (and, in 1947, the distribution and sale) of carbonated beverages.[32] Although President Avila Camacho undertook other measures to foster import substitution by Mexican companies, such as the extension of import licenses, no further formalization of the rules on foreign investment took place during his administration.

Regulation by the state not only affected ownership but also provided protection to foreign patents and trademarks. In 1942, a thorough and well-drafted law (not decree) was passed governing patents, trademarks, and licenses. For the most part, this legislation was consistent with the international standards of the Convention of Paris for the Protection of Industrial Property of 1883, to which Mexico adhered. Patents were protected for fifteen years, reduced to twelve years if the patent was not industrially applied in Mexico; industrial designs were protected for ten or seven years under the same conditions. Standards of novelty were established for patents, and the priority of foreign patents was accepted in accord with the Paris Convention (or by reciprocity with states not members of the Convention). The most notable restriction was the exemption of chemical products from patentability, but chemical processes were patentable.

Trademarks were protected by the law for ten years, with unrestricted renewals; advertising slogans were granted one-time protection for ten years. Trademark protection could be canceled for nonuse if the trademark was not applied for five years. Both patents and trademarks were registered in offices of the Ministry of Industry and Commerce (earlier the Ministry of National Economy). Licenses governing their use were not controlled at all, however. By administrative practice, the ministry required the registration of agreements as proof of use of trademarks, but this was overturned in a case taken to the Mexican Supreme Court in 1959. Private contracts for the use of trademarks were thus unregulated at this time.[33]

President Miguel Alemán (1946–52) was the most active president in the postwar period in the development of policies on industrialization. Among the most important measures for industry were the decree on Executive Discretion (1948), which allowed administrative determination of all products subject to import and export licenses, and the Law on Economic Powers of the President (1950, regulated in 1951), which most notably established state control of prices.[34] Toward foreign investors, Alemán continued and extended the policies of his predecessor. In 1947, he established an interministerial commission on investment, with representatives of the presidency and six ministries. The commission met irregularly and ceased to function altogether under President Adolfo Ruíz Cortines (1952–58). During the time it functioned, however, it ratified the measures taken by the Ministry of Foreign Relations and extended the list of industries that required the Mexicanization of new enterprises to include shipping, rubber, international as well as domestic air transport, and fruit juices and noncarbonated beverages as well as carbonated soft drinks. Manufacturing imports were limited; foreign investment was encouraged.

Regulation of importers constituted promotion for foreign-owned producers.

Extended State Intervention in the 1950s

The major lasting contribution to development policy during the Ruíz Cortines administration was the enactment of the law on the Development of New and Necessary Industries, passed at the end of 1954 and in force for over two decades. This law relied on incentives rather than restrictions as a way to encourage investment in industries classified as "new" or "necessary," producing goods inconsistently or briefly available. Both new and necessary industries should fulfill the needs of industry and agriculture or supply food, clothing, and shelter. Together, the new and necessary industries were classified as "basic," "semibasic," and "secondary," with different provisions and exemption periods for each.

The package of measures (specified in extensive detail in regulations to the law) was aimed not at changing the ownership of enterprise but at regulating their operational practices or behavior. Foreign-owned firms were fully eligible if their production met the requirements. One of the major aims was to increase the "local content" of goods assembled in the country: industries in which imported materials exceeded 40 percent of the total were excluded from the benefits (article 6). The incentives were powerful not only because of the financial savings but also because they were designed to facilitate the supply of production equipment and raw materials, both of which could and did cause production bottlenecks. The exemptions on taxes of imported machinery and intermediate components were widely used; in time, this would undermine one of the goals of import substitution, namely, an improvement in the balance of payments. Ironically, import substitution would come to mean the substitution of one kind of imports for another.

Thus, by the late 1950s, following a mild recession and a major devaluation in 1954 (the last until 1976), Mexico was moving into the second stage of import substitution, producing consumer durables such as automobiles and some machinery as well as nondurable consumer goods. Barriers to imports of finished goods were maintained and increased, and tax subsidies were provided for the importation of intermediate and capital goods. A sophisticated set of monetary and fiscal policies held inflation to under 5 percent, thus ensuring a stable exchange rate. In this protected environment, subsidiaries of foreign enterprises in manufacturing industries increased their number and thrived.[35]

At the same time as these incentives were extended to manufacturing firms, both domestic and foreign owned, other policies aimed to complete the nationalization of utilities and some natural resources and to Mexicanize others. President Adolfo López Mateos (1958–64) took several important steps in this direction, ruling "on the extreme left within the Constitution."

This policy orientation accentuating not only nationalism but statism more generally was controversial. In particular, as Roger Hansen reported, national private capital did not appreciate the attitude of López Mateos, and "shortly after his term began in December 1958, approximately U.S. $250 million from the Mexican private sector fled the country in a matter of days; this was one of the major factors that led the president to soften both his words and actions very soon afterward."[36] Thus limited in the domestic changes he could pursue, López Mateos, moving more actively in the control of foreign investment, garnered broad support. Whereas antibusiness measures were divisive, nationalism served as a unifying ideology for the state, the local private sector, and labor and popular sectors.

During the López Mateos *sexenio*, the Mexican government extended state ownership of the energy industry in Mexico, including electric power and petroleum. In the last days of his administration,[37] Adolfo Ruíz Cortines had approved a regulation of article 27 of the Constitution extending state control not only to petroleum but also to primary petrochemicals, and expanding the powers of PEMEX, in effect granting greater powers of expropriation to the state-owned enterprise. In the next year, López Mateos followed this with an amendment to article 27 that reserved to the state all mining in petroleum-related areas. But the largest single move of his administration was the purchase of the major electricity producers, the Mexican Light and Power Company and the American and Foreign Power Company. Like petroleum, electric power was critical for development, both for industry and for domestic consumption. A series of rate conflicts had ensued between the state and the companies, since the state wanted low utility rates to encourage industrialization while the companies wanted higher rates not only for profits but also to expand capacity to meet demand. As the companies eventually saw elsewhere regarding investments in Latin America, rate conflicts have no easy or permanent solution, and the firms began to look for a way out.

For the López Mateos administration, torn by business opposition on the Right and pressures on the Left to support the new regime in Cuba, the nationalization of electric power was a dramatic and unifying measure that had the support of Left and Right alike.[38] In 1960, the state acquired the American and Foreign Power Company for 70 million dollars. The purchase was financed in March 1960 with credits from the Prudential Insurance Company of America, the "first long-term credit granted to Mexico since the Porfiriato by a foreign private financial institution without prior conditions for its use."[39] This started a trend. The outlay would, however, cause a negative balance in the flow of foreign investment for the year (see table 3.2). The beneficiary of the operation was the Federal Electricity Commission, which originated during the *maximato* of Calles and which became the second largest state-owned enterprise after PEMEX. The nationalization was celebrated as a historic event, with posters reading "Land—1917, Oil—1938, Electricity—1960."

Mining also came under increased control during the López Mateos administration with the 1961 mining law.[40] The 1930 mining law had set aside certain areas as "national mining reserves" subject to special regulations and granted the president the power to declare what lands would be included in the law. The 1961 law formalized the Mexicanization of the industry, requiring majority Mexican ownership. Requiring Mexican ownership had previously been only an informal practice. At least 51 percent of each new mining enterprise had to be owned by Mexicans, and on national mining reserves, 66 percent. The law was not retroactive—existing firms were given twenty-five-year concessions from the date of the law—but such large tax rebates were offered to companies that voluntarily Mexicanized that most firms found it more profitable to be a minority shareholder than to maintain majority ownership. Forestry and real estate ownership were also further restricted under López Mateos.[41]

In manufacturing, the López Mateos government was faced with the need to extend import substitution in order to expand industrialization. Since automobiles and parts constituted a significant part of Mexico's import bill (11 percent at the time) and because of the extensive forward and backward linkages of automobile manufacture, the auto industry was a prime candidate for regulation. The Automobile Manufacturing Decree of August 1962 required at least 60 percent local content (not just offering optional incentives) and reserved auto parts manufacture to domestic firms, limiting the operations the foreign firms could carry out. But other restrictions proposed by the national development bank, NAFINSA, and supported by some technocrats were *not* adopted by the state: strict limitations on the number of firms, required Mexicanization of ownership, and restrictions on model changes and product differentiation.[42]

The case is discussed in more detail in chapter 7. The point here is that the limits on regulation in the automobile industry must be seen in the context of other extensive interventions in the economy under López Mateos. The net effect of his administration was a substantial increase in state ownership and regulation.

Mexicanization in the 1960s

Foreign concern over the extension of Mexicanization, even when not retroactive, was not unfounded. Indeed, López Mateos had extended Mexicanization in chemicals and in food products—both representing larger shares of foreign investment in manufacturing in 1960 than transportation equipment. With the authority of the Emergency Decree of 1944, the Ministry of Foreign Relations between 1960 and 1963 extended the list of industries in which the formation or acquisition of majority foreign-owned enterprises would not be approved to include fertilizers, insecticides, and chemicals and the packing of marine products and the packing and preservation of food products.[43] Thus, although neither legislation nor decrees were adopted for these industries, the quiet intention to control the future expansion of majority foreign-owned firms was clear.

The effectiveness of these policies was weakened, however, by their shaky legal base. In 1961, the Ministry of Foreign Relations ruled that Química Industrial de Monterrey, S.A., would have to Mexicanize to obtain permission for the requested increase in capital. The Mexican Supreme Court granted relief to the company, supporting the claim that the Ministry of Foreign Relations did not have the authority to require evidence of majority Mexican control of the board of directors. Though this decision only applied to the company in question, it opened the door to the possibility of similar *amparo* (relief) suits and weakened the Emergency Decree as the basis for future policy.[44] Political and legal constraints limited presidential discretion.

Gustavo Díaz Ordaz (1964–70) has come to have a reputation as a pro-business and a law-and-order president. In the area of foreign investment he continued to extend the restrictions on foreign investment in many areas of the economy while welcoming new foreign investment in others. Certain actions of the new president indicated that he would favor new foreign investment. The extensions of the Mexicanization list of the Ministry of Foreign Relations to include fertilizers, insecticides, basic chemicals, and food products, adopted under López Mateos, were dropped. He also rescinded the requirement that Mexican companies investing in restricted industries must have a clause excluding foreigners—a requirement aimed at eliminating foreign investment in restricted industries through holding companies but lacking legal grounding. As a result of the lifting of these restrictions, a wave of new investment came into Mexico, with food products prominent among them.[45]

In one area Díaz Ordaz was an especially active promoter of foreign investment. For years Mexican workers had traveled legally to the United States under a binational agreement known as the Bracero Program. When that program was terminated in 1964, Mexican policymakers looked for a way to provide employment for the former migrants.

Observing the experience of Puerto Rico under Operation Bootstrap, which enabled U.S. firms to assemble manufactured goods abroad and re-import them to the United States, Mexico developed a similar option, known as the Maquiladora Program. Under the U.S. tariff code (sections 806.30 and 807), U.S. firms setting up assembly operations (e.g., in textiles, plastics, and electronics) were allowed to export components from the United States and re-import finished goods, paying duty only on the value-added. On the Mexican side, no tax was charged on the imported components, and firms were completely exempt from Mexicanization regulations.

Other measures taken by Díaz Ordaz were more consistent with economic nationalism, however. Following reports that several large foreign banks were negotiating the purchase of controlling shares of Mexican banks, a series of decrees was proclaimed in December 1965 forbidding any type of foreign participation in the capital of Mexican banks, insurance companies, bonding companies, or investment companies.[46] The president made clear that this was not designed only to protect Mexican industry, which might lose the preferential financing it received from Mexican banks under government stimulus, but to extend control over the financial industry more generally. The 1982 "nationalization" of the banking system was thus the extension of state control over Mexican-owned banks; foreigners (with the exception of Citibank) had long since been excluded.

Mexicanization was extended, in 1967, to 66 percent of the companies mining sulphur in Mexico, especially the majority foreign-owned subsidiaries of Pan American Sulphur and Texas Gulf Sulphur. Sulphur is an important raw material for the chemical and fertilizer industries, and in the first half of the 1960s it experienced a rapidly growing world demand. A number of foreign companies interested in exporting Mexican sulphur were anxious to enter Mexico and willing to Mexicanize in accord with the 1961 mining law, but they were not admitted. Mexican reserves had not expanded and in fact had declined. Thus the state wanted to prevent exports of Mexican sulphur. When the existing companies (which had not voluntarily Mexicanized) began to expand their planned exports, Mexican officials began to worry about future national needs and to encourage the firms to diversify into fertilizers and chemicals for the national market. But the two major companies increased their exports in 1964 to a level that, if continued, would have exhausted the existing Mexican reserves in nine years, and the state imposed export ceilings.

In another example of negative foreign reactions to nationalist policy, the foreign press and Senator Russell B. Long of Louisiana began to argue that the export limits were designed to force the U.S. firms out of business, and Senator Long argued for the application of the Hickenlooper Amendment and the reduction of Mexico's sugar quota. The result was the opposite of that intended. As Miguel Wionczek wrote, "If anything had been necessary to mobilize Mexican public opinion in support of state actions in sulphur, these attacks and threats served the case perfectly."[47] Though several new finds expanded the reserves, international prices remained high and foreign political pressures strong, and in October 1966 the Mexican government, together with a group of Mexican investors, made an offer to buy 66 percent of all the subsidiaries of Pan American Sulphur.[48] The offer, with adjustments, was accepted in 1967; and a similar arrangement was made with Texas Gulf Sulphur. Though the companies denied that there was Mexican pressure to accept the offers, the companies clearly would have preferred majority ownership, certainly at least as long as world prices remained high. Nevertheless, Mexican public opinion was against them, and other firms were willing to come in as minority partners in joint ventures. In contrast to the electric power case, sulphur can be considered a case of forced Mexicanization in which preferences were successfully translated into policy, even though no ultimatum was given specifying the consequences of refusal.

President Díaz Ordaz continued the policies of his predecessors in pushing for national control of natural resources and utilities and ensured continued national control of banking and insurance. Though he opened the way to the entry of foreign enterprise in some manufacturing industries at the beginning of his administration, at the end he closed the road to majority ownership of new ventures in several others. By a decree of June 1970, new companies in steel, cement, glass, fertilizers, cellulose, and aluminum were required to have at least 51 percent Mexican ownership and control.[49]

Perhaps more important in the long run was an administrative change in 1967 whereby the president removed sole authority for foreign investment decisions from the Ministry of Foreign Relations. After that date, every application for foreign investment was first submitted to the Ministry of Industry and Commerce for their determination of the amount of foreign ownership to be allowed.[50] This was a logical change, since Industry and Commerce was more likely to have the appropriate specialists and had already been involved with the regulation of foreign investors through its control of import permits and the evaluation of production plans (*programas de fabricación*) submitted to obtain the import permits. But it was also a change with far-reaching implications, for it gave the Ministry of Industry and Commerce the mission of regulating foreign investment, a mission they were to pursue actively in the next administration.[51]

Conclusion

By 1970 basic industries of power, natural resources, and transportation were under state ownership. Both ownership and performance were regulated in many others. But existing foreign enterprises in manufacturing industries were allowed to maintain their level of foreign ownership. And in some areas new foreign investment was actively promoted.

Four

Nationalist Regulation of Foreign Investment in the 1970s

MEXICO DEMONSTRATED consistent patterns of state intervention in the economy, as owner (through expropriation), as regulator, and as promoter of foreign investment, in the decades following World War II. In the 1970s these patterns were formalized, codified, and to a large extent enforced. Those actors with a nationalist development vision continued to dominate, increasing their ability to translate meta-preferences into policy and law. Foreign investors became the lightning rod for nationalism, in the context of a pragmatic acceptance of some foreign presence in Mexican industry. This chapter presents further evidence for state action consistent with a nationalist meta-preference. After discussing the problems of foreign investment as they were analyzed at the time, I discuss the 1973 foreign investment law, which officially oriented Mexican policy through the 1980s. In accordance with Krasner's analysis in *Structural Conflict*, the foreign investment law represents not only a nationalist metapreference but metapower: the ability of the state to change the rules of the game. The case is an early example of nationalist/statist preferences prevailing. It shows that the state had sufficient strength, bargaining power, and autonomy to design and implement a policy for which foreign firms, their home governments, and some within Mexico had no desire, eroding the liberal international regime, at least in one country. Its eventual reversal should not obscure the importance of nationalist regulation in Mexico's development.

Problems of Foreign Investment

By the time Luis Echeverría Alvarez (1970–76) assumed the presidency of Mexico on December 1, 1970, the country had been following a policy of import substitution industrialization (ISI) for three decades. In the course of this process, the country had changed from a predominantly rural society to a predominantly urban one, and manufacturing industries had assumed increasing importance in the economy. State policies had encouraged both the growth of industrialization in general and the development and strengthening of the national private sector. Although a series of policies adopted under previous administrations had restricted the role of foreign investment in nonmanufacturing sectors of the economy (excluding their participation altogether or limiting it to minority participation), foreign investment in manufacturing had for the most part been welcomed as complementing national private capital. As a consequence, by 1970 the largest part of foreign investment was located in manufacturing industries.

As table 4.1 shows, the share of subsidiaries of transnational enterprises in the value of production had increased from one fifth to more than one quarter from 1962 to 1970; the share of foreign-owned firms in both production and value-added had increased for the manufacturing sector as a whole and for each of the major industries within manufacturing. Nevertheless, the development pattern had not solved fundamental structural problems in the economy. Two problems in particular threatened to undermine government efforts to strengthen the national economy and national private capital: (1) the rapid increase in acquisitions of national manufacturing firms by foreign enterprises and (2) the increasing deficit in the balance of payments. Regional concentration and job creation for the burgeoning

TABLE 4.1 Foreign Share (Percentage) in Value of Production and Value-Added, Selected Manufacturing Industries

	Foreign Share of Value of Production		Foreign Share of GDP (Value-Added)	
	1962	1970	1962	1970
Food	4.9	8.6	3.4	6.1
Beverages	10.4	19.0	8.4	15.4
Tobacco	65.0	79.7	64.7	84.6
Chemicals	58.4	67.2	57.8	72.5
Electrical machinery	58.3	79.3	43.4	62.6
Transportation	42.6	49.1	33.3	35.5
All manufacturing	19.6	27.6	17.6	22.7

Source: Sepúlveda and Chumacero, *La inversión extranjera en México* (1973), appendix, tables 15 and 17.

population were other problems involving foreign investment, though for these issues the impact of foreign investment was less.

In this chapter, I emphasize the autonomous nature of the state action. But it should be clear from the outset that the conditions for complete autonomy were not met, and this discussion of policy choices must necessarily be complemented by a later discussion of constraints. Let us begin with some of the more salient problems observed in 1970 as a result of the process of ISI through DFI (direct foreign investment): the denationalization of industry through the acquisition of controlling interests in Mexican firms by foreign investors; declining balance of payments, exacerbated by foreign investment; and regional concentration, especially in Mexico City, made worse by the locational preferences of the foreign firms. Each of these problems contributed to a nationalist policy response.

Acquisitions

When transnational enterprises established subsidiaries in Mexico, the Mexican government expected these undertakings to contribute new capital, technology, and skills to the Mexican economy. As government pronouncements indicated, foreign investment was welcome precisely because it complemented the capabilities of existing national enterprise.[1] This expectation was called into question when, instead of establishing a new subsidiary "from scratch," the transnational enterprise acquired a previously existing Mexican firm. The advantages of acquisition for the transnational enterprise were clear: they were able to build on a base of existing productive capacity, knowledge and experience in the local market, and known and accepted products. But from the perspective of the national economy, the benefits of new capital were greatly diminished when that capital replaced rather than supplemented existing national investment. Moreover, when the nationally owned firm had been successful under its old owners, the contributions of technology and managerial expertise brought by new foreign owners were likely to be marginal. Rather than decreasing the concentration of industries, the acquisition of existing firms tended to increase that concentration and to give the new transnational subsidiary a head start in the industry. An acquired subsidiary combined local experience, trained workers, and established clientele with the technical, managerial, and financial resources of the parent firm. The foreign firm would thus begin its Mexican operations with an advantage that could be threatening to the remaining national firms in the industry.

Both the rate of entry into the Mexican market and the likelihood of entry via acquisition were increasing at the start of the 1970s. Data on the Mexican subsidiaries of both U.S. and non-U.S. parent companies from the Multinational Enterprise Project at Harvard University confirm that the number of subsidiaries in Mexico had been increasing steadily since before World War II (see table 4.2). A majority of the 322 subsidiaries reported by U.S. parent companies in 1975 were formed after 1964. The non-U.S. parent companies surveyed in 1971 reported that 60 percent of their Mexican subsidiaries were established after 1965. Of the subsidiaries reported in those samples, 50 percent of the U.S. subsidiaries, whatever their date of establishment, were newly formed (see table 4.3). Of those manufacturing subsidiaries of U.S. companies in Mexico, 30 percent had been directly acquired and 18 percent had been acquired through another subsidiary. This latter figure probably reflects the fact that the informal policy adopted under President Díaz Ordaz discouraging acquisitions of majority shares in existing firms by foreign enterprises had left open the possibility of their acquisition by other companies already established in Mexico, whatever their ownership structure. Manufacturing subsidiaries of non-U.S. parents were more likely to have been newly formed. In any event, more and more foreign firms were coming to Mexico, and many were buying Mexican firms.

These data do not directly demonstrate that the rate of acquisitions (rather than new formations of subsidiaries) had been increasing over time; however, other data do confirm that trend. An important study

TABLE 4.2   Entry of Foreign Firms in Mexico by Percentages, 1922–1975

Year of Entry	1975 Survey of U.S. Subsidiaries ($N = 322$)	1971 Survey of Non-U.S. Subsidiaries ($N = 96$)
Before 1922	—	1
1923–28	2	1
1929–34	2	0
1935–40	3	1
1941–46	4	1
1947–52	5	8
1953–58	11	13
1959–64	17	15
1965–70	29	60
1971–75	27	—
Total	100	100

Source: Harvard Multinational Enterprise Project, calculations by author.

TABLE 4.3   Method of Entry into Mexico of Foreign Subsidiaries in
Manufacturing, Harvard Sample of Multinational Parent Firms

	1975 Sample of All U.S. Subsidiaries (N = 317)	1971 Sample of All Non-U.S. Subsidiaries (N = 87)
Newly formed	50%	62%
Merger or breakup of subsidiaries	2%	3%
Directly acquired	30%	14%
Acquired via another acquisition	18%	21%
Total	100%	100%

Source: Harvard Multinational Enterprise Project, calculations by author.

by Newfarmer and Mueller for the Subcommittee on Multinational
Corporations of the Committee on Foreign Relations of the U.S. Senate provides the necessary evidence (see table 4.4).[2] Of 294 Mexican
subsidiaries in that sample, 43 percent had been acquired rather than
formed; this is roughly consistent with the Harvard data. However,
when one isolates the period 1966–73, the share of acquired subsidiaries rose to 67 percent; two thirds to three quarters of all the
subsidiaries established in that period in food, chemicals, and transportation equipment were acquisitions.[3] In short, as transnational enterprises increased their pace of investment in Mexican manufacturing, they were increasingly likely to do so by acquiring existing
Mexican firms.

Products produced by transnational subsidiaries were likely to be
produced by only a few other firms. Oligopoly (concentrated seller
markets) is usually measured at the level of specific product groupings.
In industrial classifications, this is usually indicated by four-digit numbers corresponding to each product class.[4]

Studies of industrial organization usually measure concentration
by calculating the sales of the four leading firms as a percentage of
sales of all products in that class. These data do not exist for Mexico.
A study based on the 1970 census, however, analyzed the concentration of production in the four leading plants in each of 238 four-digit
product classes.[5] This measure underestimates the true concentration
since several plants among the four largest may belong to the same
firm. (In food processing, for example, in seven of forty four-digit
classifications, two plants belonged to the same firm among the top
four plants, and in one class, three of the top four plants belonged

TABLE 4.4   Form of Establishment of Mexican Subsidiaries: Percentage
Acquired Rather than Newly Formed

	SRI Sample (N = 222)	Senate Sample	
		All (N = 294)	1966–73 (N = 109)
Food	35	43	77
Chemicals	33	37	68
Electrical machinery	12	28	33
Transportation	50	44	75
All manufacturing	33	43	67

Sources: Newfarmer and Mueller, *Multinational Corporations in Brazil and Mexico* (1975), pp 187–88.
SRI data are from Robinson and Smith, *The Impact of Foreign Private Investment on the Mexican Economy* (1976), p. 197.

to the same firm.)[6] Nevertheless, this study provided the best available indication of concentration and amply confirmed the correlation of foreign ownership and high concentration.

The study revealed that transnational subsidiaries owned at least one of the four largest plants in about two thirds of the four-digit product classes and owned all four in 10 percent of them. Newfarmer and Mueller summarized the Mexican data as follows:

> For manufacturing as a whole, 61 percent of MNC [multinational corporation] production was sold in markets where the largest four plants accounted for half or more of the market's total sales . . . The association between MNCs and concentrated industries can be seen in another way. Of all manufacturing sales in highly concentrated industries (with four-plant concentration ratios of greater than 75 percent), MNCs produced 71 percent while (national) enterprises produced 29 percent.[7]

Aggregate concentration of production and foreign ownership was somewhat lower. Table 4.5 presents the Mexican data on concentration of production, aggregating the various four-digit product classes for selected industries. On average, 42 percent of production in the four-digit sectors of the manufacturing industry were produced by the four largest plants. The share production by foreign subsidiaries, 34.9 percent of the total, tended to be highest in the industries where concentration was high.

The inflow of transnational enterprises was not accompanied by voluntary Mexicanization (joint ownership, with Mexicans holding a

TABLE 4.5   Foreign Ownership and Concentration of Production in the
Four Largest Plants, Aggregated for Selected Sectors

Sector	Foreignness (% Foreign Participation in Production)	Concentration (% Production in Four Largest Plants)
Food	21.5	32.2
Beverages	30.0	44.6
Tobacco	96.8	76.7
Chemicals	50.7	36.9
Electrical machinery	50.1	43.9
Transportation	64.0	55.4
Total manufacturing	34.9	42.6

Source: Fajnzylber and Martínez Tarragó, *Las empresas transnacionales* (1976), p. 186.

majority). Rather, most foreign subsidiaries in Mexico in the early
1970s were majority owned by the parent firm. Of 239 firms in a
survey conducted for the American Chamber of Commerce in Mexico,
85 percent were majority owned by foreigners. In the survey by Newfarmer and Mueller, 81 percent of 288 firms affiliated with transnational enterprises were majority owned. Moreover, in the latter
sample, 61 percent of these manufacturing subsidiaries reported 90
to 100 percent ownership of their equity by foreigners.[8] These figures
give a clear baseline for judging ownership at later dates.

The policy of ISI followed by the Mexican government resulted in
a significant internationalization of the economy. Transnational enterprises had invested in Mexican manufacturing in large numbers.
With increasing frequency they did so through the purchase of existing Mexican firms. Once established, they were likely to be producers in concentrated, oligopolistic product markets in which their
sales accounted for a significant proportion of total sales in the market.
Moreover, majority control of the equity of these subsidiaries (and
management control of the enterprise) rested with the foreign parent
corporations. This structural change in the Mexican economy represented a threat to Mexican domestic business, since the foreign firms
brought competitive advantages in marketing, technology, and fi-
nances. Evidence also began to accumulate indicating that the behavior of these foreign-controlled enterprises was contributing to other
problems in the Mexican economy. In particular, critics of foreign
investment noted that it actually worsened the balance of payments
for that country. Also, no mechanism existed to track, let alone bargain
with, the foreign firms.

Balance of Payments

The purpose of the program of ISI had been not only to build an industrial infrastructure in the country but also to reduce the imports of goods from abroad. The program in some respects had been successful. In a study of industrial policy prepared at the beginning of the Echeverría administration by the national development bank (NAFINSA) and the Economic Commission for Latin America (ECLA), a comparison of the structure of imports and exports at the beginning of the 1950s and at the end of the 1960s showed that imports of consumer goods had declined from 19 percent to 12 percent of total merchandise imports, and imports of intermediate goods (including fuels) had declined from 52 percent to 45 percent. On the export side, semimanufactured and manufactured goods as a percentage of total exports had risen from 32 percent in the 1950–52 period to 41 percent in the 1967–69 period.[9] This was cause for some satisfaction.

Nevertheless, Mexico's balance-of-payments situation was deteriorating. In only one year since 1950 had the balance-of-payments been positive. Moreover, when the balance is compared with Mexico's ability to pay (i.e., when the difference between exports and imports is divided by total exports), that ratio shows a fluctuating but steady decline. This situation was due in part to the very nature of the industrialization process: as production expanded, demand for imported components and machinery also expanded, but with no compensating exports. Capital goods had accounted for 29 percent of all imports in the 1950–52 period but had risen to 43 percent of a much higher import bill in 1967–69.[10]

Merchandise imports were not the only cause of foreign exchange outflows.[11] Remittances on foreign investments constituted the other major category of foreign exchange outflows that contributed to the growing balance-of-payments deficit.[12] (Remittances include repatriated profits as well as payments for patents, trademarks, know-how, etc.) From 1945 until about 1960, remittances on foreign investment represented about 6 percent of all outflows of foreign exchange from Mexico. But in the 1960s that share rose to 8 percent and hit 9 percent in 1969. Though foreign investment had contributed to Mexican industrialization, the cost of that contribution seemed to be rising.

On the basis of the usually published Mexican figures, it was difficult to know how much of the total amount remitted abroad was remitted as profit and how much as other payments. However, a 1971 study,[13] using data from the Bank of Mexico and the World Bank, broke down the payments abroad for the period 1960–69. Those data showed that payments for interest, royalties, technical assistance, and other payments were growing at a much faster rate than remitted profits: 13.1 percent for the ten-year period, compared with 3.5 percent for profit remittances. Moreover, precisely when the Mexican balance-of-payments was worsening in the last half of the 1960s, those remittances grew at almost 18 percent per year. This trend could be explained in part by preferential tax treatment to promote technical assistance. Until 1970, technical assistance was taxed on a sliding scale with a maximum of 20 percent, whereas royalty payments for patents and trademarks were taxed on a sliding scale with a maximum of 42 percent, the same as the tax on profits. Thus, the inflated figures were most likely in technical assistance payments.[14] A later study confirmed this: from 1960 to 1970, inclusive, technical assistance payments grew from U.S. $24.4 million to $85.5 million (15.4 percent); payments for licenses grew from $18.7 million to $40.2 million (8.0 percent).[15] Parent companies were well able to manage their accounts in order to take out profits under one category rather than another, and the data indicate that they were doing so.

The differential tax rate could be corrected with relative ease and this was done soon after President Echeverría took office. But the Mexican officials realized that they had almost no idea what they were getting for the $177.8 million paid in 1969 for "interest, royalties, and other payments." No systematic review or required registration of contracts existed in Mexico. There was no way to know what Mexican affiliates received or what contribution to the Mexican economy was obtained with these payments. Nor was it possible to evaluate whether less expensive alternatives were available.

By the mid-1970s, when the Fajnzylber and Martínez Tarragó study was completed, there was ample documentation for the fact that transnational enterprises were having a negative net impact on the balance of payments.[16] In the manufacturing sector foreign subsidiaries accounted for over one half of all imports, over one third of all imports by the private sector, and about half of all private sector imports of capital goods.[17] Of greater concern, repatriated profits and interest, royalties, and other payments constituted a growing net outflow of funds. Although the data for the early 1970s reported in that study were not yet available at the start of the Echeverría administration, the concern about the impact of transnational enterprises on the balance of payments had reached sufficient proportions for new policies to be considered.

The attitude was less one of hostility than one of pragmatism, at least in official circles, though confrontation was not uncommon. Without denying the contribution of transnational enterprises to the import substitution process that the government itself had encouraged, the problem of extending Mexican industrialization without worsening the balance-of-payments was considered to be the pressing issue. As the authors of the 1976 study put it, "What is important is to adopt measures to confront the commercial deficit that transnational enterprises actually generate . . . This is the reason the analysis . . . concentrated on the evaluation of the real situation and . . . avoided the question of what could have occurred if transnational enterprises had not participated in the industrialization of Mexico."[18]

Regional Concentration

Though not directly related to foreign investment per se, the concentration of industry in major urban areas, and especially in Mexico City, was an important policy concern at the beginning of the Echeverría administration. As a result, decentralization became one of the goals that would be pursued in later regulation of transnational enterprises in Mexico. Industrialization had been concentrated in three regions: Mexico City, Monterrey, and Guadalajara. Migration, as well as population growth, had caused an increasing concentration of population in urban areas: Mexico City had been growing at almost twice the rate of the rest of the country. The metropolitan area of Mexico City accounted for 14 percent of the total population in 1950, 17 percent in 1960, and 20 percent in 1970 (including the Federal District and the contiguous municipalities of the state of Mexico). Thirty percent of the industrial work force was already located in the capital in 1950, increasing to almost 36 percent by 1965. More significantly for industrialization policy, the share of the Federal District and the state of Mexico in total industrial production had grown from one third in 1950 to 53 percent in 1965. The second major industrial city of the country is Monterrey. When the state of Nuevo León (of which Monterrey is the capital) is added to the Federal District and the state of Mexico, the share of national industrial production of these three entities grew from 49 percent in 1950 to 64 percent in 1965.

At the same time, not only the poorest states but also the states at intermediate levels of development lost relative shares in national industrial production. Jalisco, Veracruz, Chihuahua, and Coahuila declined from 28 percent of the total to 18 percent in 1950, with the rest of the country accounting for only 18 percent in 1965.[19] Concentration continued to increase in the next decade as well; in 1975, two thirds of the value-added in manufacturing industries was located in the Mexico City and Monterrey metropolitan areas.[20] As industrialization proceeded, the largest and wealthiest areas of the country grew at the expense of other areas. In the absence of effective state policies to encourage decentralization by national and foreign enterprise, the process of regional concentration continued.

Regional disparities in Mexico during the period of postwar industrialization were documented by a joint study of NAFINSA and ECLA devoted to industrial policy and economic development in Mexico. That analysis emphasized the attraction of large consumer markets, skilled labor, technical assistance, and transportation and communications facilities. Business executives need to have easy access to government policymakers. Enterprises in Monterrey, the second largest manufacturing facility in the country, usually maintain offices in Mexico City, and Monterrey executives often spend one day a week or more in the capital. The NAFINSA/ECLA study suggested that the problem has tended to be self-reinforcing: "Industrial concentration increased demographic concentration and tended to attract infrastructure facilities and services in increasing volumes, which in turn contributed to increase the rhythm [of concentration]."[21]

Foreign investors were more concentrated geographically than other industries in Mexico. According to a 1967 study of the U.S. Department of Commerce,[22] of 837 subsidiaries of U.S. firms in Mexico in 1967, 645 (77 percent) were in the Federal District and the neighboring state of Mexico; another 79 were in Monterrey and the state of Nuevo León; and only 113 (13.5 percent) were in other states. Transnational enterprises contributed significantly to Mexico's regional concentration.

The Law to Promote Mexican Investment
and to Regulate Foreign Investment

The Law to Promote Mexican Investment and to Regulate Foreign Investment was approved by the Congress on February 16, 1973. (Excerpts from the law are given in appendix 2.) The law was published in the *Official Daily* in March and went into effect on May 9, 1973. This action occurred less than two months after a technology transfer law had been approved (see chap. 6). This foreign investment law codified existing regulations of ownership in Mexican industry and extended the norm of majority Mexican ownership to the entire manufacturing sector. This law responded to the growth of foreign investment in Mexico, the increase in acquisitions of existing Mexican firms by transnational enterprises in the 1960s, and the associated problems with the balance of payments.

Changing the Rules of the Game

Both the Mexican private business sector and the state were reacting strongly to the internationalization of the Mexican manufacturing industry. Although some businesses responded to the competition of transnational enterprises as early as the 1940s, most national firms had been willing to accept foreign investment as complementary to the capacity of domestic firms. However, acquisitions began to affect even the largest firms in Mexico, and competition increased as the concentration of industry grew. With these changes, support for an extension of Mexicanization increased.

Clearly, the businesses that sold out to foreigners were satisfied with their deals, but those national firms that remained were resentful. Even those Mexican businessmen who had been tolerant of foreign investment in the past came to share this point of view. Flavia DeRossi interviewed the head of one of the largest Mexican food-processing firms as part of her study of Mexican entrepreneurs. The firm had a long-standing licensing agreement with a large U.S. food processor but no foreign ownership of capital. DeRossi reports that this entrepreneur

> will never sell out and has turned down many offers, the most recent one for two hundred million pesos from an American concern; he had made his sons swear to him that they too will hang on . . . . He does not fear competition, although his competitors are world giants, such as Del Monte, Heinz, General Foods, United Fruit, Kraft, etc. He does not favor government protection but he is not overenthusiastic about the purchase of Mexican companies by Americans and considers the acquisition of the long established firm of Clemente Jacques, S.A., by the United Fruit Company . . . as particularly untimely.[23]

This Mexican entrepreneur is representative of those who felt that something had to be done. This attitude constitutes support for nationalist, not statist, policy—that is, for preserving local private ownership.

In a survey of Mexican entrepreneurs interviewed by Cinta, over 95 percent had relations of some kind with foreign firms, yet almost all supported restrictions on foreign investments.[24] Forty-seven percent thought these restrictions should be extensive and should limit the activities in which foreign investment would be accepted. As acquisitions increased, more and more Mexican businessmen came to believe that such acquisitions were not only "untimely" but should be restricted by the government. In 1966, at the twenty-first meeting of the Bilateral Businessmen's Committee, the proposal was made to study the benefits of foreign investment and "likewise the possible harm, if such were to exist, for the people and the country from where the investments originate and for the people and country that receive the investments."[25] The outcome of this proposed study, dubbed the "Fausto Miranda study" after its principal proponent, indicated the difference in perception between American and Mexican businessmen. Rather than a single report, each of the committees commissioned separate reports of their own. Herbert May undertook the U.S. section's report, and a committee undertook the study for the Mexican section. Fausto Miranda described the two reports:

> The difference in the two studies is that whereas the United States section study endeavors to prove quantitatively that direct private investment has been good for Mexico, the Mexican study wanted to investigate not only the quantitative aspects but also the qualitative aspects; and . . . more than anything else—some of the reasons why we consider that though all direct private foreign investment and the transfer of technology are beneficial under certain conditions, Mexico has historically decided and endeavored to base its economy principally, though not exclusively, on its own means and manner.[26]

Well before either of those studies was published (in 1971), a prominent Mexican lawyer, José Luis Siqueiros, published an article in a legal journal in which he called for a new law to regulate foreign investment. Criticizing the existing conglomeration of rules and regulations based principally on the 1944 Emergency Decree, Siqueiros concluded that the

> present legislation is from any light obsolete, heterogeneous, and in many cases unconstitutional. With a new law on foreign investment the disparate and imprecise administration policies would be fortified; the systemization and homogeneity that is required would be maintained, abating their content. What is more important, one of the postulates of law [del Derecho] would be achieved: juridical security.[27]

Academics such as Pablo González Casanova, of the National University, and Daniel Cosío Villegas, founder of El Colegio de México, had been calling for increased regulation of foreign investment for several decades. When the primary responsibility for decisions on foreign investment passed from the Ministry of Foreign Relations to the Ministry of Industry and Commerce at the behest of President Díaz Ordaz in 1967, that ministry began to study ways to systematize the regulation of foreign investment. By the time Luis Echeverría assumed the presidency in 1970, a growing national consensus was building in support of regulating new foreign investment in Mexico, though there was still disagreement concerning the exact form the regulation should take. In his inaugural address on December 1, Echeverría emphasized the belief of the Mexican government, already well established in practice, that foreign investment should complement and not displace national business. He also criticized those Mexican businessmen who sold their enterprises to foreigners and echoed, in a more moderate way, the challenge that Lázaro Cárdenas had offered to businessmen who were tired of struggle. Cárdenas had suggested that businessmen who did not wish to negotiate with labor could turn their enterprises over to the state; Echeverría suggested that businessmen who sold their enterprises to foreigners should turn them over instead to Mexican entrepreneurs willing to carry on.[28] Two days later, on December 3, 1970, in a private Mexican home, the new president addressed a group of sixty businessmen (twenty-three Mexicans and thirty-seven foreigners) on the subject of foreign investment:

> For the international industrial and economic struggle and because of the increase of our population (and I want to say it without circumlocution), to progress we need great national and foreign capital and great technology . . . We think that investors and creators of technological innovations must certainly obtain a fair contribution for their creative efforts and for their risks, but Mexico needs to compensate that explainable outgo of currency with exports and new investments . . . To this end there is a good panorama in Mexico. We do not have an expropriating mentality. There will not be any modifications in the rate of exchange. This government will be a government of guarantees. Our friends who come to share responsibility in investment and in industrial production should be at ease, and we expect of them the feeling that all must cooperate toward a solid Mexican economy.[29]

The new president was able to keep his word regarding the free convertibility of currency and undoubtedly would have liked to have maintained the exchange rate, which finally fell in the last months of his administration.[30] However, as the Mexican lawyer Siqueiros had pointed out several years earlier, a new law on foreign investment would not be inconsistent with a "government of guarantees."[31]

Nationalism and the Private Sector

During the Echeverría administration, the level of conflict between the state and private business escalated. On the issue of the regulation of foreign investment, however, the local business community generally supported state regulation. Both points are illustrated by the Guajardo Suárez affair. In the first month after Echeverría took office, a dramatic conflict developed between the president and the private employers association COPARMEX. On December 16 and December 17, COPARMEX issued several public statements criticizing both the policies of the new administration and the way in which those policies were being adopted.

The policies that most disturbed COPARMEX were the proposed increases in the budgets of state-owned enterprises, price controls, a proposed tax on luxury items, the elimination of a tax deduction for 50 percent of advertising expenditures, and an increase in the tax on payments for technical assistance to the same level as the tax on dividends. The COPARMEX statement of December 17, 1970, proclaimed that "in effect, a mistaken fiscal policy, an unfounded control of price, and exaggerated interventionism of the state constitute factors that have seriously threatened national progress."[32] COPARMEX noted with approval the "healthy custom" of previous administrations of discussing policy initiatives with the national business sector before submitting them to the Congress. COPARMEX cited with approval the practice of the Ministry of Finance with respect to the income tax law, profit sharing, and value-added tax, and the practice of the Ministry of Labor with respect to the Federal Labor Law. In the latter case, COPARMEX noted that the ministry had "established a constructive dialogue that allowed the accomplishment of substantial modifications to [the labor law initiative] before it was sent to the legislature."[33]

On January 28, 1971, President Echeverría held a meeting with representatives of COPARMEX. Without prior warning to the representatives of private industry present, the president had invited the press to cover the meeting, including live television coverage. Subsequent commentaries suggested that the text of the prepared COPARMEX statement had been leaked to the president, who was in a combative mood. The president of COPARMEX, Roberto Guajardo Suárez, began by praising the initiatives of the new administration, including the formation of organizations "worthy of applause" (including the Mexican Foreign Trade Institute [IMCE] and the National Council on Science and Technology [CONACYT]); the selection of cabinet ministers; and government campaigns against corruption, bureaucratization, and contraband. But most of his comments were directed against the reliance of the government on personal friends in the private sector rather than on business organizations, and at specific criticism of new policies proposed by the government. Implicit in the criticisms was the suggestion that such policies could result in a decline in private investments in the economy.

Among the conclusions presented by Guajardo Suárez were the suggestions that ministers of the Echeverría administration should hear the recommendations of business organizations and that a publicity campaign should be undertaken "to encourage national and foreign investment." It is relevant to note that although none of the top officials of COPARMEX were affiliated directly with foreign investors, eleven out of fifty board members and advisers held their primary positions in firms associated with transnational enterprises, including the Mexican affiliates of Pepsi Cola, Kimberly Clark, Hooker Chemical, Sears Roebuck, and Phelps Dodge. The Phelps Dodge board member Jorge Sánchez Mejorada later became the president of CONCAMIN (the national chamber of industry). The interests of private business, both national and foreign, were vigorously promoted by the private association.

The president responded aggressively. He defended the practice of Mexican functionaries who consulted their friends in the private sector and, with respect to consultations with business organizations, commented that "you may be sure that if the Constitution of the Republic ordered me to send my proposals for laws to the Employers Confederation of the Mexican Republic [COPARMEX], you would have had them from the very beginning." The president then addressed the leader of COPARMEX:

> I have never heard you, sir, demonstrate disapproval of Mexican businessmen that sell their enterprises to foreigners. I believe that a businessman or a director of businessmen, such as you are, who wants to be really influential with ideas that are always affirmative of the welfare of Mexico should be recommending, rather than unjustified criticisms of the government (for much of the recommendations of this document are unjustified), should be recommending that his associates in the organization care for the patriotic interests represented by each Mexican industry. It is not possible that contradictory interests, some of which really affect the economic future of Mexico and others that show a healthy nationalism, can be made to coexist within an organization such as the one you direct.

Roberto Guajardo Suárez tried to clear his name of the charges made by the president that he was not a nationalistic Mexican businessman. In February 1971, COPARMEX circulated a booklet that reproduced the exchange between the president of the Republic and the president of COPARMEX. It also included a summary of recommendations that had been made at a meeting of COPARMEX in 1967 in which the necessity of foreign investment was confirmed, but public policies were recommended to ensure that foreign investment would complement national investment; to avoid the "de-Mexicanization" of industries through foreign acquisitions; to avoid the "case-by-case and discretionary treatment" of foreign investors by the public sector, unless the opinion of the business sector were taken into account; and to "limit and reject foreign investments that endanger the sovereignty, economic, political, and monetary stability, the balance of payments, and in general the economic and social development of the country." In addition, statements by Guajardo Suárez himself supporting these positions between 1967 and 1970 were reproduced.[34]

During the first two years of his administration, Echeverría and his ministers continued to exchange vigorous criticisms with the private sector, both national and foreign. The commitment of the government to pursue the regulation of foreign investment became clearer. Indeed the president became a spokesman for such regulation internationally when he proposed the Charter of Economic Rights and Duties of States to the third session of the United Nations Conference on Trade and Development (UNCTAD) in Santiago, Chile, on April 19, 1972. By the last quarter of that year, the intention of the government to regulate foreign investment more explicitly and the transfer of technology were evident.

Challenging U.S. Preferences

The concern generated among foreign enterprises and the Mexican intention to carry out more systematic regulation were both evident in an exchange between the U.S. ambassador and the undersecretary of industry and commerce. Some who are inclined to folkloric explanations of policy cite this exchange as the proximate cause of the 1973 foreign investment law. At the U.S.-Mexican Bilateral Businessmen's Committee convention in Acapulco in October 1972, the ambassador of the United States, Robert H. McBride, asked if the rules of the game were changing:

> As part of my job I am frequently in contact with business representatives both from the United States and from Mexico. Allow me to say with much frankness that I have noted an attitude not of

alarm but of a certain concern. Many are no longer certain whether foreign investment is wanted or unwanted and whether the rules of the game may change—not only as far as new investments but also with respect to already established firms. I hope that this committee with all its richness of knowledge and experience in relation to business both in the United States and in Mexico can assist in the clarification of this important topic of economic activity between our two sister countries.[35]

In response, the undersecretary of industry and commerce (soon to become secretary), Lic. José Campillo Sáinz, answered, "Sí, señores, estamos cambiando las reglas del juego! (Yes, gentlemen, we are changing the rules of the game!)." The theme of the undersecretary's talk was Mexicanization: "We want—as I said in a talk before the American Management Association—Mexicans to be partners, not employees [*socios, no empleados*], of foreign capital; co-participants and friends, not subordinates."[36]

Campillo Sáinz went on to specify the regulations of foreign investment that Mexico proposed. It was clear that his remarks were not in specific response to Ambassador McBride's questions, for his description closely paralleled the text of the new law that would be sent to Congress in December 1972. The undersecretary gave an extensive justification for Mexican policy toward foreign investment. His comments are worth citing at length, for they illustrate clearly the Mexican philosophy of state intervention in the economy and the metapreference for the regulation of foreign investment. This philosophy, with roots going back to Cárdenas and the 1917 Constitution, perhaps better termed an ideology, suggests that the state must intervene in economic relations between unequal parties on the side of the weaker:

> Not only in Mexico but in the whole world, the topic of foreign investments should be raised, asking ourselves if the investments coming from abroad should be determined exclusively by the results or the profits that the foreigner hopes to gain from them, or whether they should also and fundamentally be considered an instrument that aids the development of the countries which receive them.[37]

He went on to say to the assembled businessmen in Acapulco:

> No one any longer debates the legitimacy of the principles that justify a minimum wage, a maximum working day, and a social security system. And that is because we recognize the necessity to

regulate the relations between the strong and the weak, in order
that it should be the law that establishes equality and justice between
them, and this [principle], which is applicable as an indisputable
principle of social justice in the internal politics of each country, in
yours and in ours, is also applicable in international relations.[38]

In the process of industrialization in Mexico, the Mexican private
sector was weak and transnational enterprises were strong; the state
stepped in to even the balance.

Regulation under the 1973 Law

The Law to Promote Mexican Investment and to Regulate Foreign
Investment established the National Foreign Investment Commission,
including the ministers of the Interior, Foreign Affairs, Treasury,
National Property, Industry and Commerce, Labor, and the presidency.[39] The commission was charged to establish general criteria for
foreign investment and evaluate the applications of foreign individuals, foreign corporations, other foreign entities, and Mexican companies in which foreign capital represented a majority. A registry was
also established in which the names of all foreign investors, the amount
of their investments, and any management agreements would be
recorded, as well as the applications for exceptions to the law and the
decisions of the commission. An executive secretary served the commission and headed the registry. (Appendices 2–4 include the text of
several of the most important articles of the foreign investment law,
the technology transfer law, and the Law on Inventions and Trademarks.)

The foreign investment law specified those industries reserved exclusively for the state on the basis of past expropriations, nationali-
zations, or policies. These industries fell into three principal categories: transportation, communications, and energy (see article 4).
Those activities not reserved for the state in these three categories
were reserved for Mexicans or for 100 percent Mexican companies.
Foreigners were prohibited from owning more than 34 percent of
mining operations on national mineral reserves or more than 49 percent elsewhere; in the secondary petrochemical industry and in the
manufacture of automobile components, a maximum of 40 percent
capital could be held by foreigners. In all other industries, foreign
investment was allowed up to 49 percent, unless the permission of
the National Foreign Investment Commission was obtained to allow
ownership to exceed 49 percent.

The 1973 law on foreign investment expanded the scope of past policy by extending to all industries the norm of minority foreign ownership. Only by application and negotiation with the National Foreign Investment Commission was it possible for a foreign individual or enterprise to achieve majority ownership of a Mexican firm. Permission was required for the acquisition of more than 25 percent of the capital or more than 49 percent of the fixed assets of any company.

The law did allow for exceptions. Article 13 provided seventeen guidelines for the decisions of the commission. Nevertheless, the major concern of the 1960s, the acquisition of Mexican companies by foreigners, had been addressed. The law brought under the control of the state any foreign acquisition of a majority share in a Mexican company.

Besides the seventeen guidelines for exceptions, the major loophole was the automatic approval of existing foreign investment at the current levels of ownership. The law was only applicable to new investments; this grandfather clause seriously weakened the law. All enterprises existing prior to the effective date of the law in which foreigners held majority shares were allowed to continue to exist and to increase their capital as long as the proportion of foreign to national capital remained the same. In contrast to the law on mining, which required Mexicanization after twenty-five years, and unlike the "fade-out" norms established for the countries of the Andean Common Market in their Decision 24, no fade-out provisions were included in the law. The concern of Ambassador McBride for already-existing companies proved unwarranted. Moreover, the activities of firms in which foreigners owned less than 49 percent did not fall under the authority of the commission; only registration, not permission, was required. Although the law stated that decisions by the commission were required when effective control of a company was in foreign hands, even though a minority of the capital was held by foreigners, there was no mechanism for determining the actual control of a company. The law was thus based on the assumption that Mexicanization of a majority of capital entails the retention of management control by Mexicans, a presumption yet to be supported. Several researchers have questioned this presumption for Mexico and for other countries.[40]

The Mexicanization provisions of the law were reinforced by the incentive structure of Mexican industrial policy. Registration with the foreign investment registry was required in order to enjoy the benefits provided by tax and import incentives. Provisions for evasion of the law included fines as well as the loss of such incentives. Most documents in Mexico were required to be notarized, and notaries that approved documents without the required proof of registration risked their licenses. Nevertheless, a major enforcement loophole still existed. In Mexico, shares in companies had long been anonymous "bearer" shares. Although it was proposed that all shares should become nominative in order to ensure the identification of foreign investors, this provision was not adopted, due to the opposition of the Mexican private sector. Only foreign-owned shares were required to be registered, thus leaving open the possibility of evasion through the use of Mexican fronts, or *prestanombres* (literally, name-lenders). Although there is little direct evidence that major foreign investors utilize *prestanombres* to evade Mexicanization requirements for new investment, rumors still circulate about the existence of such illegal arrangements. Several small-scale foreign investors explained to me quite openly the arrangements they had with their Mexican partners.[41] Mexican lawyers routinely serve on the boards of directors of foreign firms to satisfy the majority Mexican management requirement.

The law gave considerable leeway to the commission, reflecting the ample executive discretion that is part of Mexican politics and was part of the law itself. One lawyer critical of the commission commented to me, "They could have simplified the law by having it read only, 'The Commission can do what it wants, when it wants, and how it wants.' " Nevertheless, the commission was limited by the text of the law, and firms had access to the Mexican courts to challenge its decisions.

Corruption is always a potential problem in the implementation of laws and policies. The structure of the commission was designed to minimize this problem, however. One argument for having a foreign investment commission composed of seven secretaries, who met once a month whenever a quorum of four secretaries or undersecretaries was present, was that such a group would be more immune to corruption than a single minister. As one technocrat in the Ministry of Industry and Commerce (now Commerce and Industrial Development) suggested, "With such massive investment decisions in the hands of one minister, the temptations would be too great for any man to resist." The commission and the foreign investment registry initially shared the good reputation that the technology transfer registry achieved. One low-level employee in the registry was dismissed for accepting bribes, but the problem was endemic here as elsewhere in Mexico. Some officials complained that certain lawyers representing foreign investors were more likely to propose improprieties than the executives of the firms themselves, who hardly ever made such proposals. Some even suggested that this was the major service that lawyers offered. Corruption extended to judicial proceedings. More than one official pointed out to me one of the country's most prominent lawyers who always won his cases before certain judges. This same lawyer spoke on the law at a meeting I attended; he proposed a collection from the lawyers present to create a fund to buy information from within the registries. In an earlier essay, I wrote that the foreign investment and technology transfer offices seemed exempt from corruption. Upon reading it, a former high official in the ministry commented that the compliment was unwarranted (*fuera de justicia*).

Outcomes of the Regulation of Foreign Investment

Acknowledging the limitations of Mexico's regulations on foreign investment, including the grandfather clause and the possibilities of corruption, should not deter us from an appreciation of the magnitude of the change from an unregulated to a regulated environment. All foreign investment was now required to register the details of their activities and ownership structures with the National Registry on Foreign Investment. The majority-owned enterprises, new establishments, new lines of business, and transfer of shares among majority foreign-owned enterprises all required the approval of the National Foreign Investment Commission. What effect have these regulations had on the profile of foreign investment in Mexico? The data presented in tables 4.1–4.5 allow several conclusions. First, foreign investment has continued to flow into Mexico, although the rate has varied. Second, there has been a notable shift away from majority ownership and a corresponding increase in minority partnerships. Third, there has been a marked shift away from the United States as the main source of foreign investment. Fourth, foreign investment continues to be an important source of employment, disproportionate to its share in the economy. Fifth, these gains in Mexico's development goals notwithstanding, the first dozen years under the regulatory regime produced little progress toward the major objective, namely, an improvement in the balance of payments. It was not until 1986 that the performance of foreign enterprises on the external account turned positive, and by then policy had shifted toward export promotion.

The first and most striking result of the regulation of foreign investment in Mexico is that, contrary to dire predictions, the flow of foreign investment capital into Mexico was not deterred. In every year from 1971 through 1987, net inflows of direct investment capital have gone to Mexico. At times, the rate of increase in new investments has slowed (see table 4.6). However, the accumulated stock of foreign

TABLE 4.6   Value of Accumulated Foreign Investment (in Millions of
Current U.S. Dollars)

Year	New Investment	% Change	Accumulated Investment	% Change
1973	287.3	51.3	4,359.5	7.1
1974	362.2	26.1	4,721.7	8.3
1975	295.0	−18.6	5,016.7	6.2
1976	299.1	1.4	5,315.8	6.0
1977	327.1	9.4	5,642.9	6.2
1978	383.3	17.2	6,026.2	6.8
1979	810.0	111.3	6,836.2	13.4
1980	1,622.6	100.3	8,458.8	23.7
1981	1,701.1	4.8	10,159.9	20.1
1982	626.5	−63.2	10,786.4	6.2
1983	683.7	9.1	11,470.1	6.3
1984	1,442.2	110.9	12,899.9	12.5
1985	1,871.0	29.7	14,628.9	13.4
1986	2,420.9	29.4	17,049.8	16.5
1987[a]	3,877.2	60.1	20.927.0	22.7
1988[a]	1,943.3	—	22,870.3	—

Source: Dirección General de Inversiones Extranjeras y Transferencia de Tecnología, *Anuario es-*
tadístico (Mexico City, 1989). Preliminary data for 1989 showed $2,476 million in new investment,
and 1990 was estimated at $4 billion (Diane Lindquist, "Can Mexico Draw Foreign Investments?"
San Diego Union, January 13, 1991, p. I–1.)

[a]Preliminary data; information to September 1988.

Note: Certain changes to take capital adjustments into account were made for 1984 and 1985 but
not for subsequent years, according to the source document. Changes in new investment for 1971
and 1972 were 16.3% and 12.9%, respectively. Changes in stocks for those years were 4.5% and
4.9%, respectively.

investment has increased every year at rates ranging from 6 percent
to over 23 percent. Every year since the law was passed in 1973, the
stock of foreign investment has increased at a faster pace than the
increases of 1971 and 1972. Several trends stand out. First, the rate
of increase after 1979 has been much more rapid than during the
1970s. Second, the rate of increase has slowed in the years leading
up to major devaluations (1976 and 1982). But the weight of the
evidence suggests that foreign direct investors were not deterred by
Mexico's regulations.

A second major result of foreign investment regulation was that
foreign investment increasingly went to Mexico in minority shares.
As we have already demonstrated, prior to the regulations the great
majority of foreign investors were majority or sole owners of their
subsidiaries. By 1988, as table 4.7 illustrates, only 40.7 percent of the
8,316 firms with foreign investment owned more than 49 percent of

TABLE 4.7   Mexican Enterprises Registered in the National Registry on Foreign Investment by Sector and Percentage of Foreign Ownership, 1988

Sector	Number of Enterprises	Up to 24.9%	25.0%– 49.0%	49.01%– 100%	% of All Firms
Agriculture	40	2	18	20	0.5
Mining	307	22	267	18	3.7
Manufacturing	4,443	325	2,078	2,040	53.4
Commerce	1,595	140	771	684	19.2
Services	1,931	220	1,093	618	23.2
Total	8,316	709	4,227	3,380	100.0
Share of total		8.5	50.8	40.7	100.0

Source: Dirección General de Inversiones Extranjeras y Transferencia de Tecnología, *Anuario estadístico* (Mexico City, 1989).

Note: The total does not reflect firms that were eliminated from the registry in 1986 and 1987 due to Mexicanizations, liquidation, etc. Data are current through September 30, 1988.

the capital of the subsidiary. Over half, 50.8 percent, of the firms held between 25 and 49 percent, while the remainder, 8.5 percent, held less one quarter of the capital of their firms. Mexicanization clearly affected large numbers of foreign investors.

Over the last fifteen years, we can observe a sharp decline in the dominance of the United States and the accumulated stock of foreign investment (see table 4.8). In 1973 U.S. firms held 76.6 percent of the stock of foreign investment in Mexico. Over the next fifteen years, this declined to 65.5 percent. Given the preponderance of U.S. investment in the past, however, this gradual reduction in the U.S. share is due to much more marked reductions in the annual flows of investment.

Although foreign investment tends to be capital intensive on the whole, nevertheless it has provided a significant number of jobs in the Mexican economy. As table 4.9 illustrates, from the sample of firms registered with the Mexican Social Security Institute, firms with some degree of foreign investment accounted in 1986 for approximately 12 percent of the 6.2 million jobs that the sample registered. Since the numbers do not match those reported by the National Registry on Foreign Investment, it is difficult to know if the proportion of all jobs in Mexico is this high; but at least for a set of industrial enterprises, it seems that the foreign share of employment generation is growing. The probable explanation is both the rapid increase in recent years of foreign investment, at a time when general investment

TABLE 4.8   Origin of Accumulated Foreign Investment (Percentage by Country), 1973–1990

	1973	1978	1983	1987	1990
United States	76.6	69.8	66.3	65.5	63.0
West Germany	4.2	7.3	8.5	6.9	6.3
Japan	1.5	4.8	6.3	5.6	5.0
Switzerland	3.9	5.5	5.1	4.4	4.5
Spain	0.4	1.4	3.1	2.9	2.6
Great Britain	4.1	3.6	3.1	4.7	6.7
France	1.3	1.3	2.0	2.8	2.9
Sweden	1.7	1.5	1.5	1.4	1.3
Canada	2.2	1.8	1.4	1.4	1.4
Netherlands and Belgium	1.2	1.8	1.0	1.0	1.0
Italy	1.6	0.6	0.3	0.2	0.2
Others[a]	1.3	0.5	0.9	3.2	5.1
Total	100.0	100.0	100.0	100.0	100.0

Source: Dirección General de Inversiones Extranjeras y Transferencia de Tecnología.
[a]Includes Denmark, Norway, Finland, etc.

TABLE 4.9   Employment: Distribution by Sector of Firms with Foreign Capital, 1986

	Total		Firms with Foreign Capital		
Sector	Firms	Workers	Firms	Workers	Participation in Sector (%)
Agriculture	25,449	200,275	19	653	0.33
Mining	1,094	45,701	111	9,298	20.35
Manufacturing Industry	89,087	2,574,034	1,441	506,596	19.68
Construction	14,683	150,535	43	4,212	2.80
Trade	144,548	1,345,833	492	43,411	3.23
Transportation, communications	20,791	412,746	53	43,083	10.44
Other services	78,358	1,058,104	1,057	148,348	14.02
Subtotal	374,010	5,787,228	3,216	755,601	13.05
Other activities without foreign investment participation	49,790	435,388	—	—	—
Total	423,800	6,222,716	3,216	755,601	12.14

Source: Dirección General de Inversiones Extranjeras y Transferencia de Tecnología, Anuario estadístico (Mexi City, 1989). The estimates for the total numbers of firms and workers are derived from data compiled by t Mexican Social Security Institute.

in Mexico has been stagnant, and the especially rapid increase of export-oriented production and more labor-intensive segments of industry.

The indicators of continued flows of foreign investment, control of acquisitions and majority ownership, diversification of sources, and job creation all point in the direction of successful implementation of the foreign investment law. However, a major goal of the regulations was to improve the performance of the foreign-owned sector in the balance of payments, and here the record was negative. The period 1973–74 marked a shift in the composition of outflows, indicated by

1. an acceleration in long-term trends toward fewer remitted profits and more interest payments;
2. reduced payments for royalties and technical assistance and increased payments for miscellaneous charges such as technical visitors, commissions, and so forth;
3. increased total outflows of payments on foreign investment and increased reinvested profits.

Indeed, for every year after 1973, outflows as a share of the stock of foreign investment, reinvested profits, and the sum of the two reached record levels. Outflows increased by approximately 25 percent between 1972 and 1979; total outflows plus reinvested profits increased from 16.6 percent to 24.5 percent over this period.[42] This result seems to suggest that firms maneuvered financial flows among categories and regarded the regulatory environment as a risk to be compensated for by additional financial rewards. If this is a fair conclusion, the impact of the regulation of foreign investment had precisely the opposite effect than was intended in one area of prime concern to the policy designers.

Table 4.10 reflects the changes that have taken place in the overall foreign exchange operations of firms with foreign capital. For the period 1978–82, foreign firms showed a net negative balance of trade; a negative outflow of remitted profits, royalties, interest, and reinvested profits; and a net negative balance of current and capital accounts. These discouraging outcomes, combined with the crisis of 1982, led to a liberalization of trade and investment policies during the De la Madrid (1982–88) and Salinas (1988–) administrations. By 1986 the trade balance had turned positive; by 1987 the positive balance of trade was sufficient to offset other current outflows and produce a positive balance in the current account, amounting to over 1 billion dollars. At the same time, net flows of foreign investment on the capital account were accelerating rapidly, and the overall balance

TABLE 4.10 Foreign Exchange Operations of Firms with Foreign Capital (in Millions of U.S. Dollars)

Concept	Cumulative 1978–82	1983	1984	1985	1986	1987ᵃ	Cumulative 1983–1987ᵃ
Current account	-22,564	-968	-954	-1,943	-133	1,110	-2,888
Trade balance	-13,249	225	236	-915	896	1,886	2,328
Exports	6,453	1,673	2,780	3,430	5,520	6,829	20,232
Imports	-19,702	-1,448	-2,544	-4,345	-4,624	-4,943	-17,904
Tourism revenue	443	98	117	103	108	136	562
In-bond industries	2,140	474	670	735	919	1,116	3,914
Others	-11,898	-1,765	-1,977	-1,866	-2,056	-2,028	-9,692
Remitted profits	-2,236	-184	-241	-386	-335	-385	-1,531
Royalties, other	-1,917	-235	-265	-273	-356	-303	-1,432
Interest	-3,724	-1,149	-1,256	-975	-778	-678	-4,836
Reinvested profits	-4,021	-197	-215	-232	-587	-662	-1,893
Capital account	9,420	537	490	574	2,116	3,504	7,221
Foreign investment	9,420	537	490	574	2,116	3,504	7,221
New investment	4,010	70	543	270	1,307	2,386	4,576
Reinvestment	4,021	197	215	232	587	662	1,893
Intercompany accounts	845	193	-368	-11	-9	200	5
Others	544	77	100	83	231	256	747
Balance	-13,144	-431	-464	-1,369	1,983	4,614	4,333

Source: Executive Secretariat of the National Commission on Foreign Investment with data from the Bank of Mexico and the Ministry of Tourism.
ᵃPreliminary figures.

of current account and capital account was positive for both 1986 and 1987. Regulation increased perceived risk and worsened outflows; liberalization accelerated investment and improved performance.

Conclusion

In conclusion, the Mexican government fundamentally changed the rules of the game for foreign investors in 1973, subjecting them to registration requirements in all cases and to negotiating requirements for all cases of majority ownership. The effect was positive for several of the goals of the regulations, especially control of foreign acquisitions and diversification of sources. But the short-term effect of the new regulatory regime was to exacerbate the drain on the balance of payments represented by foreign-owned firms. This situation was reversed only with the more open policies toward foreign investment pursued after 1982. It is important to emphasize that these new policies did not entail the repeal or reversal of the foreign investment law. Rather, a more open attitude was communicated and implemented in the application of the seventeen guidelines for exceptions to Mexicanization and in the negotiation of investment in particular industries, as we will see in part III. By May 1989, regulations were issued significantly liberalizing the treatment of foreign investment. The law itself will surely be revised as part of the negotiations for a North American Free Trade Agreement. In foreign investment, the failure of the nationalist policy to achieve its goals and the opportunities of liberalization combined to shift policy. Similarly, in the next chapter, the limitations of Mexico's regulations on technology transfer provide a good example of the constraints of a liberal international regime on the nationalist metapreferences of Mexican regulators.

Five

Technology Regimes, Patents, and Trademarks

Technology

Technology is useful or productive knowledge. It is the ability to put abstract, scientific knowledge to practical human use. In contrast to a definition of technology as knowledge with commercial application,[1] this definition is consistent with the etymology of the word, the dictionary definition, and common usage. The existence of the technology or know-how to apply scientific knowledge to human needs does not imply that it is commercially viable; this definition thus enables us to make sense of the expression "The technology exists, but it is not economical."

Nevertheless, technology can be, and frequently is, a commodity: it can be bought and sold, transferred from one person or organization to another. When useful knowledge is widely known, it is usually free, available to anyone who wishes to learn. But when useful or productive knowledge is scarce, and especially when it is new, technology is likely to be treated as an expensive commodity.

When produced by private individuals or firms, technology tends to serve as a commodity rather than a free good. When developed by the private sector, it differs markedly from knowledge produced by men and women working in public institutions or in academe, although the methods used and even the knowledge produced may be the same. Usually in academe and public institutions (though not in public firms), the goal is to make a contribution to general knowledge and to publish and/or make public the results. In private enterprise the goal of producing useful knowledge is to make a profit on what is produced and to keep the results a secret for as long as possible. Jorge Sábato has described this difference as follows: "Although the scientist in the laboratory rules his behavior according to two cardinal principles: 'don't plagiarize' and 'publish the results of your research,'

108

one who works in a technological enterprise considers it natural to appropriate indiscriminately the results of others and to hide carefully his own. What for one is sacrilege, for the other is a virtue that is often generously rewarded."[2]

When technology is developed by a firm, the knowledge produced becomes proprietary and may be retained, transferred, or sold as the firm sees fit. When a firm decides to acquire technology and possesses full knowledge of the alternatives available, the price may be fixed in comparison with other similar technologies or with alternative methods of production. In developing countries, however, market information on technology is frequently scarce, and the search costs are high. When the acquiring enterprise is a subsidiary of a foreign enterprise, the search costs are minimized by utilizing the technology already known and used by the parent corporation. In this situation, when technology is transferred, it is a commodity, but the price of that commodity is not a market price; rather, it is an accounting price fixed by the supplier.

Two legal instruments, patents and trademarks, lie at the center of the liberal international regime and became the focus of Mexico's national efforts to change that regime.

Patents

One of the principal ways in which technology has become a salable commodity is through the patent system. The original phrase, *letters patent*, referred to an open letter from the monarch in which the crown gave public assurance that all others except the holder of the patent would be prohibited from producing a given good. Thus the patent is from its inception a creation of the state.

The patent regime is an anomaly in the free market, for it creates a monopoly in the name of fairness. According to the Paris Convention, industrial property "is concerned with patents, utility models, industrial designs, trademarks, service marks, tradenames, and indications of source or appellations of origin, and the repression of unfair competition" (article 1). Industrial property is occasionally joined with copyrights and other literary protections under the more general heading of "intellectual property." Although the patent does not confer an absolute monopoly on its holder, since similar but not exact products may be available that serve as effective substitutes in the market, the entire system is based on the assumption that no other producers will compete with the patent holder in the production of the goods it covers for the period that it is in effect.

In developing countries, most patents are held by foreigners. This is due in part to the low level of scientific and technological research undertaken domestically in these countries. It is also encouraged by the patent system, specifically by the Paris Convention, and by bilateral agreements, which ensure reciprocal treatment for patent holders in different countries, and grant priority—that is, recognize the date of discovery—in all countries on the basis of a patent developed in any one. The benefits of being first extend throughout the system.

Trademarks

Like patents, the trademark represents a legal monopoly granted by the state for a word or identifying mark used by a producer on its products. In contrast to patents, however, this protection is not limited in time. Rather, it is a permanent exclusive right to use the identifying mark. (The trademark protection is usually granted for a specific period but is indefinitely renewable.) Trademarks had their origin many centuries ago when artisans placed their signature or identifying mark on their products. Since that time the trademark has served to distinguish a product from others of its kind.

Several theories of the function of the trademark have been proposed. The trademark is at once a communications device and an item that itself represents economic value to its owner. All agree that trademarks provide distinction. The original function of that distinction was to identify the origin of the product, that is, to enable the consumer to identify the specific producer of the product. However, as the practices of firms changed and products were produced by a variety of contractors, subsidiaries, and licensees, the trademark no longer identified exactly the producer of the product. With the internationalization of production, identically marked items could be produced in various places around the globe. Ladas describes the shift away from the "source of origin" theory:

> It is now generally recognized today that the old theory that a trademark represents to the consumer the source of origin of the products to which it is affixed is wholly without basis in fact. This is not only because the source is uncertain, varied, or fluid. More realistically we find that the consumer is concerned with the quality of the goods he purchases, and the assurance of that quality. This had come to be known as the guaranty function of the trademark . . . The source theory has been broadened to include not only manufacturing source but also source of standards and specifications of the goods bearing the trademark.[3]

Ladas goes on to point out that the acceptance of the guaranty function by courts in various countries has given legal protection to a practice that had already become widespread before World War II, namely, the licensing of trademarks to producers other than the producer that first obtained the trademark. Thus, trademarks facilitated internationalization.

The economic function of the trademark for the firm that owns or licenses it is to protect the goodwill associated with the trademark over time through its use and its promotion in advertising. Goodwill is a complex notion that does not have exact equivalents in other languages. In Spanish the term used is *clientela*, referring to the clientele assured by the trademark. In French, the term *fonds de commerce* is used but is even less exact. Ladas quotes a certain Lord Lindley speaking in the House of Lords in 1901 as offering the best definition of goodwill.

> Goodwill regarded as property has no meaning except in connection with some trade, business, or calling. In that connection, I understand the word to include whatever adds value to a business by reason of situation, name and reputation, connection, introduction to old consumers, and agreed absence from competition, or any of these things, and there may be others that don't occur to me.[4]

The trademark thus protects the goodwill of the enterprise and in fact represents the market share of the firm for the product produced under that mark. It is for this reason that goodwill is listed by corporations as an intangible asset on their books and can be valued and sold by the enterprise. An estimate widely cited in the 1960s indicated that the trademarks Coca-Cola and Coke had a goodwill value of some $3 billion.

The goodwill represented by the trademark must be located in one or several national markets. Lord Lindley went on to say,

> In this wide sense goodwill is inescapable from the business to which it adds value, and, in my opinion, exists where the business is carried on. Such business may be carried on in one place or country or in several, and if in several, there may be several businesses, *each having a goodwill of its own* (my emphasis).

For products produced by foreign corporations, although the products may first have been produced abroad and imported into a host country and later produced within the country, the goodwill associated with the products sold in a given country must nevertheless represent the clientele for the product in that country. For consumer goods in general, trademarks are much more important than patents to the firm. As table 5.2 shows, food, beverages, pharmaceuticals, and automobiles (transportation equipment) have many more trademarks than patents. In summary, the primary function of trademarks has come to be the protection of goodwill and market share for the firms that own them.

The Global Technology Regime

Global efforts to protect property rights in technology constitute one of the oldest international regimes. Many of the norms and principles of the present-day technology transfer regime were laid down over a century ago at the international conference of 1883—the Paris Convention. This conference was called by the French minister of commerce for final approval of the text that had been drawn up at an 1880 conference. The countries that signed on March 20, 1883,[5] agreed to abide by the provisions of the convention, which went into effect on July 7, 1884. They then constituted the International Union for the Protection of Industrial Property (or simply the "Union").[6] In 1963, the bureau overseeing both the Paris Convention and the Berne Copyright Union began to take an active role by publishing model laws that were intended as guidelines for the formulation of national policies. The Eighth Conference of Revision at Stockholm in 1967 brought about significant administrative reforms. Until this time, the bureau had been independent of the union's member states. As early as 1952, some member states had expressed a desire for more control over the bureau's affairs.[7] The Stockholm revisions designated an assembly composed of all member states as the superior organ of the Union, giving it the power to direct the development and implementation of the Paris Convention and guide both the director-general and the bureau.

The World Intellectual Property Organization (WIPO) was also established at the Stockholm Convention and formalized on April 26, 1970. The existing Bureau of the Paris and Berne Unions was merged into WIPO's International Bureau. The stated objectives of WIPO are the promotion of intellectual property protection, the assurance of administrative cooperation among the various unions or agreements, and the provision of legal-technical assistance. Since its inception, WIPO has had special working arrangements with various UN bodies, particularly the UN Industrial Development Organization (UNIDO) and the UN Conference on Trade and Development (UNC-

TAD). WIPO itself became a specialized agency of the UN in 1974. By the mid-1970s, eighty-seven states, including Mexico, had signed the constituent agreement.[8]

The fundamental assumptions of the technology transfer regime preceded, and were included in, the Paris Convention. First, the protection of industrial property guarantees rewards to inventors, who have a "natural right" to their inventions and, thus, to derive value from them.[9] Second, this protection promotes research and innovation, since research requires significant inputs of time and capital, which few would invest if they were not assured of receiving protection and/or compensation for their successful efforts. Third, this protection provides the confidence necessary to stimulate foreign investment, trade, and licensing of foreign technology. And fourth, this protection encourages disclosure of information, which is useful to other researchers and enterprises and, in the case of trademarks, to the consumer public.

Several norms reinforce these primary assumptions. An important norm of the regime is that of uniformity and harmonization. Increased uniformity of patent laws has always been desired. The First International Congress on Industrial Property at Paris in 1873 tried to unify the myriad national laws on industrial property. Eventually, the more realistic goal of harmonization became the task of the Union. Attempts to make patent and trademark registration procedures more uniform have resulted in the Patent Cooperation Treaty, which provides international patent and trademark applications through WIPO and encourages regional attempts at uniformity such as the European Patent.

The Paris Convention of 1883 agreed that members of the convention should grant foreigners the same protection and rights they grant to their nationals. The norm of a right of priority also is provided, ensuring that if an application for protection is filed in one member state, applications by the applicant in any other member state within a certain period are regarded as filed on the date of the first application. This is intended to give the applicant time to decide in which countries protection is desired and how to proceed. Finally, there is the relation between international and national legislation; although the convention specifies rules that member states must follow, certain areas have traditionally been left to national discretion. The assumption is that although harmonization is desirable, states should be allowed to legislate according to their own situations. For example, one area left exclusively to the state is the definition and regulation of "exploitative" licensing.[10]

These various norms are upheld by rules and procedures, some formalized in the common rules of the Paris Convention. There are many, but the principal ones are listed below.

1. An inventor must apply for protection in each country in which protection is desired. The norms of national treatment and right of priority apply here.
2. Applications must be filed with the appropriate national or international office and include a description of the invention or trademark and claims. The application may be published before or after protection has been granted.[11]
3. The application for a patent is examined for the requirements of patentability: novelty, inventive step (does not follow obviously from the state of the art), and industrial applicability.
4. The importation by the patentee of articles covered by the patent does not entail forfeiture of the patent.
5. The patentee has the right to exclude all others from manufacturing, using, or selling the patented product or process, or from using a registered trademark or service mark. The patentee can license others to use it at his or her discretion.
6. Different countries may legislate regarding these licensing agreements to guard against abuses. They may also pass legislation on the duration of protection and compulsory licensing.

Challenges to the Global Regime in the 1970s

The 1970s brought about several changes in the international arena, and the technology transfer regime faced challenges to its norms as well as its rules. The developing countries voiced their interests and concerns at the new forums on international property protection. WIPO and UNCTAD held debates on the value of the international patent system and on the international protection of industrial property generally for developing countries. In 1975, UNCTAD and WIPO jointly published "The Role of the Patent System in Technology Transfer," which reexamined the issues covered in a bureau study undertaken in the 1960s. The earlier study had identified national legislation as an obstacle to the free flow of technology. The new study pointed up the dependence of developing countries on foreign technology by quoting an 84 percent figure for patents held in developing countries by foreigners. It also spoke of the "widespread" abuses in licensing agreements such as limitations on purchases and sales.[12] The study mentioned that the norm of equality of foreigners was an important factor in strengthening foreign dominance of patents.

The revisions of the Paris Convention, stated the report, had not affected its primary provisions; and although it left much to national legislation, most national laws (of member states and nonmembers) had "by and large incorporated its major provisions."[13] This and subsequent UNCTAD documents called for some sort of international agreement to promote the flow of technology to developing countries. They also strongly recommended the development of a general national policy on technology transfer in less-developed countries (LDCs). Mexico's laws were cited as examples of the kind of legislative and administrative undertakings suggested.

The voices of the developed-country experts in these and other UNCTAD conferences were heard throughout the decade lamenting the technology transfer process on quite different grounds. They claimed that their property rights were unsatisfactorily protected in LDCs and that problems existed for enterprises in attempting to secure an adequate return on technology transfer.[14]

UNCTAD did not publically examine the role of trademarks in developing countries until 1979, when it published a report stating that although countries derived benefits from the identification function of trademarks, the social costs of its other significant function—creating market power—far outweighed them.[15] It recommended policy options such as abolition of trademark protection in certain sectors, revocation, compulsory licensing, and combined trademarks. The Mexican law, examined below, requiring linkage of a foreign with a domestic mark (though never implemented and later overturned) was cited as an example of positive action.[16] Throughout the seventies, the number of foreign trademarks registered in LDCs increased; by 1974, 50 percent of trademarks registered in LDCs were foreign.[17]

In 1975, a series of draft conventions on a possible "international code of conduct" on the transfer of technology was initiated under UNCTAD. Two initial draft outlines were presented at the first session of the Committee on Transfer of Technology of UNCTAD, one put forth by the so-called Group of 77, which called for a legally binding set of rules, and the other submitted by Group B, which called for flexible and voluntary guidelines. The Group of 77's outline mentioned "taking into consideration particularly the needs of developing countries," and Group B's draft spoke only of the "legitimate interests of source and recipient enterprises and their governments."[18] An intergovernmental group of experts failed to develop fully a composite text of these and the draft outlines submitted by other groups. Although the principles of facilitating access to technology under fair terms, fostering negotiations between contracting parties, and assisting the growth of the technological capabilities of nations were agreed upon, an outstanding area of dispute was the extent of the application of the draft rules regarding restrictive business practices.[19] The code of conduct did not contain specific provisions that contradicted the norms of the regime, but it discussed areas previously left to national regulation. However, it was never finalized.

Mexican Nationalist Policy

By the start of the Echeverría administration in late 1970, the issue of technology transfer had come to the fore in Mexico because of concern about the balance of payments. Although issues related to technology in general and to patents and trademarks in particular had become the subject of studies in some international bodies and in a few developing countries, little attention had been paid to these topics in Mexico until the mid-1960s. Nevertheless, in the short time between 1967 and 1970, technology and technology transfer came to be major objects of national policy in Mexico, and the regulation of technology transfer, patents, and trademarks became central pieces of national policy toward foreign enterprise. Later, the Mexican experience provided a more general challenge to the liberal regime in technology.

At the end of the 1960s, few studies of technology transfer in Mexico existed. One early study brought the issue to the attention of the UN Economic and Social Council in 1968. The author was Miguel Wionczek, who was to be a key adviser to Luís Echeverría on the regulation of foreign investment and technology. Another was an unpublished study by Mauricio de María y Campos, who would be a key player among those developing the nationalist vision over the next two decades.[20] In 1969, the Ministry of Finance produced a study analyzing the high-technology component of foreign remittances by subsidiaries of foreign enterprises in Mexico. The findings dramatically raised the level of official concern regarding technology and technology transfer. The ministry study emphasized the foreign exchange cost of technology and the fact that since the government had no records of technology transactions, there was no way to determine if the price paid by Mexican firms and foreign subsidiaries in Mexico was high or low. In the same year, an UNCTAD study suggested that there were costs other than price involved in the acquisition of foreign technology. In a survey of a small sample (109) of licensing agreements for patents, trademarks, and know-how, the UNCTAD survey found 126 restrictive clauses limiting the behavior of the recipient firm. Most of these restrictive clauses limited the export of goods produced with the acquired technology: 106 of the 126 restrictive clauses limited exports in one form or another. In 53 of the clauses, exports were prohibited completely. In others, the restrictive clause specified enterprises to which exports could be made, established export quotas, required the approval of the technology provider to export, or prohibited the use of trademarks for export. Other clauses restricted the level or form of production by the acquiring firm. Although the sample was small, the large number of restrictive clauses suggested that the phenomenon was widespread, and the findings were especially disturbing to the Mexican government because the restrictions on exports ran counter to a major goal of government policy, namely, to diversify and increase manufactured exports.[21]

It was soon evident, moreover, that most imports of foreign technology (including patents, trademarks, know-how, and technical assistance) were made by affiliates of foreign enterprises. Data in 1971 reveal that the major industries of the manufacturing sector in which foreign investment was important—food, chemicals, electrical machinery, and transportation equipment—accounted for a large majority of all foreign payments for technology (see table 5.1).

Payments by foreign affiliates in all manufacturing, valued at $114.8 million, accounted for 79.8 percent of all technology imports in the manufacturing sector. In food, beverages, and tobacco, the foreign share ranged from 90 to 100 percent; in chemicals, electrical machinery, and transportation equipment, the foreign affiliates accounted for 81–87 percent of all payments for the importation of technology.

A few comparisons indicate the relative importance of these payments. Fifty-three percent of payments by affiliates of foreign enterprises were in the durable and nondurable consumer goods industries. The payments for foreign technology in consumer goods exceeded Mexico's total expenditures for scientific research and technological development in 1971. Payments for technology by foreign affiliates in the pharmaceutical industry approximated the payments by all private national enterprises in the entire manufacturing sector.[22]

Fortunately, good data exist to demonstrate the predominance of foreign patent holders in developing countries, especially in Mexico. Stephen P. Ladas, in his magisterial work *Patents, Trademarks, and Related Rights*, presented data for patent applications filed and patents granted during 1969 for a large number of countries. In the United States, 30 percent of all patents filed that year were filed by foreigners, and foreigners received 25.4 percent of all patents granted. In West Germany, 30.7 percent of applications came from foreigners, and 28.2 percent of grants went to foreigners. In Brazil, the corresponding

TABLE 5.1   Sectoral Structure of Payments for Importation of
Technology (Patents, Trademarks, Know-How, and Technical Assistance)
in Mexico, 1971

Sector	Foreign (%)	Private National (%)	State (%)	Total (%)
Food	7.6	2.7	3.0	6.6
Beverages	6.3	3.0	—	5.6
Tobacco	0.4	—	—	0.4
Chemicals (industrial)	12.8	12.3	2.0	12.6
Chemicals (pharmaceuticals)	23.9	15.9	—	22.2
Electrical machinery	11.7	9.7	—	11.3
Transportation equipment	9.9	5.2	1.4	8.9
Other manufacturing	27.4	51.2	93.6[a]	32.4
Total, all manufacturing	100.0	100.0	100.0	100.0
(millions of U.S. $)	114.8	28.1	0.9	143.7

Source: Fajnzylber and Martínez Tarragó, Las empresas transnacionales (1976), pp. 325, 344–45.
[a]Most payments in the state sector were in basic metals (68.1%) and in petroleum and coal derivatives (25.4%).

figures were 62.5 percent of applications and 51.2 percent of patent grants. Few countries, however, showed greater foreign dependence than Mexico. In 1969, 90 percent of all patent applications filed and 92.6 percent of all patents granted went to foreigners rather than nationals.[23] Table 5.2 gives a sectoral breakdown of patents and trademarks registered by the 196 foreign manufacturing subsidiaries in Mexico in the Fajnzylber and Martínez Tarragó sample.

On the nearly 13,000 patents registered by these foreign enterprises in Mexico prior to 1970, most were in the chemical industry, followed by the electrical machinery industry. Within chemicals, patents were much more important for industrial chemicals than for pharmaceuticals. In general, patents were more important in technologically advanced industrial sectors, while trademarks were more important for consumer goods industries. In Mexico, in practical terms, compliance with the international regime in patents meant reliance on foreign technology.

Although the issue of technology became a matter of national policy concern in 1970, there was some precedent for this focus on tech-

TABLE 5.2   Total Number of Patents and Trademarks Registered by the Fajnzylber and Martínez Tarragó Sample of 196 Foreign Manufacturing Subsidiaries in Mexico before 1970

	Patents		Trademarks		% of Total Manufacturing	
		% of Total		% of Total		
Sector[a]	No.	PAT+TM	No.	PAT+TM	Patents	TMs
Food (16)	278	16.6	1,397	83.4	2.2	11.4
Beverages (3)	12	5.7	199	94.3	0.1	1.6
Industrial[b] chemicals (69)	4,249	62.9	2,508	37.1	33.2	20.4
Pharmaceutical[b] chemicals (69)	2,788	39.4	4,280	60.6	21.8	34.9
Electrical machinery (29)	2,707	76.3	839	23.7	21.2	6.8
Transportation equipment (15)	663	40.8	961	59.2	5.2	7.8
Total, all manufacturing (196)	12,782	51.0	12,281	49.0	100.0	100.0

Source: Fajnzylber and Martínez Tarragó, *Las empresas transnacionales* (1976), pp. 348–49.
[a]The number of firms is given in parentheses.
[b]No breakdown in the number of firms was given for the subdivisions of the chemical industry.

nological dependence. In 1935, Lázaro Cárdenas founded the National Council on Higher Education and Scientific Research. In 1942, the Commission for the Development and Coordination of Scientific Research was established, and in 1950, the National Institute for Scientific Research (INIC) was founded. These early efforts pushed science more than technology. According to the self-criticism of the INIC, "the actions of these bodies for the benefit of the country . . . have been very limited."[24] In 1967, two meetings bringing together academics, researchers, and business representatives were held to discuss science and technology. On the basis of these conferences, the Ministry of the Presidency charged INIC in 1968 to formulate a national science and technology program. The most distinguished scientists and researchers in every area of the country were assembled to produce a national policy statement.

   Among the shortcomings of science and technology in Mexico pointed out by the INIC study was that Mexico's total expenditure on scientific and technological research amounted to only 0.13 percent of the gross national product (GNP). The 2,400 full-time researchers and 1,300 part-time researchers amounted to only 0.6 researchers for each 10,000 inhabitants, compared to 26 for the United States in 1965, 15 for Japan in 1969, 11 for West Germany in 1967, and 4 for Italy in 1967. The expenditure per researcher was also inferior to the level not only of developed countries but of other developing countries. The analysis of the volume of foreign payments for technology transfer by affiliates of foreign enterprises and the poverty of national research and development efforts resulted in the creation of the National Council on Science and Technology (CONACYT), one of the first acts of the Echeverría government in December 1970. Although CONACYT itself began with a small budget, it provided a center in which work leading to additional policies could be developed. Both Miguel Wionczek and Mauricio de María y Campos worked there.

Patents, trademarks, and technology and its transfer were all regulated by new laws passed in Mexico in the 1970s. Initially, what would become three separate laws on technology, foreign investment, and patents and trademarks was all designed as a package.[25] In the course of debating the issues, the regulation of technology transfer was the least controversial and the first passed into law.

The Law on the Transfer of Technology

The Law on the Transfer of Technology and the Use and Exploitation of Patents and Trademarks was passed by the Mexican Congress on December 28, 1972. First published in *Diario Oficial* on December 30, 1972, the law became effective on January 29, 1973. It had its origins in the late 1960s in the meetings of INIC, the study of foreign payments by the Ministry of Finance, the UNCTAD study on restrictive business practices, and the Wionczek study on technology transfer.

This law represented the first major attempt in Mexico to regulate technology, patents, and trademarks imported from outside Mexico. A study was begun within CONACYT by Gerardo Bueno, the director, and Miguel Wionczek, an adviser to the director and to the president. Nevertheless, primary responsibility for the elaboration of the regulation of technology transfer was given to the Ministry of Industry and Commerce. This was consistent with the policy begun by Echeverría's predecessor to concentrate responsibility for foreign investment and national industrial development in that ministry.

The law on technology transfer was designed primarily to provide a mechanism for monitoring the flow of technology and to reduce its cost. Appendix 3 gives the major articles of the law. The law established a registry with authority to review and approve, after negotiation if necessary, all contracts with foreign entities. The principal operational instrument of the law is article 7, which specifies the conditions under which registration may be denied. The law provided a means whereby the state could not only collect information on the technology transfer process as reflected in contracts with foreign firms but also could interpose itself as a third bargaining agent between the supplier of technology and the acquiring firm.[26] Enforcement was made possible by denying legal protection and effect to unregistered contracts and by requiring registration to obtain the benefits of various industrial incentive programs. In addition, fines were specified for noncompliance. The state thus made use of both its coercive legal power and its ability to offer positive incentives.

Because all technology contracts must be registered, including contracts between nationals, the law is not discriminatory against foreigners, satisfying a major norm of the global regime. However, foreign suppliers were without doubt the main object of the legislation.

The second major purpose of the law was to eliminate restrictive business practices contained in the contracts that limited the development of technology locally or that limited the export of goods produced under the technology license. Provisions for "grant-backs"[27] of newly developed technologies to the foreign licensor, management control, contract terms exceeding ten years, limits on research and development, prohibition of the development of complementary technology, and limits on price levels or volume were prohibited. Many of these restrictive business practices would be regulated by antitrust legislation elsewhere, but such controls are weak in Mexico.

The law had its limitations. No industry-specific regulations were included, and neither in the law nor in administrative practice were there specified strict limits on the level of technology payments that would be approved. This meant that each case would be negotiated on an individual basis. The built-in flexibility of the law and the case-by-case approach meant that firms were almost always able to arrive at an acceptable compromise. Two provisions protected the firms from bureaucratic inefficiency. One specified that approval of the contracts would be automatic after ninety days if no decision was forthcoming from the registry in that time. A second allowed firms to request reconsideration of any decision and that a decision on the reconsideration request would be reached within forty-five days or else would be automatically approved.

During the first five-years under the law, the National Registry on Technology Transfer faced the massive task of registering and negotiating all technology contracts for the first time; after that initial spurt of activity, renewal and review became more important. Many contracts were presented to the registry several times: first, for information purposes; after that or directly for the first time, contracts were presented for their inscription in the registry. If the initial opinion was negative, the contracts were often modified and resubmitted. The registry did not maintain a record of how many contracts were not resubmitted after an initial negative decision. But officials of the registry contended that very few contracts were canceled, since negotiation with the registry has been able to resolve most prohibitions that presented a problem for the firms.

Almost 7,000 contracts were given a positive decision by the registry in the first years; this includes contracts that received an initial negative decision by the registry and were resubmitted and approved in a modified form. Only 200 contracts received a negative final decision. Excessive payments were involved in the denial of 85 percent of these 200 contracts. Nearly 31 percent of the negative decisions were exclusively for excessive payments. Roughly 38 percent of the negative decisions cited limitations on the volume of production or limits on the sale price for national production or export. About 37 percent of the negative decisions were due in part to excessive duration of the contract, exceeding ten years; 22 percent cited the intervention of the licensor in the administration of the acquiring enterprise; 21 percent cited the impermissible subjugation of the contract to foreign laws or tribunals; 20 percent cited grant-backs to the licensor of patents, trademarks, inventions, or improvements made or obtained by the licensee; and 17 percent of the negative decisions cited limitations on exports. The predominance of excessive payment as a reason for initial refusal of approval reflects the prevailing orientation of the law and of the registry to limit the cost of technology transfer, based on its concern with the impact of technology transfer on the balance of payments.

The Institutionalization of State Intervention in Technology

The institutionalization of state intervention in the technology transfer process represented a significant departure from the practice of the preceding decade. Although agreement to a contract had presumably been reached between the two parties when a contract was presented to the registry, the state was authorized by this legislation to reopen the negotiations with criteria related to the national goals and the national welfare. Thus, what was previously a two-party, private transaction became, in 1973, a three-way transaction involving the state.

Five stages of the technology transfer process can be identified:

1. The identification of the technological needs of the acquiring firm
2. The identification of alternative suppliers of the technology required
3. The selection of one of those suppliers
4. The negotiation of the terms of the contract for technology

5. The adaptation of the technology supplied to the needs of the acquiring firm

The National Registry on Technology Transfer intervened only at the fourth stage of the technology transfer process. Nevertheless, the review and evaluation of contracts by the state, the limitation of contracts to a ten-year term, and the potential for reevaluation of contracts on their expiration made clear that technology agreements were no longer an unrestricted avenue for financial transactions between parent companies and subsidiaries.

The terms of the law make clear that technology transfer was now regarded as a purchase of an intangible commodity rather than the rental or leasing of industrial property. Terms such as "importer" or "purchaser" are revealing, reflecting the explicit arguments put forward in the early proposals for the law.[28] This conception of technology transfer as a transfer, not a rental, has implications for how the state negotiated these contracts. The assumption existed that with the exception of trademarks, contracts for technology would not be renewed after their initial period expired unless new technology was supplied. Furthermore, there was often a presumption that payments for technology transfer should decline over time, since the amount or value of technology is judged to be greater in the first five years of a contract than in later years. Some contracts were renegotiated, replacing a fixed-percentage payment with a declining percentage. For example, one firm that previously had charged 2 percent of sales for a given technology contract agreed to charge 2 percent for the first three years following the registration of the contract, 1.5 percent for the next two years, and 1 percent for the final two years of the seven-year contract.[29]

Other firms argued, however, that new technology was continually supplied to their licensees and that a constant payment was therefore justified. Such firms were also concerned with the maximum limit of ten years and the assumption that licensees would retain all technology transferred at any time during the ten years. This suggested that technology transferred in the ninth year would then become the property of the licensee after only one year. Although the contract might be renewed, under the terms of the law it would be canceled upon expiration.[30] Therefore, firms that threatened to cease transferring new technology in the later years of the contract asked for additional protection for such technology supplied late in the contract. In some cases, the registry agreed to authorize clauses specifying that the recipient firm would maintain the confidentiality of technology for up to ten years after the date on which it was supplied, without regard to the expiration of the contract.

Estimates of the amount of foreign exchange saved by negotiations with the registry cannot be taken at face value, however, because many of the contracts are between parents and subsidiaries of the same foreign firms.

The administrative discretion granted to the registry under the terms of the law suggests that opportunities for corruption could abound. Initially, the registry was populated by a young group of lawyers and economists who soon gained a reputation of honesty and professionalism. Many of these young technicians were recent university graduates. Some, such as Jaime Alvarez Soberanis, came from the elite Universidad Ibero-Americana, and others, such as Mauricio de María y Campos, came from the National Autonomous University of Mexico (UNAM). Evaluations by foreign business organizations such as Business International (1978) and the Conference Board (1980) attested to the predominant honesty of the group.[31] Such a reputation was difficult to maintain, however, as inflation and budget cuts reduced the real income of the regulators; this was a lament of directors who fought unsuccessfully for expanded staff and salaries.

The 1982 Revision

At the end of December 1981, in the last year of the López Portillo administration, a new law on technology transfer was passed by the Congress, replacing the law passed in 1972. López Portillo was considered less of an economic nationalist than Echeverría. But the new law reflected the long-term continuities of Mexican development policies. In some ways, the law, which took effect on February 10, 1982, softened the requirements of the earlier law; in other respects, the law was strengthened and loopholes were closed. (Appendix 3 includes the text of selected articles of the 1982 law; the changes from the 1973 version are italicized.)

The purpose of the 1982 law moved from mere registration and negotiation of terms of technology transfer to the development of existing technologies (article 1). A statement from the preamble of the bill reflects this change: "With this bill, [we] seek to transcend a regime [limited] exclusively to registry, toward a mechanism that would establish the basis . . . for an effective transfer of technology, within a global process of assimilation, adaptation, and local technological development."[32]

The jurisdiction of the law was broadened, both in the types of agreements and the scope of persons and enterprises covered (articles 2, 4, and 5). The coverage was brought up to date to include Certificates of Invention (established in the 1976 Law on Inventions and Trademarks) and extended to include licenses for service marks and trade names, consulting services, industrial copyright licenses, and computer programs. Perhaps the most significant extension of the legislation was to include all agreements related to the border industrialization program (the Maquiladora Program), agreements involving state-owned agencies and enterprises, and agreements signed by foreigners, whether or not they lived in Mexico.

The heart of the legislation involved the conditions for refusing registration. Of the fourteen conditions for refusing registration in the 1973 law, seven were obligatory. The other seven conditions were more flexible and operated as guidelines. But even the seven obligatory restrictions were not absolute: there have been cases in which contracts containing such clauses have been approved and registered.[33]

The 1982 law retained all fourteen clauses, in one form or another, but in four of the provisions, exceptions were included to reflect the actual practice of the registry over the preceding years or to allow for more leniency. The new law reflected the judgment that in technology, import substitution cannot be pursued if new technology is not brought into the country. The rules were relaxed to continue to attract technology suppliers.

On the other hand, the 1982 law also closed some loopholes. Exclusive sales requirements (as opposed to exclusive rights of representation) were prohibited to any single customer, not only to the technology supplier. Secrecy agreements could not extend beyond the term of the contracts (or the term set "by the applicable laws"). The supplier was liable for any infringement of the industrial property rights of third parties. Perhaps the most sweeping change required suppliers to guarantee the quality of the licensed technology (article 15-XIII).

Unlike the 1973 law, none of these clauses was obligatory. Any provision of articles 15 and 16 could be waived at the discretion of the registry staff. This increased the flexibility of the law but effectively increased the bargaining power of the supplier firms.

In short, there were long-term continuities in the regulation of technology transfer, consistent with a policy of import substitution for technology. The scope of the 1982 law was broader, but the increased discretion made it easier for foreign suppliers to license technology in Mexico, if they could argue that their practices benefited the nation.

The Law on Inventions and Trademarks

As Mexican officials considered the regulation of foreign investment at the end of the Echeverría administration, the importance of patents in some industries and trademarks in others did not go unnoticed. The law on technology transfer adopted in 1972 required the registration of contracts involving patents and trademarks (as well as know-how and technical assistance) and enabled the state to prohibit certain restrictive clauses in those contracts and to participate in bargaining over the level of foreign payments. That law did not, however, alter the rules of the game for patents and trademarks, except for the rules concerning licensing under the regulation of technology transfer. The authorization of a temporary monopoly in the case of patents and a permanently renewable monopoly for the use of trademarks continued to be ruled by the 1942 law on industrial property.

An outline for a revision of that law was prepared by the same economists and lawyers of CONACYT and the Ministry of Industry and Commerce that had prepared the law on technology transfer. But the preoccupation of the private sector, both national and foreign, over the reformist proposals of the Echeverría administration caused the formulation of a new law to be postponed. It was feared that another law restricting the rights and privileges of foreign investors, following soon after the law on technology transfer and the foreign investment law, would discourage new foreign investment altogether, which was not the intention of the regulators. However, in 1975, at the direct instruction of President Echeverría, the proposals that had been readied in 1973 were resurrected, a draft was formulated, comments were solicited from the private sector, and the law was submitted to Congress, which approved the final version on December 30, 1975.[34] The law was published in the *Diario Oficial* on February 10, 1976, and became effective the following day.[35]

The 1976 Law on Inventions and Trademarks provided a complete overhaul of the 1942 law governing patents, trademarks, and other industrial property rights. Besides extensive regulations governing the registry and maintenance of such rights with the Office of Inventions and Trademarks in the Ministry of Industry and Commerce (the Ministry of National Property and Industrial Development during 1977–82), the 237-article law incorporated a number of modifications of the legal protection granted to inventions and to trademarks, and established several novel legal instruments. Some of the more important articles are included in appendix 4.

In many countries in which chemical, pharmaceutical, and other products are removed from patent protection, the processes for obtaining them are nonetheless granted patent protection. In Mexico a new legal instrument was created under the 1976 law to provide more limited protection than that granted by patents for processes to obtain chemicals, pharmaceuticals, medicines, foods and beverages, and fertilizers. This was the Certificate of Invention. It was designed to give Mexicans easy access to technology deemed important for the national welfare.

The law authorized the owner of a Certificate of Invention to receive royalties for the use of the invention but did not authorize the exclusive exploitation that patents provide. The owner of the Certificate of the Invention was free to invent and to exploit the invention, and any other interested party could exploit the invention as well after concluding an agreement for the payment of royalties to the owner of the certificate. If no agreement on payment of royalties was reached, the National Registry on Technology Transfer was authorized to intervene at the request of the interested party and establish the level of royalties to be paid. The inventor was required to submit to the registry sufficient information on the invention to make possible its exploitation and commercial production.

Many large corporations traditionally registered large numbers of patents that they had no intention of exploiting in order to remove potential competition to products that they did produce. Under the old law the term of patent protection was reduced from fifteen to twelve years if industrial exploitation of the patent was not undertaken. The 1976 law reduced to only three years the period within which exploitation of the patent was required.

Most of the innovative provisions of the Law on Inventions and Trademarks, however, restricted rather than extended the legal protection granted to trademarks. Obligatory licenses "for reasons of public interest" were authorized for both trademarks and service marks. The registration of a trademark was reduced to a term of five years, though this change was much less important than in the case of patents, since indefinite renewals for additional five-year periods were authorized for trademarks and service marks. Like patents, however, use of the trademark was required in order for legal protection to be continued. If the trademark was not used at least for one of the product classes for which it was registered, within three years of its registration the registration ceased to be valid.

Though these modifications are important, the most controversial part of the new law was without doubt the so-called trademark link provision. Article 127 provided that "every trademark of foreign origin or the rights of which correspond to a foreign or legal person, . . . must be used jointly with a trademark originally registered in Mexico. Both trademarks must be used in an equally visible manner." Article 138 further specified that any licensing agreement for the use of a foreign trademark must contain the obligation to link that trademark in use to a second trademark originally registered in Mexico. Failure to specify the obligation in a contract would result in the refusal to register that contract in the National Registry of Technology Transfer and thus would render it without effect. Article 128 granted a term of one year for the obligation to begin use of the linked trademark and granted the Ministry of Industry and Commerce the authority to extend that period for one additional year.[36]

What did Mexico hope to gain by requiring the use of two trademarks, one foreign and one registered? Trademarks like Coca-Cola, Ford, Volkswagen, Arrow Shirts, etc., would have had to be linked to a trademark originally registered in Mexico. General Electric had linked its trademark to the trademark of the firm with which it had a joint venture: General Electric/Esamex. Their trademarks had been linked voluntarily before the passage of the 1976 law. A few similar examples existed internationally. In his testimony before the Senate on December 23, 1975, Secretary Campillo Sáinz cited another case. In India, Mercedes-Benz had produced trucks in a joint venture with a local firm called Tata. They produced trucks called Tata-Mercedes; people became accustomed to hearing about Tata-Mercedes trucks. When the joint venture broke up, Tata dropped the name Mercedes. However, he implied that the prestige and market position conferred by the linked mark were retained because Tata trucks continued to be successfully sold.[37]

The trademark link idea was intended to negate some of the power foreign parent companies wielded over their Mexican subsidiaries. If the local firm attempted to reduce its payments to the owner of the trademark, the foreign firm would threaten to withdraw the use of the trademark. This would mean that export markets would be lost and the position of the local firm in the Mexican market could be seriously weakened. It was hoped that the obligatory linking of trademarks from abroad to trademarks that were originally registered in Mexico would avoid this dependence of Mexican firms on foreign firms. An example may illustrate the idea—and its limits.

When implementation of the trademark link provision seemed imminent, Procter & Gamble, the owner of the Camay trademark, registered the word *Royal* as a trademark for soap. Since this word satisfied the provisions of the law, the trademark Camay Royal was an acceptable linked trademark. (Symbols, color combinations, distinctive packaging, and other items may be registered as trademarks, but only words could be used to satisfy the trademark link provision. It was

In late 1990, the Salinas administration began to develop new policies to protect intellectual property, overturning the nationalist regulations of the previous twenty years. Both the 1972 Law on Technology Transfer and the 1976 Law on Inventions and Trademarks were replaced, and Mexico's policies were largely brought into line with policies in the U.S. and other developed economies.

The initiatives were considered by the Mexican Congress during the spring of 1991, as the U.S. Congress was debating "fast track" authority for the Bush administration to begin negotiations with Mexico. Shortly after "fast track" was approved in the U.S., the new "Law for the Promotion and Protection of Industrial Property" was approved in Mexico. (This law was published on June 27, 1991, and entered into effect the next day. Copyright law was modified in August 1991.) The main provisions include the following:

—Patents are authorized for both products and processes, including previously excluded chemicals, pharmaceuticals, biotechnology, and plant varieties.

—The term of patents is extended to twenty years from filing; "utility models" for improvements are protected for ten years from filing; industrial designs are protected for fifteen years.

—Patent protection in Mexico is extended, upon application, to inventions already patented in other countries and not previously produced or imported into Mexico.

—Importation will constitute "use" under the terms of the patent law, eliminating the major basis for compulsory licensing.

—Trade secrets are protected; violation of confidentiality agreements is a criminal offense.

—Trademarks and service marks can be registered for protection for renewable terms of ten years from filing; commercial names can be protected for renewable terms of ten years from date of publication.

—Franchising agreements, including trademarks and commercial names, may be registered with minimal disclosure requirements.

—Licensing agreements do not require any government approval.

—Under the amended copyright law, computer programs are protected against unauthorized copying for fifty years. Sound recordings are protected from unauthorized duplication.

—Sanctions and penalties are strengthened, including confiscation of counterfeits.

The liberal metapreference links the free flows of goods, capital, and technology. Although the Law on Foreign Investment of 1973 remained in effect during the U.S.–Canada–Mexico free trade negotiations, its replacement is probable by the time a free trade agreement is reached. Thus, Mexico would liberalize the protection of investment and technology in return for assured trade access to the U.S. market.

FIGURE 3. The Modernization of Intellectual Property in Mexico

hoped that the use of a Spanish word of equal size would emphasize the national character of the second trademark.)

Some officials who entered the government with the López Portillo administration were not enthusiastic about the linked trademark idea, especially in the face of widespread and vigorous opposition by both national and foreign firms. Nathán Warman, the undersecretary of industry under López Portillo, held up a bar of Camay Royal during an interview and asked, "What does Mexico gain with this?" The bargaining power of a Mexican licensee seemed abstract compared to the reality of foreign opposition and threats of investment boycotts.

Outcomes

The repeal of the Law on Inventions and Trademarks took fifteen years. In 1991, at the start of negotiations with the United States for a free trade agreement, a new law on Industrial Property was passed, voiding the entire package of nationalist regulations on technology, inventions, and trademarks (see box, fig. 3). The opposition to the linked trademark provision, in particular, is an instructive case of the failure of a nationalist challenge to liberalism.

Although some protests were made by foreign enterprises and their representatives and by national firms over the new exclusions from patentability, shorter patent terms, extension of obligatory licensing, and Certificates of Invention, it appears that these new regulations were accepted by the Mexican private sector. Some lawyers and businessmen predicted that patented technology would cease to be transferred to Mexico. Others responded that patents were relatively unimportant in the areas that were excluded from patentability. (Pharmaceuticals are an exception.) In any case, industrial secrets maintained within the firm and not formalized in contracts or protected by patents have come to be used increasingly by foreign enterprises and their subsidiaries, since this intrafirm mechanism provides even greater protection from competition than the use of patents. The filings of patent applications did decline immediately after the law was passed; in 1975, 4,962 applications for patents were filed; in 1976 the figure was only 3,436, and in 1977 applications were submitted at about the same rate.[38] However, patent office officials argued that some of the patent filings were replaced by filings for Certificates of Invention. Both private lawyers who handled the applications and representatives of the Office of Inventions and Trademarks indicated that firms that could no longer apply for patents did apply for Certificates of Invention in large numbers. Requests for multiple licenses and obligatory licenses initially were few, and it appeared that the Certificates of Invention had been accepted. However, pharmaceutical firms were not pleased with the regulatory innovation, and when an industry-specific regulation was attempted, they fought back vigorously.

The opposition to the regulation of trademarks was widespread and can only be described as ferocious. Reactions to these regulations, and especially to the trademark link provision, began immediately in 1975 when the law was proposed and continued unabated for more than ten years, until the law was finally changed in 1986. During that time, the trademark link provision was never implemented. Opposition peaked each year in January and February prior to the anniversary date of the law on February 11. In 1977 application of the trademark link requirement was postponed for an additional year, utilizing the option provided in the law. In 1978, application appeared imminent. In late 1977 the director of the Office of Inventions and Trademarks, Eusebio Arteloitia, made a public statement on the law. He suggested that although many firms had assumed that the provision would be dropped when the López Portillo administration took office, no such miracle occurred. A leading patent lawyer circulated a memorandum reporting on this statement to his clients; he recommended that firms prepare to comply with the law by February 11, 1978. Informally he commented, "I have an arrangement with the church around the corner: I take care of patents and trademarks; they take care of miracles." Yet in February 1978 a partial miracle was accomplished: application of the law related to the linking of trademarks was postponed once again.

Ninety-six contracts had been denied registry for failure to include the required provision on trademark links, but this was only a tiny fraction of the firms that would be required to comply with the law. The crucial implementation was not the revision of contracts but the effective requirement for linkage. During 1978 the state was in a position of not enforcing a law that it had strongly defended. In 1979 the anomaly was formally corrected by the introduction and approval of a legislative amendment leaving the trademark provision on the books but providing for its indefinite postponement. An official for economic affairs in the foreign ministry suggested that this was only a tactical retreat. By leaving the law on the books the regulation of trademarks and the use of the trademark link provision became, he said, like the neutron bomb: "We have it ready, but we have not deployed it." Although a few firms like Procter & Gamble had anticipated the application of the law and had produced products with linked trademarks, most firms had waited for the miracle. Finally, in

1986, following intense pressure from firms and from the United States, the miracle happened. To use the Mexican official's analogy, it was unilateral disarmament. The revised 1986 law dropped the trademark link requirement altogether.

Legal, economic, and political arguments were put forward in opposition to the obligatory linking of trademarks. These arguments came in a formal diplomatic note of protest from the United States in 1977, as well as in legal arguments from lawyers for the affected firms. Legal arguments proceeded along various lines. The strongest position suggested that the obligatory linking of trademarks diminished the goodwill of the firm that owned the foreign trademark and thus constituted an expropriation of assets without compensation. A second argument asserted that the law was contrary to the Paris Convention, of which Mexico was a signatory. Some asserted that the trademark link constituted discriminatory action against foreigners, contrary to the international convention that required equal treatment of foreigners and nationals. Finally, several legal arguments criticized the technical aspects of the law. For example, it was argued that compliance was impossible for majority foreign-owned subsidiaries of foreign corporations, since even the second trademarks would be the property of the entity identified as foreign under the terms of the law. The second trademark would thus be subject to linkage to a third trademark, the third to a fourth, and so on endlessly.

Economic arguments were advanced energetically by firms obliged to place a second trademark on all their products. The Mexican bottlers of Coca-Cola were vociferous in their opposition, even more than the parent company itself (whose main worry, according to a confidential survey, was its "imperialist" image). Significant costs would be incurred in market research to find a compatible trademark, in design costs to redesign all packaging materials, and in inventory costs to replace all of the bottles with single trademarks. These arguments carried considerable weight and helped account for the first two postponements of the application of the law. They do not in themselves account for its abandonment, however.

The most effective arguments against the Law on Inventions and Trademarks and specifically against the trademark link provision were the political arguments that the law did not contribute to the objectives of industrial policy endorsed by the state. The major objectives of this law, like the law on technology transfer and the law on foreign investment, were to bring about an effective transfer of technology and an increase in technological progress in Mexico; to protect the local economy and local firms from abuses and unequal competition from foreign firms; to encourage exports; and to avoid excessive payments abroad. The law's specific goals were to increase the volume and prestige of Mexican exports; limit changes in consumption patterns, termed "mental colonialism" by proponents of the law; and increase the negotiating power of the Mexican licenses.[39] The law's opponents argued that these goals would not be met.

Some opponents argued that the law might actually obstruct the aforementioned objectives; others argued that the foreign investment law and the law on technology transfer were sufficient to accomplish these goals. It was feared that the trademark link requirement would force some producers to withdraw from the Mexican market. Coca-Cola joined its bottlers as one of the principal opponents of the law.

Although an increase in the prestige and eventual volume of exports was one of the goals of the trademark link provision, it rapidly became clear that this benefit would not be realized. Many firms made it clear that they would not export products from Mexico on which linked trademarks were displayed; production for export would simply be shifted to other countries. Firms want the same trademark on all their products. In the 1976 regulation of the law, this threat was recognized by allowing exemption from the linkage requirement for firms whose products were exported. This potential benefit was thus rapidly eliminated.

The cost of payments for technology, patents, and trademarks would not be affected by the Law on Inventions and Trademarks, including the trademark link provision. Thus the foreign trademarks would be retained and payments could be continued for their use. In that case, the National Registry on Technology Transfer—which already existed—was empowered to review and control the cost of foreign payments. Questions were raised about the effectiveness of the trademark linkage in modifying consumption patterns. The National Commission on Foreign Investment already had the ability to prevent the expansion of foreign-owned enterprises into new product lines, potentially limiting new consumption habits. Although multiple trademarks for identical products could be prohibited under the inventions and trademarks law, neither this law nor the law on foreign investment effectively prevented product differentiation, the variation-on-a-theme that producers use to sell in different market segments.

This left the protection of Mexican firms from the eventual withdrawal of the trademark by its foreign owner as the main benefit of the trademark link provision. Some small Mexican firms favored this protection, but large Mexican firms utilizing foreign trademarks did so precisely because it enabled them to share in the oligopolistic advantages that use and promotion of prestigious trademarks provide to their users. These firms thus had common interest with the foreign firms from which they licensed foreign trademarks and were not willing to jeopardize their profitable arrangement.

Flexibility is a distinguishing characteristic of successful economic policies in Mexico. Both the law on foreign investments and the law on technology transfer left considerable leeway for bargaining and discretionary application. In contrast, the trademark link provision in the Law on Inventions and Trademarks was obligatory. The provision had been successful in individual cases of joint ventures: Tata-Mercedes in India, General Electric/Esamex and IEM-Westinghouse in Mexico. The provision of the 1976 law, however, was not limited to joint ventures but was applicable to all foreign trademarks. Nor was it limited to a single industry. Some industries were more easily able to comply with the linkage requirement than others; but its obligatory application to all industries meant that a formidable array of the largest and most powerful foreign and national firms in Mexico opposed the law. Some proposed that the linkage of trademarks should become optional, required only at the request of the licensee. Such requests would be likely only when conflicts arose between the foreign owner of a trademark and the Mexican licensee, however. Thus, without the benefits of a gradual creation of goodwill (the buildup of consumer recognition of both names), the double trademark would not provide the increase in bargaining power that the obligatory linkage would have provided.

The trademark link provision of the 1976 Law on Inventions and Trademarks was an effort to challenge a liberal global regime and to regulate the power of foreign corporations in the economy. It identified trademarks as a major structural element of the power of foreign firms in Mexican markets. In the long run, it promised an increase in the bargaining power of Mexican firms affiliated with foreign enterprises and held out the possibility of an economy less dependent on the international economic system. Nevertheless, trademark owners, backed by their governments, were able to make an effective argument that the long-run benefits of the provisions were outweighed by its disadvantages. Under these circumstances it is perhaps surprising that the provision was ever incorporated in the law. The law was not repealed until 1991, and the trademark link provision caused serious friction for ten years.

Conclusion

How can we explain the adoption of and subsequent shift from nationalist policies? In part the explanation lies in the structural characteristics of the international economy and the position of foreign corporations in the Mexican economy. The position of the Mexican private sector, the influence of international organizations and of other states, and the enforcement capacity of the Mexican state contributed to the outcome. The reasons for the success or failure of the three policies discussed in this chapter and chapter 4 can be summarized briefly.

The law on foreign investment institutionalized the policy of Mexicanization for new instruments. The policy was not obligatory. Not only were all existing enterprises exempted from the Mexicanization requirement, but the application to new investments was explicitly made flexible and subject to bargaining. The provisions regulating new establishments and new lines of business were not immediately enforced, thereby defusing the potential opposition of existing foreign subsidiaries in the years when the law was new. Precedent existed for Mexicanization in policies toward specific industries (such as mining) in Mexico and requirements in other countries for minority ownership by foreign enterprises. The Mexican law did not itself serve as a ground-breaking international precedent. Perhaps more important, the law did not immediately affect the control of affiliated enterprises by foreign investors, with the possible exception of completely new investments. And in the case of such investments, Mexican vulnerability was low because the attractiveness of the Mexican market and the growing strength of European and Japanese home economies combined to provide alternative investors for any given project.

In the case of the regulation of technology transfer, in spite of the fact that several regulations of restrictive clauses were labeled obligatory, only the requirement for submission of contracts to Mexican legal jurisdiction was strictly enforced. The main focus of the regulations was on the level of payments, and the negotiations of those payments were quite flexible. By 1990, only registration was required (and in 1991 the law was finally overturned). Moreover, investor firms themselves had flexibility in the way in which profits were taken out of the country because of the convertibility of Mexican currency. Like Mexicanization, the regulation of technology had precedents in other countries, and the Mexican law did not break new ground. Finally, although search procedures were not well developed in the Mexican industry, alternatives for all but the most complex technologies were available from a variety of suppliers, and Mexican vulnerability was therefore low.

In contrast, the attempt to regulate trademarks through linkage to a second mark was obligatory. A specific compliance date was set, and there was no provision for flexible application either by industry or by firms. Although isolated precedents existed for linked trademarks on a firm-specific basis, there was no precedent for a general regulation of trademarks in all industries. Because of this, the Mexican law would have served as international precedent, and the specter of linking their trademarks to a different mark in every host country horrified foreign enterprises. The regulation did increase the control of local enterprises in those cases in which the trademark represented an important aspect of oligopoly market power. Mexican alternatives were not clear. No foreign firms of any nationality came forward to express their willingness to link their trademarks to a Mexican mark. Brand loyalties of Mexican consumers were firmly established through long exposure to heavy advertising. (Advertising in Mexico amounted to 0.60 percent of the GNP in 1974, several times the level of total expenditures on research and development.)[40] The *Malinchista* mentality[41] that had led Mexicans to believe that foreign goods are superior had not been overcome, and the long border with the United States allowed for the possibility that smuggling goods identified by foreign trademarks would become an even greater problem.[42] Most important, Mexico's need to export and to integrate into the global economy meant that nationalist metapreferences were prevented from becoming policy.

By 1991, Mexico was proposing a free trade agreement with the United States and Canada. A new law on industrial property was prepared in late 1990 and submitted to the Mexican Congress in March 1991. After the U.S. Congress approved the "fast track" procedure for free trade negotiations, Mexico approved the new law, which entered into effect on June 28, 1991. It superseded both the 1972 technology transfer law and the 1976 Law on Inventions and Trademarks and brought Mexican legislation much closer to international liberal standards.

In the next chapter, we look more generally at the failure of nationalism in Mexico to provide a viable alternative to international liberalism.

Six

The Limits of Nationalism

Industrial Strategies and the Roles of the State

Mexico has pursued diversified development strategies: commodity exports, import substitution, and export promotion. The nationalist era coincided with the period of import substitution, as earlier chapters have shown. The nationalist state tried to assume most of the functions of foreign investment in the economy. The state played five roles: owner, regulator, promoter, innovator, and financial manager. Some of these roles were played quite poorly, and this contributed to the failure to realize the nationalist metapreference.

Dependency, statism, and liberalism each claims to characterize accurately foreign investment and the role of the state. In this chapter I distinguish three different patterns of state action toward development, suggesting that these three types are responses to different patterns of international trade and foreign investment. None of the three theoretical perspectives is capable of effectively analyzing all three patterns of foreign investment. It is not just intellectual fashion that has led dependency to be supplanted by statism, and statism, in turn, by liberalism; rather, it is changes in the relative importance of different types of foreign investment in global economic relations. This chapter will synthesize the Mexican experience presented in the preceding three chapters, identifying three distinct patterns. Then I shall analyze the five roles of the nationalist state. The state was able to own, regulate, and promote, but it failed to innovate or finance industrialization from domestic sources.

Developing countries bring diverse advantages to the bargaining table when foreign investment is considered. Some countries are rich in natural resources. They may wish to make large one-time investments in mines or in infrastructure projects. Other countries have large markets sufficiently attractive for global firms to establish productive facilities in order to serve that market. In other cases, countries offer inexpensive and disciplined labor forces to firms looking for manufacturing sites for their global markets. Some countries, including Mexico, have all three advantages.

Global corporations likewise bring diverse advantages. Access to capital makes possible massive investment projects, such as mining, railroad construction, and power generation facilities. Technological skills, based on experience in the home country and other developed markets, give some firms the ability to produce manufactured goods efficiently. Global marketing networks make available markets that might otherwise be closed to developing countries' products. Management skills combined with these other factors give firms a competitive advantage. There is no reason, however, why all of these factors should unite in equal proportion in every investment project. In fact, as we shall see, the dominant combinations of country attractions and investor advantages vary.

Three Patterns

In Mexico, three strategies of industrialization have characterized the twentieth century. The first, a development strategy based on the export of primary materials, gave way to a manufacturing strategy based on the substitution of imports. This, in turn, has been supplanted by an export promotion strategy. Now, export promotion has come to dominate primary exports and import substitution in strategic importance and has led to the current push for regional integration.

Industrialization based on primary exports began during the Porfiriato, with the development of mining, petroleum exploitation, and railroads. After the Mexican Revolution, Mexico was the largest foreign producer of petroleum for the United States, and not incidentally the largest single host of U.S. foreign investment.

During the interwar years, the economy began to include more manufacturing enterprises producing goods for the local market, but import substitution industrialization (ISI) did not take off until after World War II, when the government adopted the 1955 Law on New and Necessary Industries. Direct foreign investment (DFI) was welcomed as part of the strategy of ISI, though the later reaction seems to indicate that the extent of foreign investment in manufacturing industries was unanticipated. Indeed, the pattern became one of import substitution industrialization through direct foreign investment: ISI through DFI.

If reliance on foreign investment to replace imports with local manufactures was only partly a conscious strategy, there was no such ambiguity about the use of foreign firms to promote manufactured exports. In 1965, the year after the termination of the special bilateral Bracero Program for migrant workers and just as the negative consequences of import substitution were beginning to be felt, a special program was set up to entice foreign producers to use Mexican labor for the labor-intensive part of their operations. As electronic equipment has become one of the fastest-growing industries in the United States, the in-bond and production-sharing arrangements on the border have grown as well. Moreover, as increased restrictions have been adopted on existing foreign investors, the border industrialization program has been exempted.

Although the three patterns of industrialization were introduced to Mexico in historical sequence, they now coexist. Mexico exports oil, encourages the replacement of imports in many areas, and promotes the export of manufactured goods. But the role of foreign trade and investment is different in each of these sectors of the economy, and the role of the state varies from owner to regulator to promoter.

Let us begin by looking at the patterns of trade that link developing countries to the world economy. The first pattern is one characterized by Peter Evans as "classic dependence." The developing countries are the "hewers of wood and drawers of water" for the global economy. Primary commodities needed by firms in the advanced industrial countries are available in the developing world, and foreign investment is a method to extract them. Those elites within the host country who benefit and have access to foreign exchange also have access to the luxury products of global consumption. Elites emulate the lifestyle and consumption patterns of the industrialized world. However, not only automobiles and grand pianos but tools and equipment—indeed, most manufactured items—must be imported. The wealth generated by commodity exports results in a pattern of inequality within the country and a reliance on imports for all of the products necessary for industrialization and growth.

A second pattern of trade relations is in part a response to the first. High and growing levels of imports of manufactured products were combined with price instability and often long-term declines in the prices earned for commodity exports. In response, the state often regulates imports, using tariffs and quotas to limit importation to those items most necessary for industrialization. For the rest, local and foreign firms can be invited to produce within the local economy those goods that had previously been imported. ISI is thus a strategy made possible by the power of the state to protect the local market and is a response to dependence and to the changing terms of trade in the global economy.

Import substitution is hardly a panacea. In Mexico, local production tended to be inefficient and prices were high. More troublesome, import substitution did not generate exports. In the third strategy of industrialization, which characterizes the late twentieth century, manufactured exports are produced in developing countries for consumption in the industrialized countries, and indeed throughout the world. This third pattern has two components: first, global demand for nontraditional exports and, second, state policies to promote exports. The structure of global industry, and particularly the competitive needs of firms in the developed countries, produced the internationalization of production. Global competition has led to increased competitiveness in the main countries of the industrial world. The automobile industry is a clear example of this: European and Japanese products, with greater efficiency, higher quality, and lower cost, brought intense pressure on the big three auto makers in the United States. Globalized competition meant that old production patterns were inadequate. Antiquated plant facilities and rigid production processes had to give way. The response was a shift away from the continuous assembly line combining raw materials and producing a finished product. Instead, the final product has been divided into components, and those components are produced in sites around the region or around the world. From the perspective of the developing country, gaining a share of this global market in manufactured goods and components was attractive in part for the employment it generated but even more for the foreign exchange it brought.

The transformation of industrial structure, considered in detail in part III, shifted the incentive structure for nationalism and liberalism. When the United States was hegemonic and most industries were stable oligopolies, nationalism had an appealing logic. After the limits of nationalism became more obvious, U.S. preeminence declined, and global industries became both internationalized and highly competitive, liberalism became attractive to the new industrial countries—more attractive, indeed, than to the new nationalists in the North.

Foreign investment has been an important part of each of the three development strategies. Moreover, in each case, the state intervened in the process of development. In each case, market characteristics of the sector in question influenced the role of the state. During the nationalist period, the Mexican state tried to be simultaneously owner, regulator, promoter, innovator, and financier.

The State as Owner

The initial forays of the state into enterprise ownership were a reaction to direct foreign investment. DFI first came to Mexico in large quantities before the revolution, as Mexico was in the process of modernizing and as U.S. enterprises were just beginning to expand abroad. Investments were concentrated in mining, agriculture, railroads, and petroleum. Over time, the power of the state grew, reducing or eliminating DFI in each of these sectors. The nationalization of the railroads began even before the Mexican Revolution. The Cárdenas administration extended the power of the state over the railroads and took over the oil industry in 1938. The trend continued in subsequent administrations; for example, electric power was nationalized in 1960 under the administration of López Mateos. The last major expansion of state ownership, which went beyond the core definition of strategic industries established by the earlier patterns, was the expropriation of the banking system in 1982.

There has been an easily discernible shift in the sectoral locus of U.S. direct investment, at the same time as the total volume of investment grew (with the exception of the 1930s). This gradual shift out of railroads, oil, mining, and utilities was accompanied by an expansion of the role of the state as owner and manager of those same sectors. PEMEX (Petroleos Mexicanos, the oil monopoly) and CFE (the Federal Electricity Commission) are the two largest state-owned enterprises in Mexico; the state owns the railroads and is a majority owner of most of the mines in the country.

The model of the obsolescing bargain fits these industries well. As indicated by Vernon's general argument, by Moran's study of copper in Chile, and by Tugwell's study of oil in Venezuela, among others, the original deals between foreign enterprises and the state in natural resources and basic infrastructure industries became obsolete, with the power of the state increasing. As they also point out, the shift was not a rapid one. Only gradually did the state move up the "learning curve" (to use Moran's phrase) and take over complete control.[1]

Under the Mexican regulations summarized in the 1973 law on foreign investment (see appendix 2 and chap. 4), only the state may engage in productive activities in petroleum, basic petrochemicals, nuclear energy, electricity, railways, and radio and telegraph communications. Only Mexican nationals (private or state) may be active in radio and television, transportation, forestry, and gas distribution. The sphere of action of the state is circumscribed but extensive.

In each of these activities (but notably not in banking), access to the land or natural resources of the nation has been crucial for the success of the enterprise. Although state enterprises in these sectors have continued to rely on imports for intermediate and capital goods, large enterprises such as PEMEX and CFE have become more self-sufficient in technology and have either owned or obtained locally many inputs for the industry. Because of sectoral characteristics of the investments and because of the strategic importance of the state, the relationship of investors to the state is well described in this sector as an obsolescent or obsolescing bargain: the power of the state has increased over time and foreign ownership has been phased out.[2]

State-owned enterprises in Mexico are of major importance in the economy, especially in energy, transportation, communications, and fertilizers. PEMEX absorbs more than a quarter of all investment by the state. CFE absorbs more than 14 percent of total state investments. CONASUPO is a large diversified enterprise in the food area, though its major activities involve support prices, supplies, and distribution, rather than the manufacture of processed food products. The workers' housing fund (INFONAVIT) is the major governmental institution for the building and financing of workers' housing. It receives its funding from obligatory contributions by employers and undertakes research in housing design and construction as well as the financing of workers' homes. The state owns all railroads, and during the oil boom engaged in a massive effort to update and improve them. The state is also active in hospitals and welfare services operated primarily through the Mexican Social Security Institute (IMSS). None of these major state entities were touched by privatization in the 1980s.

Leaving aside debates over the inherent inefficiency of state-owned enterprises, there were problems with the state as owner. First, some enterprises were created with an explicit social function, such as providing social and industrial infrastructure. These state enterprises are similar to regular government offices: they are net users of funds. The same cost/price pressures that kept foreign electric power firms from making money operated with greater effect on state-owned firms. Second, some enterprises were taken over precisely because they were losing money—to preserve jobs, for example. Third, even in those areas that should generate earnings, namely, commodity exports, state enterprises became subject to the cyclical variations of global commodity markets. Global trends worked against the state: prices for primary commodities other than petroleum have been in decline for most of the period after 1970. Petroleum prices rose dramatically in real terms after 1970, fueling the 1977–81 oil boom in Mexico, only to crash unceremoniously in 1981–82 and 1985.[3] In other words, ownership did not insulate the state from either social pressures or global trends.

The State as Regulator: Import Substitution

The decline of DFI in industries oriented toward the export of primary materials was more than offset by the expansion of industries designed to satisfy the domestic consumer market. ISI relied heavily on foreign direct investors, who accepted the implied invitation of high tariffs to invest in the most dynamic industries in Mexican manufacturing: automobiles, chemicals and pharmaceuticals, electrical equipment, and food processing.

Raymond Vernon has suggested that the obsolescing bargain holds for manufacturing industries as well as for raw materials industries (although he conceded that the fit may be somewhat tighter in the latter).

> There is a basis for picturing the development of overseas manufacturing facilities in the following terms: To begin with, U.S.-controlled enterprises generate new products and processes in response to the high per-capita income and the relative availability of factors in the United States; they introduce these new products or processes abroad through exports; when their export position is threatened they establish overseas subsidiaries to exploit what remains of their advantage for a period of time, then lose it again as the basis for the original lead is completely eroded.[4]

Given the continued and expanding presence of foreign investors in manufacturing industries producing for the domestic market, I argue that the relationship in manufacturing for the domestic market is better characterized as a "renewable" bargain,[5] with the state as regulator.

What are the characteristics of the renewable bargain? It is most appropriate for an understanding of manufacturing industries. It is particularly appropriate in industries that produce consumer goods, whether those are consumer durables like automobiles or nondurables like food products. According to the renewable bargain, firms enter a new market in a relatively weak position, since their established clientele is small. If there is little competition, the firm may rapidly establish a strong position in the market; if many other firms also produce the same product, the firm will have to work harder to establish the prestige of its products and to ensure its share of the market. It is for this reason that many firms are willing to establish a base in a country that presents an attractive market potential, even though the firm may absorb losses for many years.

Since firms want access to local markets and the state controls that access, state regulatory potential is likely to be greatest on the entry of firms into markets. At that point firms are anxious to establish a foothold and to begin to create goodwill for their products. However, precisely because the market is undeveloped and the new producers promise to produce goods that were not previously available or were previously imported, the state is not likely to restrict entry. Once foreign enterprises in the consumer goods industries are well established behind the tariff walls, and particularly if the market for specific goods can be characterized as a protected oligopoly in which trademarks and product differentiation serve as major barriers to the entry of new firms, displacement of the industry leaders by competition or by state action is difficult. New firms must compete for the attention and product loyalty of consumers whose preferences have already been influenced, and there are strong international norms against the limitation or nationalization of trademarks and the goodwill they represent.

Unlike cases of investment in raw materials where the value of the initial investment declines over time, the value of goodwill as an asset tends to increase over time. Because trademarks in every country are indefinitely renewable, there is no reason to expect firm power to decline. Enterprises in the food-processing industry, for example, often favor contracts for technology and trademarks for which the term is indefinite.[6] This suggests that in some cases the renewable bargain may even become a self-renewing permanent investment (i.e., automatically renewed without explicit bargaining).

The renewable bargain is consistent with the behavior of foreign enterprises described as "oligopolistic reaction." Consumer goods producers are anxious to get established in large markets, and if one firm threatens to establish a large market share or to increase its share, other foreign enterprises want to establish themselves as well, in order to stabilize market shares within the oligopoly. Work by Thomas Horst has shown that firms for which trademarks and advertising expenditures are important are among those firms in the manufacturing sector most likely to invest abroad.

Bennett and Sharpe suggested that the renewable bargain functions in the automobile industry; other studies indicate results compatible with this model for the pharmaceutical industry and for the tobacco industry. Bennett and Sharpe concluded one study of the automobile industry in Mexico as follows:

> In a high-technology, consumer-goods manufacturing sector, such as the automobile industry, the situation (of the obsolescing bargain) is often reversed. Access to the domestic market is the state's principal basis of bargaining power, and can be used most effectively at the point of initial investment. After that, the firms are entrenched in the host country through their relationships with suppliers, distributors, labor and consumers. Because such manufacturing en-

terprises are integrated in the local economy to a far higher degree than resource extractors, they establish relationships within the host country which significantly enhance their bargaining power, both by reinforcing the host country's needs for their kind of production and their products and by being able to mobilize domestic allies, and so long as the industry is dependent upon external sources of technology, the possibility of nationalization by the host country is not a credible threat.[7]

Though Bennett and Sharpe point to consumer loyalty as an element of the strength of foreign enterprises in consumer goods manufacturing, their primary emphasis is on technology. As part III will show, evidence from the food industry indicates that marketing and trademarks can be as important as technology or capital. The food-processing industry is not a high-technology industry. If technology were the crucial variable, foreign enterprises producing food products would have been displaced long ago. Both the obsolescing bargain model and Bennett and Sharpe's model emphasizing technology predict that producers of canned fruits and vegetables, canned milk products, breakfast cereals, and pasta products would have been displaced from the Mexican market. They have not been displaced: Del Monte, Nestlè, Kellogg's, and other well-known brands all continue to prosper in Mexico and in many other developing markets.

The state became more active in its regulation of foreign manufacturers, especially by establishing Mexicanization as the norm for new investments after 1973 and by reviewing and negotiating contracts for foreign technology. The law on technology transfer increased the intervention of the state: agreements that previously had been two-party transactions between private firms were now three-party transactions involving the state.[8] For the first time contracts were required to be filed with a state agency, and state approval was stipulated. But the state only intervened after a contractual agreement had been drawn up; it was thus most effective in reducing the payments abroad by local licensees for certain services (such as trademarks or technical assistance) and in eliminating clauses containing some restrictive business practices. The regulation was not designed to create an effective national technological search capacity, let alone to replace foreign technology with national or state-generated technology.[9] The role of the state in this area was clearly regulatory, not competitive.

Few if any manufacturing firms have been required to pull out due to state regulations. There has been some bargaining over technology contracts and some increase in joint ventures, but most foreign investors in the major manufacturing industries aimed at the domestic market are still actively operating in Mexico. The bargain may have changed at the margins, but it is renewed and does not result in fade-out as occurred in the raw materials industries. The state as regulator may slow the flow of DFI or it may change behavior, but it does not replace foreign investment.

The State as Promoter: Manufactured Exports

A completely different pattern operated in the manufacturing industries integrated into the international operations of foreign firms. Most of these firms are in electronics or textiles and were set up as part of the Maquiladora Program, an in-bond industrialization program.[10] The growth of these industries has been extraordinary since 1965: from a dozen plants to over 1,100; from 3,000 employees to more than 400,000. (See table 6.1.)[11] This program has grown to include about 10 percent of all manufacturing jobs in Mexico.

Special provisions of the U.S. tariff code allowed for the entry of goods assembled from components originating in the United States, with tax only on the value-added abroad. Mexico has been the primary beneficiary of these provisions, followed by the Asian "gang of four": Taiwan, Singapore, Hong Kong, and South Korea, in decreasing order. Most of the value-added has been in the electrical and electronic products area (and within this, televisions and television parts were most important). Following in terms of dutiable value-added have

TABLE 6.1   General Data on In-Bond Processing Plants in Mexico, 1965–1990

Year	No. of Plants	No. of Workers	Workers Per Plant
1965	12	3,000	250
1970[a]	120	20,000	167
1975	454	67,000	148
1980	620	120,000	193
1985	760	212,000	279
1990[b]	2,077	467,808	225

Sources: Unless otherwise indicated, data are from Manuel Martínez del Campo, "Ventajas e inconvenientes de la actividad maquiladora en México: Algunos aspectos de la subcontractación internacional," *Comercio Exterior* 33 (2) (1983): 148. Data for 1985 are from *El Mercado de Valores* 49 (9) (1989): 7.
[a]Other official figures are 108 plants and 15,858 workers.
[b]Data for 1990 are from the American Chamber of Commerce of Mexico.

been automotive products, office machines, apparel, and toys and games.[12] By the late 1980s, the dominance of electronics was still notable, but automobile parts and components had grown to nearly one quarter of the total.

In the *maquila* industry, production is geared to exports, and the Mexican government benefits by having increased foreign exchange. (The *maquila* industry, or *maquiladora*, derives its name from the verb used to describe the grinding of grain brought by farmers to a mill. It has primarily been an assembly industry.) Little of the process is controlled by Mexico. Under the special regulations that govern this sector, foreign ownership of 100 percent is allowed, although Mexican entrepreneurs can also participate in the program. (About 40 percent of the *maquiladoras* are Mexican owned.) Most of the technology is foreign, since the processes are integrated into home company operations. And few of the inputs are produced locally: only 1 or 2 percent initially, up to 4 to 6 percent more recently.[13] The production process is integrated, production is shared, and the industry as a whole is accurately described as foreign. The role of the state is that of promoter for DFI, but the intention was to create an isolated export enclave while pursuing a nationalist development strategy domestically.

The three strategies of development provide evidence of alternative visions or orienting preferences (*rectoría*, in the Mexican idiom) of the state, to which foreign investment should respond. The nationalist metapreference did not apply equally to all sectors. As nontraditional exports grew in importance, the liberal promotional role of the state did not remain an enclave strategy, but became a dominant metapreference.

Why did the liberal strategy of integration with the United States and the world economy, initially developed as a specialized and limited program for maquila assembly operations along the border, become the dominant strategy in Mexico for the 1990s? The answer lies in part in the transformation of the global industrial structure, explored in detail for three industries in part III. But the failure of the nationalist vision was also the product of the failure to replace foreign capital and technology with a coherent domestic development strategy. An analysis of Mexico's weak indigenous technological capacity illustrates the problem with the state as innovator.

The State as Would-Be Innovator

Technological autonomy, even under conditions of interdependence, requires the effective integration of three institutional vertices. The

Argentine scholar Jorge Sábato has identified three institutional bases of technological development, which have come to be known as the Sábato triangle: government, productive enterprises, and centers of technological research. Miguel Wionczek gave the nationalist rationale for technological development, not only for autonomous development but also for absorption of foreign technology: "The incorporation of [transferred technology] into the productive structure and its positive effect on the social organization of the receiving country depends almost exclusively on the ability of the host country to establish its own capacity to absorb the technological knowledge received, in accord with the priorities indicated by its development model."[14] Thus, as Moran and Stepan emphasized regarding the success of expropriation, the success of a nationalist project in the area of technology and industrial development depends on the ability of the state to develop its replacement capacity. A critique of the liberal vision is as strong as the viability of the alternative.

The Institutional Development
of the State as Innovator

Mexico has a limited innovative past and the effort to create state agencies to replace foreign technologies failed. The country has a relatively small number of full-time researchers, and that number in turn is highly concentrated in a few institutions. In 1974 approximately 17 percent of the country's 5,352 researchers were at the National University (UNAM), with another 8.6 percent at the Mexican Petroleum Institution (IMP), the largest single research institute in the country. At the time of a CONACYT study done in 1976, nearly one third of the labor devoted to research and development in Mexico was done by personnel in the ten largest research institutes, and the thirty largest accounted for over half of such labor.[15]

Some of Mexico's research institutions and some offices and departments within governmental ministries and educational institutions have research and development as their main activities (see table 6.2). Besides the Mexican Petroleum Institute for oil-related research, important centers exist for agriculture studies (INIA and CIMMYT); for the social sciences, especially anthropology, history, and rural development (CIESAS); for research on nuclear energy (INEN); for nutrition studies (INN); and for health and welfare studies (IMSS and ISSSTE). These research institutes depend on the federal government for their budgets even though they are administratively autonomous, and their policies are normally coordinated with the state-owned enterprises and government ministries with which they are associated. Several federal government ministries sponsor research within their various offices, as well as through their support of the autonomous research institutes.

UNAM is the largest single educational institution in the country. With more than three million university students in Mexico, however, other institutions have begun to share the burden of higher education; the system of regional and state universities, for example, has grown rapidly in recent years. The National Polytechnic Institute (IPN), founded by Lázaro Cárdenas in the 1930s, is a major center for technical training and research in Mexico City, as is the Autonomous Technological University of Mexico (UTAM), founded by the government in the mid-1970s. El Colegio de México and the Center for Advanced Studies and Research in Social Anthropology (CIESAS) both specialize in social science research and training. The Monterrey Technological Institute, modeled after MIT in the United States, has an excellent reputation for technical training, and many businessmen and technicians in the private sector having received their training there. The Chapingo Agriculture School, like the National Institute for Agriculture Research (INIA) and the Wheat and Corn Research Center (CIMMYT), has achieved an international reputation. The rapidly increasing demand for education has placed the system under strain, but Mexico has a tradition of respect (sometimes honored in the breach) for independent, quality education.[16]

One of the weaknesses of science and technology in Mexico has been the lack of coordination between research centers and industry. In looking at the linkages described by the Sábato triangle, we find a fairly strong connection between government and research; but the technological links between research and industry and between government and industry are quite weak.

The founding of CONACYT in 1970 was directed at raising the level of priority placed on science and technology and at providing an institution that could coordinate the governmental, industrial, and research sectors in Mexico. Through organizations such as Información Técnica (INFOTEC-CONACYT, which offers information and advice to Mexican businesses seeking technology) and Mexicana de Tecnología (charged with fostering the export of technologies developed in Mexico), CONACYT attempts to fill gaps by providing linkages among the various sectors. The creation of a series of national testing laboratories was another step toward the integration and coordination of technologically related activities at the national level. Nevertheless, research centers in Mexico were not sufficiently linked to existing industry to make fruitful use of underutilized factors of production.

TABLE 6.2   Institutional Composition of the Mexican Technology System

Governmental Institutions

Regulatory
Undersecretariat for Foreign
  Investment and Technology Transfer
  (includes Office of Inventions and
  Trademarks, SECOFI)
Ministry of Foreign Relations
Ministry of the Interior (residence
  visas)
Ministry of the Treasury and Public
  Credit (foreign remittances, taxes,
  and tax exemptions)

Promotional
Informational, discussion,
matchmaking:
  Ministry of Foreign Relations
  Ministry of Commerce
  Ministry of Planning and Budget
  CONACYT
  NAFINSA
Financial, participatory:
  NAFINSA
  Bilateral commissions
  SOMEX
  Trust funds (FOGAIN, FOMIN,
  FOMEX, FONEI, FONEP)

Productive Institutions

Technology Consumers/Recipients
Private:
  "Monterrey Group" (Alfa, VISA,
  etc.), ICA, etc.
Mixed enterprises:
  NAFINSA and affiliates
  SOMEX and affiliates
  Coinvestments, joint ventures
State-owned enterprises:
  PEMEX (oil and petrochemicals)
  CFE (electricity)
  CONASUPO (food)
  INFONAVIT (housing)
  IMSS (health and welfare)

Informational/Bargaining Groups
Ad hoc commissions, committees
Institutional private bargaining—
Business Coordinating Council (CCE):
  CONCAMIN (industry)
  CANACINTRA (manufacturing)
  COPARMEX (industry)
  CONCANACO (commerce)
  Mexican Businessmen's Committee
  ABM (banking)
  AMIS (insurance)
  ANADE (business lawyers)
  CEMAI (international affairs)
  More than forty bilateral
  businessmen's committees

Scientific and Technological Institutions

Research Institutes
IMP (oil, gas, petrochemicals)
INIA (agriculture)
INAH (anthropology, history)
INEN (nuclear energy)
INN (nutrition)
IMSS (health and welfare)

Private Research
International firms with local in-house
  research and development
Foreign consulting firms (both sales
  offices and direct investments)
Local firms

Educational Institutions
Universidad Nacional Autónoma de
  México (UNAM)
Instituto Politécnico Nacional (IPN)
El Colegio de México
CIESAS
Instituto Tecnológico de Monterrey
Regional universities

Coordinating Institutions
CONACYT-INFOTEC
UNIDO-NAFINSA
President and advisory commissions
Ministry of Programming and Budget

Source: Whiting, "The Politics of Technology Transfer in Mexico" (1983), with modifications.

CONACYT, as an autonomous council, enjoys an advisory relationship to all bodies dealing with topics of science and technology. Its status as an independent council not tied to any ministry gives it increased flexibility, but that same independence isolates it from intra- and interministerial and private sector activities relevant to its mission. CONACYT's most important single mission so far is training (the development of human resources), and a large part of its budget is spent on scholarships for Mexican students both in Mexico and abroad. As foreign exchange became scarce, CONACYT suffered.

CONACYT is not the only institution engaged in the coordination of various sectors and activities. NAFINSA has been especially important in planning and coordination at the national level in its work with the UN Industrial Development Organization (UNIDO), headquartered in Vienna. Two UNIDO officials, Enrique Aguilar and Fernando Fajnzylber, played particularly important roles in pushing Mexico's autonomous technological development. Aguilar, a Mexican national employed in Vienna, helped design Mexico's law on technology transfer, returned to Mexico to be the first director of the technology transfer registry, and was UNIDO's liaison with Mexico on matters of technology. Fajnzylber, a Chilean economist representing UNIDO in Mexico, worked for some time with NAFINSA on a massive NAFINSA-UNIDO study of Mexico's capital goods industries in various priority sectors. But the same irony of ISI through DFI applies to capital goods: it is foreign investors, not the state, that have the technological capacity to stimulate Mexico's capital goods industry.

In coordinating activities of different ministries and sectors, Mexico's president and the office of his advisers are particularly important. Since Mexico has a strongly presidential system, the president's interest and the efforts of his advisers are perhaps the most effective means for bringing about the coordination of activities or the creation of new institutions and patterns of behavior. Furthermore, in the presidential system, the initiative and full support of the president are necessary for the successful implementation of plans and programs.

Interministerial commissions are important instruments through which Mexico's president can formulate policies that cross areas of responsibility as defined by existing ministries or institutions. The National Foreign Investment Commission, formed in 1973, and the National Commission on Industrial Development and the National Commission on Agroindustrial Development, both formed in mid-1979, are important examples of institutional mechanisms for high-level consultations and decision-making at the interministerial level.[17]

Although these three commissions have been important, the existence of a commission does not necessarily mean that it has great power, that it in fact determines policy, or that it will endure. Much depends on the priority given by the president to the commission's area of responsibility and, in turn, the importance given to the commission by the ministers who compose it. (For example, depending on their priorities, ministers may attend a commission meeting themselves, send a subsecretary, or send another alternate.)

Other government institutions explicitly tried to promote transfers of technology judged necessary for national development, providing information, conducting discussions or negotiations, and at times matchmaking between potential suppliers of foreign technology and national enterprises or institutions. The Ministry of Foreign Relations at times tried this, and Mexican embassies abroad, responsible to the ministry, certainly served as sources of information for nationals of other countries. However, the missions and embassies were low on the "need to know" list. The Ministry of Commerce, which also engaged in informational activities relevant to technology transfer, was less likely to become involved in specific discussions or negotiations on technology. The Mexican Foreign Trade Institute (IMCE) had offices abroad in many countries and provided information to interested firms or parties regarding possibilities for technology agreements.[18] But even taken as a whole, these activities could at best complement, not replace, foreign investment.

More specialized and relevant for technology transfer, however, are the activities of CONACYT and NAFINSA. CONACYT, working in conjunction with the Ministry on Foreign Relations, has successfully concluded a number of bilateral agreements in the area of science and technology. Like many other governmental institutions, NAFINSA is quite active in providing information to potential suppliers of technology. However, NAFINSA is most likely to be helpful when it might finance the project itself, either alone or through a coinvestment. Bilateral commissions such as INGERMEX have expanded the role of NAFINSA in this area. While serving as secretary of finance, David Ibarra described NAFINSA's role this way: "Industrial development forms without a doubt the very center of the responsibility of Nacional Financiera. Here the selection of the best foreign technologies should be combined with the activities which are prompted with priority" (NAFINSA promotional materials). As part of its international expansion, NAFINSA opened offices in London, New York, Washington, and Tokyo.[19]

The mixed public and private bank SOMEX did not have the extension and reach of NAFINSA, particularly in international activities.

However, because of its merger with Banco Mexicano and its expansion of industrial development activities (through purchasing shares of existing companies and by organizing new firms), SOMEX could, like NAFINSA, become more active in the international search for and contracting of foreign technology.[20]

Finally, it is worth noting that a series of special-purpose trust funds (usually established under either the Bank of Mexico or NAFINSA) were created to offer information, advice, and assistance to Mexican entrepreneurs with regard to technology as well as finance. These trust funds, or *fideicomisos*, have been founded at various times during the past several decades, some as early as 1953 (FOGAIN); and they have continued to grow. They include FOGAIN (Fund for the Development of Small and Medium Enterprise); FOMIN (Fund for the Development of Industry), which has operated since 1972 to encourage decentralization, import substitution, and export promotion; FONEI (Fund for Industrial Equipment), which has contributed to studies of industrial equipment; FOMEX (Fund for the Development of Exports of Manufactured Products); and FONEP (National Fund for Preinvestment Studies). Besides aiding in the selection of foreign technology, these trust funds are supposed to promote the export of Mexican technology.[21] Some of them have been eliminated or consolidated with the privatization drive since 1983, but others have been created. After José Warman failed to get his computer policy established as law (see chap. 8), he went on to head the Center for Electronics Technology and Informatics. Unlike the earlier *fideicomisos*, this center relies upon financing from participating private companies. But the general purpose of linking the institutional capacity of the state to the private sector is the same.

The problem with most of these organizations is that they are easy to create, hard to pay for, and harder still to kill. The major institutions of development in Mexico have shown considerable continuity over time, continuing to expand their function and role in the economy from one decade to the next. Although some institutions develop more rapidly than others under a given presidential administration, the state has been slow to withdraw from a particular form of intervention once it has established the institutional apparatus with which to intervene. Many of the touted reductions in state entities were in fact consolidations and rationalizations.

The Failure of the Statist/Nationalist Model

The array of technological institutions just described does not constitute a replacement for foreign technology. Sábato's industry–government–research institute model describes a national or sectoral technological system. For some sectors or industries, or even for entire countries, the triangle may not exist, or the sides of the triangle may be weak or nonexistent.[22] Mexico has not succeeded in producing an indigenous technological capacity, even by Latin American standards (see tables 6.3 and 6.4). As figure 4 shows, foreign technology creates a series of external linkages to the Mexican triangle that are strongest between the foreign supplier of technology and the national recipient firm.

Indeed, Sábato argued that it is the availability of foreign technology that keeps the national triangle weak. National enterprise accepts available foreign technology, government avoids defining or implementing a policy of technological development, and the national research establishment, to the extent that one exists, dedicates itself to complementary activities rather than developing an independent research capacity. He describes a vicious circle, which "accelerates progressively: dependency (the 'technology should come from abroad')—lack of local innovation ('why generate innovations if you can buy them?')—inferiority complex ('we cannot create')—('we don't know how to create') and so on."[23] Sábato laments the fact that insti-

TABLE 6.3   Investment, Technology, and Industrial Property in Mexico: Foreign Participation, 1983–1987 (Percentages)

Origin	Amount of Investment	Technology Contracts	Patents and Certificates of Invention	Registered Trademarks
Total	100.0	100.0	100.0	100.0
National	91.0[a]	67.8	6.0	48.0
Foreign	9.0[b]	32.2	94.0	52.0
of which:				
United States	65.5	75.0	56.4	51.2
Federal Republic of Germany	6.9	3.1	7.9	8.7
Japan	5.6	2.3	6.5	4.4
Switzerland	4.4	1.3	3.6	4.8
United Kingdom	4.7	2.2	3.6	5.3
France	2.8	3.4	6.9	8.8
Other countries	10.1	12.7	15.1	16.8
Total foreign	100.0	100.0	100.0	100.0

Source: Executive Secretariat of the National Foreign Investment Commission, *Summary of the 1983–87 Report* (Mexico City, 1988).
[a]Gross fixed capital information (Secretariat of Planning and Budget).
[b]Financial flows of new investments and reinvestments (Bank of Mexico).

TABLE 6.4   Research, Development, and Patents in Argentina, Brazil, Chile, and Mexico

Scientists and Engineers Employed in Research and Experimental Development

Country	Year	Scientists and Engineers in R&D	Scientists and Engineers in R&D per 10,000 People
Argentina	1982	10,486	3.6
Brazil	1982	32,508	2.6
Chile	1984	1,587	1.3
Mexico	1984	16,679	2.2

Expenditures for Research and Experimental Development

Country	Year	Expenditures on R&D (in Millions of 1982 Dollars)	Expenditures on R&D as a Percentage of GDP	Expenditures on R&D Per Capita in 1982 Dollars
Argentina	1981	561.40	0.77	19.57
Brazil	1978	1,592.84	0.75	13.75
Chile	1980	139.59	0.63	12.52
Mexico	1984	881.50	0.50	11.37

Patent Applications in Selected Countries of Latin America

	Patent Applications			
	1980		1985	
Country	Total	Applications by Residents (%)	Total	Applications by Residents (%)
Argentina	4,332	29.3	3,838	30.8
Brazil	8,377	25.7	8,379	23.3
Chile	825	17.0	687	19.9
Mexico	5,472	12.9	4,048	16.0

Patents Granted in Selected Countries of Latin America

	Patents Granted			
	1980		1985	
Country	Total	Patents Granted to Residents (%)	Total	Patents Granted to Residents (%)
Argentina	4,570	34.8	1,677	30.4
Brazil	3,843	9.1	3,934	15.4
Chile	817	8.7	455	9.7
Mexico	2,552	6.8	1,374	6.6

Source: InterAmerican Development Bank, Social and Economic Report, 1988 (Washington: IDB, 1988).

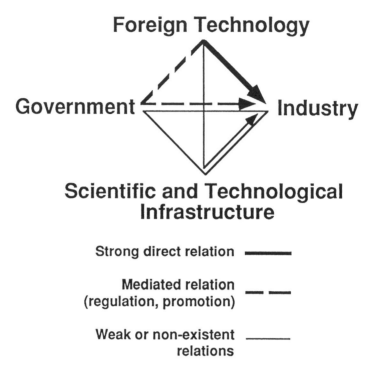

Strong direct relation ━━━

Mediated relation ━ ━
(regulation, promotion)

Weak or non-existent ━━━
relations

FIGURE 4. Technology Transfer in Mexico: External Relations and the
Sábato Triangle
Source: Van R. Whiting, Jr., "The Politics of Technology Transfer in Mexico."
Research Report Series, 37, Center for U.S.-Mexican Studies, University of
California, San Diego, 1984.

tutions and individual officials often are actually unaware of the problem of technological dependence and its associated costs: the high
cost of imported technology, inadequate absorption and adaptation
of imported technology, and forgone opportunities for the development of new, appropriate, and needed products and processes. By
implication, the way out of the vicious circle is initiated by *concienti-
zación*: waking up, coming to an awareness of the problem. But those
whose nationalist metapreferences included technological conscious-
ness-raising have been pushed to the sidelines by those who see foreign
technology as a pragmatic alternative to nationalist wishes. The over-
whelming push for exports in the wake of the debt crisis led to increasing rather than decreasing external integration in the technological area.

The State as Financier

The most profound failure of the nationalist project was in the role of the state as financier. The story of the debt crisis is fairly clear by now. On the supply side, excess liquidity in money center banks in the 1970s resulted from a combination of dollar deposits from OPEC exporters and recession conditions in the OECD countries. Bankers rushed to lend to sovereign borrowers. On the demand side, the Mexican state engaged in a series of actions that generated a rapidly growing public external debt.

External Indebtedness

Mexico relied increasingly on commercial loans rather than on either official lending or DFI to cover government expenditures and bal-ance-of-payments shortfalls. Although unintended, the effect was to replace DFI, "unbundling" the capital from technology and manage-ment. Capital flowed directly to the state from the international com-mercial banks. During the two administrations from 1970 to 1982, five trends exacerbated Mexico's external indebtedness. First, public spending expanded. Expenditures of the central government, espe-cially on social welfare and industrialization, nearly doubled as a share of gross national product (GNP). Second, state enterprises generated massive losses. The number of state enterprises and decentralized agencies expanded dramatically (from roughly 100 in 1970 to more than 900 at the peak), and expenditures as a share of GNP doubled. Third, the petrolization of the economy induced a massive flow of financial resources into a highly cyclical industry. Fourth, conflicts with the private sector and especially the nationalization of the banks in 1982 resulted in massive transfers of Mexican financial assets abroad. This capital flight, concentrated in 1976, 1981–82, and 1986, was estimated by Morgan Guaranty Trust Company at $84 billion by the end of 1987.[24] This includes appreciated assets; net outflows from 1977 to 1987 amounted to an estimated $45 billion, or about one third of the total capital flight from fifteen major debtor countries. And fifth, heavy indebtedness, on variable terms, just as global interest rates peaked and global commodity prices fell, meant that interest payments abroad were a major and growing financial drain. Table 6.5 shows the magnitude and growth of the external debt.

There is another part to the story, however. The nationalist meta-preference was not to replace foreign investors with foreign creditors, *socios* with *prestamistas*. Rather, the plan was to tie the regulation of foreign investment to a tax reform that would have funded the state

TABLE 6.5 External Debt by Sector, at Year End, 1971–1988 (in Millions of Dollars)

Year	Public External Debt	% GDP	Private External Debt	% GDP	Foreign Official Bank Debt	% GDP	IMF	% GDP	Total	% GDP
1971	4,546	11.6	1,833	4.7	—	—	—	—	6,379	16.3
1972	5,065	11.2	1,054	2.3	—	—	—	—	6,119	13.5
1973	7,071	12.8	2,066	3.7	—	—	—	—	9,137	16.5
1974	9,975	13.9	2,224	3.1	—	—	—	—	12,199	16.9
1975	14,449	16.4	4,480	5.1	—	—	—	—	19,929	21.5
1976	19,600	22.1	6,500	7.3	—	—	—	—	26,100	29.4
1977	22,912	28.0	6,800	8.3	—	—	1,200	1.5	30,912	37.7
1978	26,264	25.6	7,200	7.0	—	—	1,200	1.2	34,664	33.8
1979	29,757	22.1	10,500	7.8	—	—	—	—	40,257	29.9
1980	33,813	17.4	16,900	8.7	—	—	—	—	50,713	26.0
1981	52,961	21.2	21,900	8.8	—	—	—	—	74,861	29.9
1982	59,730	35.0	23,907	14.0	8,531	5.0	240	0.1	92,409	54.2
1983	66,559	44.7	19,107	12.9	6,909	4.6	1,204	0.8	93,780	63.8
1984	69,378	39.5	18,500	10.5	6,340	3.6	2,433	1.4	96,652	55.0
1985	72,061	39.1	16,719	9.1	4,824	2.6	2,943	1.6	96,568	52.4
1986	75,351	58.1	16,061	12.4	5,551	4.3	4,028	3.1	100,992	77.8
1987	81,407	57.1	15,107	10.6	5,837	4.1	5,119	3.6	107,471	75.4
1988	81,003	45.8	7,114	4.0	7,481	4.2	4,786	2.7	100,385	56.8

Source: El Mercado de Valores 9 (May 1, 1989).

and its development efforts from domestic resources. That failure is worth recounting in detail, for it shows the weakness of a program to replace foreign capital with taxes on local capital. The effect was that the local capital left Mexico and became "foreign," too.

The Failed Tax Reform

Echeverría's 1972 law on foreign investment was initially paired with a tax reform to raise state revenues. In the last months of 1972, while most public attention was focused on the proposals for the new law on the transfer of technology, intensive private negotiations on the regulation of foreign investment were taking place. Under discussion were both the regulation of DFI and a major tax reform. The two were linked: the tax reform proposed that all shares in Mexican companies, whatever the nationality of their owners, should be issued in the name of their owner rather than as bearer shares. This provision would have made it possible to know with certainty the nationality of the owners of companies; it would also have made it possible to know with certainty the economic interests and tax obligations of wealthy Mexicans. At the start of the negotiations, the major agencies of the government were unified in their support for the conversion of bearer shares to nominative shares. The Ministry of the Treasury was charged with the development of the tax reform, and the Ministry of Industry and Commerce was in charge of the development of the law on foreign investment. By the time the initiatives were sent to the Congress, however, the proposal for the limitation of bearer shares had been dropped.

One interpretation suggests that this was the result of bureaucratic politics within the Mexican government. In a 1980 article by Susan Kaufmann Purcell and John Purcell, the authors argued that "during the intragovernmental bargaining over fiscal reform, major opposition to the elimination of bearer anonymous shares came from the Treasury and the Bank of Mexico. Their argument was that such a reform would damage Mexico's investment climate and would cause capital to flee abroad."[25] The private sector position prevailed, and a clearly established state metapreference was not translated into policy.

The fiscal reform and the elimination of bearer shares that it entailed is a classic case of what some call a nondecision. Neither the proposals nor the discussions surrounding them were made public at the time. They were never submitted to the Congress, and they were not adopted.[26] Fortunately, in the case of the 1972 tax reform, although the moment of final decision has not been revealed, enough information is available to show how the power of the private sector defeated the reform.

The decision not to carry out a significant fiscal reform was crucial not only for the regulation of foreign investment but for the Mexican economy as a whole. With the rapid increase in government expenditures, both by administrative government agencies and decentralized organizations, sources of government income became a critical aspect of national economic policies. As table 6.5 shows, public debt grew from 11.6 percent of gross domestic product (GDP) in 1971 to 22.1 percent in 1976. Total government expenditures, about 25 percent of all expenditures in the economy in 1970, grew to almost 28 percent by 1972 and continued to increase constantly, to 32.8 percent by the end of the Echeverría administration. Where was the financing to come from? If not from taxation, where? The answer was debt: the foreign debt of the Mexican public sector reached new levels in every year of the Echeverría administration, from about $300 million per year in 1971 to over $5 billion in 1976. Mexico's public foreign debt balance increased by more than a factor of 4 from 1971 to 1976.

In Mexico, both public officials and private businessmen and lawyers hesitate to criticize the president or to describe specific relations with the executive, except in private. But once a president has left office, participants and observers are sometimes more willing to speak. My interviews with government and business officials on the topic of the foreign investment law and fiscal reform, from the former president on down, revealed not one who thought that competition among different government agencies was the primary explanation for the failure of the fiscal reform and the elimination of bearer shares. All agreed that the measure was a crucial one. Similar tax reforms had been proposed in 1964 and had failed then. But most government officials believed that the measures had been closer to passage in 1972; a representative of the largest business confederation, CONCAMIN, believed that it had been "a close call." Most of the private business lawyers and representatives of the business confederation interviewed were relieved that the reform measure had failed, although a few were willing to concede that some of the fiscal problems that Mexico faced could have been ameliorated had the measure passed. None of those I interviewed could verify the exact point at which the measure was abandoned, but several referred to late-night meetings within the homes of ministerial officials at which the issues were thrashed out.

No one I interviewed suggested that President Echeverría had abandoned the fiscal reform willingly. The former president himself acknowledged to me in an interview the importance of the measure and pointed out that every time the elimination of bearer shares had been proposed, the proposal had been defeated. But asked directly to explain the defeat, he maintained an embarrassed silence and changed the subject. The myth of presidential omnipotence is at least as strong within Mexico as without. It was undoubtedly tactless to press the question, for if any policy of the Echeverría administration could be characterized as a failure, it was fiscal policy.

The official of the Ministry of Industry and Commerce in charge of the elaboration of the law on foreign investment was the undersecretary at the time, José Campillo Sáinz. He was one of the then rare officials who moved from the private sector to a high position in the government; before becoming the undersecretary of industry and commerce, he had been a president of CONCAMIN. Indeed, he had been the head of CONCAMIN in 1964 when the earlier tax reform failed. But he had joined the government convinced of the need for government regulation and was a forceful proponent of the foreign investment regulation.[27] Some former government officials who were not direct participants in the preparations of the fiscal reform and the law on foreign investment suggested that his former ties with the highest levels of Mexican business caused his defection from the government position at a crucial moment. But this has not been confirmed. The former undersecretary himself, while defending the foreign investment law, acknowledged to me that "the requirement that foreigners but not Mexicans declare the ownership of their shares in enterprises constituted a hole in the law [*un hueco en la ley*]." He would only comment that the measure to eliminate bearer shares was dropped "so as not to prejudice the interests of Mexicans [*para no perjudicar al Mexicano*]." Other participants could not lay the failure of the proposal at his door.

In a rare revelation of the inner workings of the economic policy-making in Mexico, one of the direct participants in the negotiations and discussions of the fiscal reform has not only recounted the process but did so in writing. Leopoldo Solís, writing from the peace and perspective of Princeton University, described the attempts at fiscal reform in which he participated as director of economic studies in the Ministry of the Presidency.[28] Because it is one of the few insider documents to describe political decision-making in detail, it is worth citing at some length.

According to Solís, the proposed tax reform was prepared rapidly. Tax reform options were first studied in mid-1972 at the order of the president. Serious discussion did not come until late October, however, when planning for the 1973 budget was under way. That October meeting was attended by the ministers of the Treasury, the Presidency, and National Property; their staff; the governor of the Central Bank; and two tax specialists who had been working with the Ministry of the Treasury. It was agreed at that meeting that tax reform was necessary, and the Treasury officials set to work to draft a project.

The proposal brought to the president in mid-November included income tax on all personal earnings, the elimination of bearer shares and bearer bonds, the elimination of various loopholes, a redefinition of the tax base, and an increase in the personal income tax from 35 to 42 percent on income over 1 million pesos. At that meeting, although there was some controversy over the taxing of interest income from financial assets, Solís reported that there was agreement among the participants from the Treasury, Presidency, and the Central Bank on the remaining provisions, including the elimination of bearer shares. The other participants did not attend this meeting. At the next meeting, Solís reports that the

> staff of the Presidency supported the full reform position, the Central Bank's Managing Director opposed it and the Treasury was in between, in favor of reform, exempting interest and dividends from accumulation but supporting the elimination of bearer bonds and shares. After a long and heated discussion it was decided to follow the Treasury's position.

By this time it was early December. The tax reform group had now reached a consensus that included the elimination of bearer shares. The tax group then combined with the working group on the control of foreign investments that had been operating independently within the Ministry of Industry and Commerce.

> Steering the foreign investment law was the Assistant Secretary of Commerce, formerly a private businessman and the leader of the association of industrialists [sic] when the 1964 tax reform aborted. He was turning more and more government control oriented, but we feared that because of his background he could disrupt the tax package. Finally, however, both bills moved together through the legal processing, the Attorney General reviewed the changes and the bills were ready to be sent to Congress.

The two groups met with the president in early December, each wanting its own bill to go to the Congress first in order to increase the chances of passage. The president, in a Solomonic decision, decided to send both together "and instructed the Secretary of the Treasury to meet with the representatives of the private sector later in the day and explain both bills to them. He called the Press Undersecretary and asked him to convene a meeting with some newspaper editorial writers to persuade them to support the proposals and to prepare the public for the changes." Then took place the private meetings to which my informants had referred:

> We met twice with the private sector representatives in the house of Secretary of the Treasury. Present were leaders from CONCA-MIN and CANACINTRA (industrialists), the bankers, Chamber of Commerce representatives and past presidents of the bankers' associations. The second meeting included attorneys, tax experts, and advisers employed by the associations. At the first meeting, we explained both bills to them, and at the second meeting three days later, a discussion of the bills took place. The private sector representatives were very critical and presented a common front against both bills. Even the representatives of small and medium industrialists, CANACINTRA, who generally cooperate with the government, joined the others in the fear of the changes. Their arguments were more over intention than substance. They saw the bills as a first step leading to foreign exchange control and argued that tax administration could be improved by using other measures that would not harm investors' confidence as the proposed ones would.

Solís reported that Undersecretary of Industry and Commerce Campillo Sáinz and Secretary of the Treasury Hugo Margain argued forcefully with the members of the private sector in their meetings. Campillo Sáinz did not undermine the tax reform, either in meetings with the Treasury officials to prepare the laws, in meetings with the president attended by the Treasury officials, or at the joint meetings with the private sector.[29] The Ministry of the Presidency, including Solís himself, strongly supported the measure; Margain (ambassador to the United States under Díaz Ordaz and again under López Portillo) strongly defended the bill that had been prepared to send to the Congress; the Bank of Mexico opposed it but in the end agreed to go along with the tax reform after the taxing of interest income from bank deposits had been modified. Solís concluded that the private sector posed a united front in opposition to a measure on which a consensus had been reached within the government. Solís was one of the four or five major participants in this reform effort. He concluded that because of the opposition of the private sector or due to reasons unknown to him, "the reform did not take effect and the budget was sent to the Congress only with the original proposition of a sales tax increase along with the foreign investment bill."

One prominent private sector lawyer working for CONCAMIN

suggested that I read a novel published in 1977 by Francisco Lerdo de Tejada entitled *El botín del tigre* (The Tiger's Booty), if I wanted to know "how it really was." The novel describes meetings between the top government officials and business representatives similar to those that actually took place. It also describes the feverish activity of business representatives to mount their arguments in the three days between the two meetings. But the novel had a different outcome: the tax reform measure passed; and after various machinations, a colonel in the military, with the complicity of the ambassador from the United States, deposed the president who had sponsored it.

The conflict between the government and the private sector during the Echeverría administration resulted in a consolidation of private sector organizations. In May 1975, the most important business representatives in the country joined to form the Business Coordinating Council (CCE). This association, which is completely outside government control, brings together at one table and on a regular basis, the major businessmen of Mexico and the presidents of every major business organization, including the industrialist associations, merchants, bankers, insurance executives, the employers association (COPARMEX), and a group of the most powerful businessmen in Mexico known as the Mexican Council of Businessmen. The association of small and medium businessmen, CANACINTRA, though formally subordinated to CONCAMIN, did not at first join the CCE.[30] In late 1977, however, the executive secretary of the CCE indicated that CANACINTRA was not in conflict with the council and had been cooperating with its members. The CCE, like the U.S. Business Round-table formed in the United States in 1972, brings together the chief executive officers of the largest corporations, provides a unified front when necessary to confront government policy, and enables its members to meet regularly for consultation and coordination. (Unlike the Business Roundtable, however, the CCE frequently takes public positions on major issues.) The statement of principles of the CCE is a classic statement of free market ideology, espousing private property as a natural right, defending private enterprise as the basis of the economy, and opposing the intervention of the state in new areas. Foreign capital is welcomed by the CCE as "a useful complement to national resources, to accelerate progress as long as the process of the development of our country is not self-generating."

Debt Swaps: The Failure to Replace Foreign Investment

The fiscal reform was a logical concomitant of the nationalist metapreference. Its failure contributed directly to the debt crisis and more generally to the failure of the nationalist project. The evidence for the reversal of policy could not be more vividly illustrated than by the so-called debt swaps that took place between April 1986 and October 1987. In that short period, nearly three billion dollars of foreign investment came into Mexico. The irony of debt swaps is that debt, used initially to fund the nationalist alternative to foreign investment, eventually became its instrument.

Debt-equity swaps are a specific type of debt conversion.[31] In this way, the investor obtains local equities with the redeemed debt. The bank gets dollars, the investor gets more pesos than otherwise, and Mexico gets foreign investment.

The program was first established in 1985 as part of a debt-rescheduling agreement. It became a reality in April 1986, when the first applications were approved. The program was established in the midst of one of the worst economic crises in Mexico's history. Notwithstanding the circumstances, a report of the Ministry of Finance claims that the results were positive, given that the program made possible a level of foreign investment comparable only to the level achieved during the oil boom.

The Mexican program included a series of important restrictions. Each application was reviewed on a case-by-case basis by the National Commission on Foreign Investments (CNIE) and the General Office of Public Credit (DGCP). First, the Mexican government never carried out debt-for-cash swaps—only debt-for-equity. Swaps were restricted to the acquisition of fixed assets, including real estate, construction or expansion of a productive plant, and the purchase of new machinery or equipment, or they were used to pay current debts to Mexican banks or the government. All the payments were for national goods and services—no payments to the exterior were allowed. These restrictions were designed to prevent speculation and create a positive impact on the balance of payments.

Furthermore, the program was restricted to foreign investors. The Mexican private sector was not allowed to participate in the debt conversion program. The government did not want to subsidize the return of flight capital, because much of it was considered illegal in the first place. The Mexican government had more faith in foreign investors than in the Mexican private sector—the opposite of the nationalist vision.

From April 1986 to October 1987 the Ministry of Finance received 404 applications for a total of $3.6 billion. Out of this total, $2.975 billion was allocated to investment rather than the payment of domestic debt. These investments were distributed as shown in table 6.6.

TABLE 6.6   1986–1987 Debt Swaps

Industry	Nominal Value (Billions of Dollars)	Percentage
Tourism	1.119	37.8
Automobile	0.628	21.2
Maquiladora	0.545	18.4
Metallurgy	0.266	9.0
Electronics	0.098	3.4
Pharmaceutical	0.064	2.2
Agroindustry	0.046	1.6
Others	0.189	6.4
Total	2.975	100.0

Source: Ministry of Finance.

Conclusions

With the liberalization of regulations on foreign investment under the Salinas administration, the failure of the nationalist project is evident: the state's effort to replace foreign investors as innovators and financial managers came to naught. The nationalists have moved into the left political opposition. The state under Salinas still regulated, but the aim was to promote investment, not to limit investment. Even when the instrument was the same, such as conditioning 100 percent ownership on exports, technology, or decentralization, the intent was different; the metapreference had changed. State ownership increased debt in the absence of sound fiscal policy. Autonomous technological development did not occur. Statist policy had led to crisis. Nationalism was not dead, but international liberalism replaced statism as the dominant strategy for national development.

Part Three

International Industrial Structure and State Policy: Three Case Studies

DURING THE 1970s the Mexican state demonstrated its proclivity for adopting nationalist policies toward foreign investment. By the early 1980s, the drive for additional regulation and control had shifted from general policies for all foreign investors, or for foreign investment in manufacturing as a whole, to the effort to develop specific policies in each of several industries. The prototype for such industry-specific policies was the automobile industry. As Bennett and Sharpe showed in their analysis of three bargaining episodes from the 1960s through the 1970s, the state often chose to reduce imports and promote exports, rather than insisting upon more structural reform. Work on the automobile industry well illustrates the delicate tension between the choices, or the political will, of decisionmakers, on the one hand, and the limitations imposed by structure, on the other. By comparing several industries, it is possible to see the constraints of industrial structure on industrial policy.

This section includes three case studies of industries in Mexico in which foreign investment is important and in which state policies have attempted to influence outcomes: automobiles, computers, and food processing. In the first two industries, specific policies for developing national capabilities and for limiting foreign participation were considered and debated and then modified or dropped. The choices of state officials on how best to pursue development were sharply constrained by the dynamics of industrial organization. The existence of policy initiatives that were not adopted or not implemented is consistent with the distinction between metapreference and metapower. The initiative is evidence of the preference; the outcome the evidence of power. In the food-processing industry, however, no industry-specific policy was adopted. Rather, it was an example of an industry governed by the general regulations on foreign investment, technology transfer, and patents and trademarks.

In terms of the three patterns of bargaining discussed in chapter 6, these cases are all examples of the "renewable bargain." In each case, regulations have modified outcomes, at least at the margins and sometimes more. However, in each case the foreign investors have been able to invest and expand in the Mexican market and to resist some of the more nationalist initiatives. In all of the cases, regulation moved first in a statist direction and then reversed to become more liberal.

International industrial organization is a specific theoretical concern within the field of political economy. Originating within economics as an institutional approach to the structure of industries, and largely identified with the efforts of Joe Bain and F. M. Sherer to analyze the structure of American industries, the field has since been broadened by Richard Newfarmer and others to take into account the internationalization of industry, which is the most prominent characteristic of global economic change in recent decades.[1] The basic argument of international industrial organization theory is that the observed outcomes or performance of an industry result from the interaction of firms within a structured market. In particular, it tests the hypothesis that industries are organized in oligopolistic fashion, such that the behavior of firms is influenced by other firms in the industry rather than by impersonal price signals, which would characterize a perfectly competitive market. The sequence of arguments in industrial organization, taking into account basic conditions in each national market, is that the structure of the market influences the behavior of firms, and both, in turn, influence outcomes or performance in the industry. The internationalized version of industrial organization takes foreign investment as one particular form of firm conduct in home markets. Investment behavior transmits patterns of investment, production, and structure from the home market to the host market. The industrial organization approach then looks at the structure of the industry in the host country. Market structure shapes firm conduct, which in turn shapes industry performance.

This economic model of industrial structure, conduct, and performance becomes politicized when state policymakers seek to influence or change outcomes in the industry. The state is faced with the possibility of trying to change market structure and/or to influence firm conduct (see fig. 5).

International industrial organization theory, as elaborated by Newfarmer, Bennett and Sharpe, and others, represents a greater specification of the general thesis of dependency, namely, that international firms make fundamental decisions that influence outcomes in the developing world. However, the industrial organization approach allows for the influence of state policy and thus makes theoretical room for the statist or bargaining approach. When policymakers attempt to implement their metapreferences, they will, according to this hypothesis, encounter the structural constraints of the industries they regulate. If the structure of industry is primarily competitive, the nationalist project will fail; if the constraints are weaker, the nationalist agenda may be fulfilled.

The next three chapters outline industrial policy for the Mexican automobile, computer, and food-processing industries. The characteristics of the industries and of the regulatory policies are summarized in tables III.1 and III.2. Only in the automobile industry has a systematic industry-specific policy been pursued over time. In all three industries, however, a group of planners and policymakers have

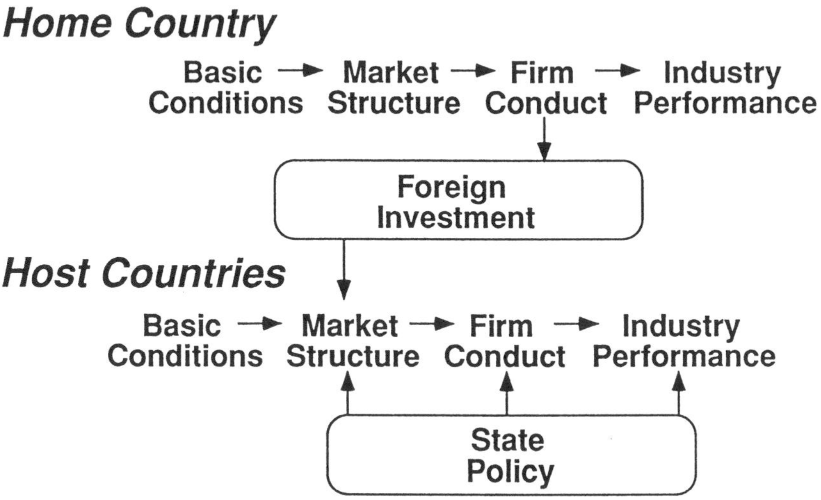

Home Country

Basic → Market → Firm → Industry
Conditions Structure Conduct Performance

Foreign
Investment

Host Countries

Basic → Market → Firm → Industry
Conditions Structure Conduct Performance

State
Policy

FIGURE 5. International Industrial Organization

shared a nationalistic metapreference, a vision of a possible future in which the market power of international firms would be reduced. In all three cases, the structure and dynamics of the international industry imposed conditions that were beyond the scope of national policy. And in each case, the advantages of cooperation with international firms were greater than the preference for nationalist controls. Those advantages, in turn, derived from the global industrial structure, which constrains nationalism and is conducive to liberalism.

TABLE III.1   Summary Characteristics of Three Industries

Characteristics	Automobiles	Computers	Food Processing
Product characteristics	Consumer durable	Consumer durable, capital good	Consumer nondurable
Industrial concentration	Medium–high	Medium–high	Low
Capital intensity	High	High	Low
Technical complexity	High	High	Low
Technical change	Medium	High	Low
Export potential	High	High	Low
Regulation:			
Ownership	Medium	Low	Low
Behavior	High	High	Low

TABLE III.2 Regulatory Summary for Three Industries

Industry	Ownership	Local Content	Export Regulation
Automobiles	Final product: majority foreign Parts: domestic	60/40%	Compensatory exports and future deficit reimbursement
Computers	Mainframes: 100% foreign Microcomputers: 49/51% until 1985, 100% foreign in 1985	65/35%	Compensatory exports
Food processing	Before 1973, 100% foreign after 1973, with exceptions 49–51%	90–100%	None

Seven

The Food-Processing Industry

FOOD PROCESSING is one of the least concentrated manufacturing industries, and Mexico is one of the strongest, most stable, and most developed of the developing countries. It should be a "most likely case" for the reduction of transnational market power. If powerful states can regulate the market strength of transnational enterprises, it should have happened for food in Mexico. In fact, the opposite occurred. In spite of popular denunciations of the foreign "monopolies" in the food industry, and in spite of occasional anticompetitive behavior, the internationalization of food processing in Mexico took place in a highly competitive environment. The response of the state was liberal rather than statist: no new policy initiatives were developed for the industry.[1]

Structural Characteristics
of the Food-Processing Industry

At the most basic level, the food-processing industry is that part of the food system that includes all economic activities by which people produce, process, and distribute nutritive biological and chemical materials needed to sustain life (as well as some nonnutritive stimulants and depressants). Specifically, the food-processing industry performs three functions: the transformation of products of the biosphere into edible form; the industrial preservation of foods and beverages; and the reduction or elimination of home preparation time. The three functions of the food-processing industry usually make it possible to transport foods more easily and to store them longer. Ease of transport and extended shelf life, in turn, have favored the growth of large firms by facilitating economies of scale and product differentiation.

Food processing dwarfs many other industries. Worldwide, more than fifty firms have annual food and beverage sales over $1 billion;

173

TABLE 7.1   Largest Global Food Firms, 1988

Rank	Parent Company	Home Country	Food-Processing Revenue (Millions)	Total Revenue (Millions)	Food Revenue as % of Total Revenue
1	Nestlè S.A.	Switzerland	24,294.0	26,497.0	91.7
2	Unilever	U.K./Netherlands	15,277.0	30,948.0	49.4
3	Phillip Morris/General Foods	U.S.	13,051.0	27,695.0	47.1
4	Kraft, Inc.	U.S.	9,876.7	9,876.7	100.0
5	RJR Nabisco	U.S.	9,420.0	15,776.0	59.1
6	Dalgety PLC	U.K.	9,005.0	9,005.0	100.0
7	Conagra, Inc.	U.S.	9,001.6	9,001.6	100.0
8	Anheuser-Busch, Inc.	U.S.	8,003.0	9,019.1	88.7
9	Occidental Petroleum—IB, Inc.	U.S.	7,681.3	15,344.0	50.1
10	Coca-Cola Co.	U.S.	7,643.6	7,658.3	99.8
11	Pepsico	U.S.	7,301.0	11,485.0	63.6
12	Sara Lee	U.S.	6,550.0	9,155.0	71.5
13	Allied Lyons	U.K.	5,943.0	5,943.0	100.0
14	Cargill	U.S.	5,735.0	31,000.0	18.5
15	Archer-Daniels-Midland	U.S.	5,400.0	5,774.6	93.6
16	BSN S.A.	France	5,118.0	5,205.0	98.3
17	Guinness PLC	U.K.	4,780.0	4,780.0	100.0
18	Ralston	U.S.	4,741.4	5,868.0	80.8
19	H. J. Heinz	U.S.	4,640.0	4,640.0	100.0
20	Borden, Inc.	U.S.	4,626.0	6,514.4	71.0
21	Campbell Soup	U.S.	4,490.4	4,490.4	100.0
22	BCI Holdings Corp.—Beatrice	U.S.	4,473.0	4,473.0	100.0
23	CPC International	U.S.	4,062.1	4,903.0	82.8
24	Bass PLC	U.K.	4,010.0	5,784.0	69.3
25	John LaBatt Ltd.	Canada	3,864.1	3,864.1	100.0

Source: Food Engineering International, June 1988, p. 40.

Notes: Breakdown by food revenue as percentage of total revenue: 80%–100.0%—16, 50%–79.9%—6, 0%﹣ 49.9%—3. Breakdown by home country: U.S.—17, U.K.—5, others—3.

Nestlè acquired Carnation and Phillip Morris acquired General Foods in 1985. Kraft was formerly Dart & Kra﹣ and RJR Nabisco was formerly RJR Industries, until it merged with Nabisco Brands in July 1985. Beatrice so﹣ its soft-drink-bottling, dairy, bottled-water, and warehousing operations and transferred fifteen operating com﹣ panies to a newly formed and publicly held company (E-II Holdings, Inc.). Beatrice has also sold many of its oth﹣ operations. LaBatt, the brewer, entered food operations with diversification throughout all sectors of the indust﹣ in 1987, after acquiring sixteen different companies.

the twenty-five largest are listed in table 7.1, which includes some of the world's largest firms.

The food-processing industry accounts for about 15 percent of manufacturing output in developed market economies, and nearly 25 percent of manufacturing output in developing countries, according to a 1980 UN study. The developed countries employed about 8 million workers in food and beverage industries, or 10.5 percent of all manufacturing employment; in the developing world, 9.7 million workers were employed in these industries, accounting for almost 19 percent of manufacturing employment. The UN study estimated that 188 large enterprises, almost all based in the developed market economies, accounted for roughly one third of total world food processing.[2]

Although some firms are primarily involved in a single food commodity, most of the major firms are diversified across the food industry, participating in a variety of commodity systems. Of the nine commodity systems identified by Domike for the UN survey (including such categories as meat, dairy, fruits and vegetables, and grains),[3] on average, the ten largest firms each participate in six systems; the top thirty firms in five; and the second largest thirty firms in four. The two largest firms, Nestlè and Unilever, are active in all nine systems.[4]

Most of the large international food-processing firms are based in the developed countries; more than half originate in the United States. Two of the very largest are European: Nestlè is Swiss, and Unilever is Dutch and British.

Among the leading firms, most enterprises have been primarily food processors, avoiding a high degree of conglomeration (reliance on nonfood activities). Of the sixty largest food-processing firms in the UN study, all but nine derived a majority of their total revenues from foods and beverages (but these nine conglomerates included such giants as Unilever, Procter & Gamble, ITT, and Mitsui). In recent years, conglomeration has been increasing, especially among food, beverage, and tobacco companies. However, widely diversified conglomerates are still the exception, not the rule, and mergers frequently take place within the food industry, such as the dramatic merger of Nestlè with Carnation, or among consumer-product firms linking beverages or tobacco firms with food processing.

The leading food-processing firms show wide diversity with respect to internationalization, the share of operations they maintain outside the home country. At one extreme, firms specializing in undifferentiated perishable commodities, such as fresh milk or beef, have few if any foreign sales. Foreign sales by brewers are also low, reflecting the difficulty of large-scale exports for a product with low value per unit of weight. At the other extreme, diversified producers of highly differentiated and processed products such as dry milk or instant coffee are more likely to have a high proportion of sales outside their home country. Nestlè, whose home market is small and which has long exported extensively, is one of the most international of firms, with 95 percent of its sales abroad. Most U.S. firms fall in the middle; even by 1988, few large U.S. firms had foreign sales over 25 to 30 percent of total sales, reflecting the large domestic market size.

History and Growth of Food Processing

Food processing was almost unknown 100 years ago. According to the biographer of H. J. Heinz, one of the pioneers of food processing, "the diet of Americans in 1869 when Heinz started out was of a dreary monotony during seven or eight months each year . . . a lemon was a luxury; an orange was something found in a Christmas stocking."[5] Today, a variety of both fresh and processed foods is now available all year long and is available to many urban people whose only relation to agricultural producers is through their participation in a money economy.

Of the social changes that have contributed to the development of the food-processing industry, the most important has been urbanization. As more and more people come to live in cities, food from the countryside needs to be preserved, stored, and transported to them. Moreover, in the urban situation, women are more likely to become involved in activities outside the home, whether or not those interests constitute wage labor; and this means that alternatives to home preparation become more socially accepted and desired. As Mexico has become increasingly urbanized, demand for processed foods has increased.

Sidney Mintz has hypothesized that industrialization and the growth of factory work have encouraged the production and consumption of products that can be easily and rapidly consumed in a variety of locations and that contain much energy, though not necessarily much nutrition.[6] Though Mintz refers particularly to the consumption of sugar and sugar products by factory workers, his argument could be extended to coffee or soft drinks with their caffeine stimulants and various other "quick energy" products that we associate with the processed-food industry.

Changes outside the food industry, especially in transportation and communication and in the chemical industry, have also helped shape the growth of the food industry. In transportation, the extension of the railroad networks across the United States made the expansion of food firms from regional to national markets possible. Later, the development of refrigerated railcars facilitated national and international shipments of frozen foods, and the more recent construction of the national highway system has led to increased reliance on trucking, in part displacing the railroad as the carrier of food products. Lined tank trucks developed for chemicals permit the long-distance transportation of bulk liquids such as corn syrups and fruit juice concentrates. Containerized shipping has made possible the integration of truck, rail, sea, and air transport for bulk shipments of all kinds. Communications technology has been important not only for mass advertising but also for communications between home offices and subsidiaries of international corporations and for rapid worldwide transmission of information on the prices of raw material commodities. All of these changes have been coming to Mexico, but mostly since 1960.

The growth of major food-processing firms has been characterized by two kinds of expansion: geographical spread from local to national to international production; and diversification of production, mostly within the food industry. As firms have grown, they have moved from specialization in single product lines (e.g., canned milk) to a complete commodity sector (e.g., dairy products) and, more recently, to a wide range of processed-food products. The growth of large food firms prior to 1950 generally involved national growth and expansion within a primary commodity sector. Internationalization and diversification across the food industry (and outside it) better characterize the last forty years. Though changes in society established the pattern of demand for processed foods, three factors within the industry and within the firms influenced the early growth of large firms: technological improvements affecting production; advertising and promotion; and mergers and acquisitions.

Technological advances in the food industry are influenced by basic product characteristics: perishability, raw material availability, and the ratio of value to weight are all important. For example, fresh milk and most bakery foods are highly perishable, making decentralized production important and inventories limited. Henri Nestlè's invention of a powdered milk food established the basis for a world-scale food firm. Many products require a specific raw material: butter requires milk, steak requires beef, and catsup requires tomatoes. Much of the technological challenge for food firms has been overcoming the limitations of these basic conditions by reducing perishability and weight and by developing substitutes for raw materials.

Technological advances, initially protected by patents, provided a competitive advantage for some firms. Advances in canning, freezing, drying, packaging, and other techniques have enabled companies to diversify their product lines and expand production. Technological advances allowed today's leading firms to establish themselves firmly in their markets.

As technology evolved and food firms diversified into other food product lines, advertising of trademarked brand names was used to promote the growth of large companies. Attention to marketing, with respect to both distributors and consumers, enabled companies to move away from single product lines; advertising and product promotion enabled Heinz to move from pickles, to fruits and vegetables, to a variety of food products. Trademarks are the basis for product identification by risk-averse consumers and hence represent the market share that advertising creates for a product. Unlike the short-term advantage of patented technology that can be copied, trademark protection is a permanent corporate asset. This was recognized long ago by Henri Nestlè when it was suggested that he should change his trademark. He replied: "I regret that I am unable to allow you to change my nest for a Swiss Cross. My product must be recognizable at first glance. Not only is the nest my trademark it is also my coat of arms (Nestlè means 'little nest' in German dialect) . . . *I cannot have a different trademark in each country*; anybody can make use of a cross, but no one else has the right to use my coat of arms" (emphasis added).[7]

As firms grew, competition increased as well. As a result, mergers and acquisitions became an important mechanism for the growth of the largest firms.[8] A first wave of mergers and acquisitions in the early part of this century saw many large single-product enterprises combine with other enterprises in similar product lines and form consolidated companies in particular product sectors. After World War II, mergers and acquisitions have resulted in diversified food companies with interests across the entire food industry, extending more recently into other nondurable consumer goods. Technological advances, aggressive marketing, and mergers and acquisitions all contributed to the growth of large firms that would outgrow their home markets.

Although a few firms confine themselves to the home market, most now are "at home abroad." Firms based in the United States often expanded across the border to Canada and Mexico; Anderson-Clayton went into Mexico in 1934, Carnation in 1947, and Del Monte in 1953. As the data in chapter 4 demonstrated (see especially table 4.2), today's largest firms often established a presence early and then continued to acquire subsidiaries. The most rapid expansion was in the 1960s.

Mergers and acquisitions are leading to fewer and larger firms; since the beginning of 1982, over 25 percent of the top food-processing companies have been merged or acquired by another major company, according to a survey by *Food Engineering*.[9] Even before this boom, food firms have been among those industrial enterprises most prone to mergers and acquisitions. Originally expanding to encompass firms outside the food industry, food processors have gradually begun to concentrate once again on their core products and to limit themselves to the food industry. However, low-cost production, abundant resources, more efficient processing techniques, increased advertising, and larger capital outlays to cover initial losses have become necessary to remain among the leaders.

Barriers to Entry

In recent years, marketing and advertising, not plant scale or research and development, have provided the most powerful barriers to entry in the industry, especially in differentiated products. Advertising increases market share and concentration; diversification facilitates massive advertising. Competition among large firms diversified across the food-processing industry makes it difficult for a new entrant to establish a significant market share without spending large sums on advertising. The largest food-processing firms have a special advantage in advertising: advertising and media firms give rates for national advertising volume even when production or distribution are regional.

In most sectors of the industry plant size is not great, and multiplant operations predominate. Research and development in the food industry is concentrated in the largest firms and for years has been primarily oriented to the differentiation of existing product lines. Even for the largest 100 firms, research and development expenditures are low, averaging between 0.4 and 0.5 percent of sales, compared with about 4 percent for all manufacturing.[10] A study of innovation in the food-processing industry showed that very few new types of food have been developed, but new brands are more frequent and "new" (differentiated) items proliferate.[11] That study indicated that in the early 1960s, a new product cost $68,000 for research and development, $26,000 for market research, and $248,000 for test marketing. *The Wall Street Journal* reported that research and development costs for an extension of an existing product are low ($20,000–$50,000) but an entirely new product may cost as much as $1 million to research.[12] Major innovations have tended to come from other industries, and in-house research of product variations allows oligopolistic competition while forcing small competitors off the shelves.

In short, concentration in home markets is increasing, in particular sectors and in the industry as a whole. Mergers and acquisitions are still speeding that process, as well as increasing diversification of product lines across the industry and into related fields. As some firms grow, potential entrants are kept out not so much by production scale economies or by the benefits of research and development as by the necessity for ample experience and large budgets for advertising. This industrial structure helps us understand the international behavior of firms as they expand beyond their home markets.

International Conduct

Structure and conduct of large firms in the food industry are closely interrelated. The food-processing industry already counts almost all U.S. citizens among its customers, and the drive for further expansion has led many firms to invest abroad. Firms first moved from their home markets to neighboring countries. They sought new markets, first through exports and then, often in the face of exclusionary tariffs, through direct investment. In a consumer-goods industry, it is natural that firms should seek investments in countries with an attractive potential market: it is in countries with high per capita income that food firms are most likely to invest. As total foreign investment in food and tobacco has grown, the share of Latin America has declined dramatically, to be replaced by Europe as the major locus of U.S. foreign investment. From 62 percent of all U.S. foreign investment in 1929, Latin America's share fell to 15 percent by 1976, whereas Canada and Europe both doubled their shares from 13 to 28 percent and from 20 to 43 percent respectively.[13] Mexico, the leading host country for U.S. food investments at the turn of the century, had fallen to fifth place by 1970; but Mexico still leads the developing countries.[14]

Foreign investment changed the structure of the food industry through interpenetration of markets. As U.S. firms expanded abroad, European and Canadian firms invested in the U.S. food industry. This increase in foreign investment in home countries meant a possible increase in competition at the level of particular product lines. But the foreign presence did nothing to slow the increase in concentration at the level of the whole industry, and indeed, the trend toward rising concentration was exacerbated when investments were made by acquisition of existing companies. Subsidiaries of international corporations are often formed by the acquisition of local firms. Since 1948, the number of subsidiaries has been increasing, but the percentage that are actually new companies has been declining. Well over half of all subsidiaries of twenty-three large U.S. food-processing firms in 1948–67 and over two thirds in the most recent part of that period were acquired rather than newly formed.[15] The expansion of food firms abroad has challenged local firms to new competition, although the competition has not made for less-concentrated markets. This, indeed, is oligopolistic competition.

In investing abroad, transnational food-processing firms are likely to earn higher profits than at home. International profits have been reported as much as 50 percent higher than home-market profits, reaching as much as 25 percent of U.S. sales.[16] According to *Survey of Current Business*, earnings of U.S. foreign affiliates in 1975 were higher in food processing than in all manufacturing (12.5 percent vs. 11.1 percent of assets); they were also higher in developing countries than in developed (15.0 percent vs. 11.9 percent of assets).[17] Horst also found foreign operations in general to be more profitable than home operations, though he did not distinguish between developing and developed countries.[18] Advertising increases concentration; both increase profits. With high profits, more mergers and acquisitions are possible. Concentration in the food industry increases as the number of firms declines. Concentrated firms with high advertising levels are more likely to invest abroad, where they are likely to make even higher profits.

Mexico is a good case for the study of foreign investment by food firms. The organization of the international food industry has affected the structure, conduct, and performance of the Mexican industry and has raised important policy issues.

The Structure of the Food-Processing Industry in Mexico

Foreign food firms have invested in Mexico since the turn of the century, but from 1950 to 1970, as manufacturing investment in general increased, foreign enterprises in food and beverages invested heavily in Mexico, growing tenfold in twenty years, from about $20 million in 1950 to $235 million in 1970. The food share of all foreign investment in manufacturing has remained fairly steady at about 10 percent.[19] Nevertheless, foreign firms represent a small share of all food processing in Mexico. Foreign firms in the food industry (not including beverages) accounted for only 8.6 percent of production and 6.1 percent of value-added in 1970; this level of foreign participation was only about one third of the manufacturing average and a small fraction of the levels for sectors such as chemicals, electrical machinery, or automobiles, where foreigners account for two thirds to over three quarters of production.[20]

The food industry in Mexico accounts for almost 15 percent of the value of all manufacturing industry. Of major manufacturing industries where foreign investment is important, the food industry has both the lowest aggregate level of foreign participation and the lowest aggregate four-plant concentration ratio. These figures would seem to belie the notion commonly held in Mexico that the food-processing industry is highly concentrated and foreign dominated. The seeming paradox of high absolute levels of foreign investment in an industry in which foreign firms do not dominate is resolved by considering the larger absolute size of the industry and by disaggregating: foreign firms do indeed dominate some specific product markets.

To take examples from the dairy industry, there are no foreign milk pasteurizers or bottlers, and only one ice cream firm was foreign in 1970. But in evaporated and canned milk, ten out of twelve firms are foreign, and they control 96 percent of invested capital, 98 percent of value-added and production, and 99 percent of profits. Though there is no evidence of explicit market sharing, evidence points to accepted spheres of influence. Even in Mexico, with ten foreign dairy firms, members of the industry seem to specialize. Nestlè and Carnation both produced canned dairy products but did not produce directly competing product lines. When Nestlè acquired Carnation, production became even more concentrated. Nestlè for a time sold baby food in Mexico but later dropped it, leaving Gerber as the sole producer. This forbearance behavior in the food industry contrasts with industries such as automobiles, in which oligopolistic reaction led to competition among many foreign firms in spite of inefficiencies due to the size of the market.

Ownership

Patterns of ownership in the Mexican food industry can be summarized as follows: most food firms are private national firms; state-owned firms are of little importance except in fishing and sugar. Foreign firms tend to dominate in specific product lines that also tend to be highly concentrated, in contrast to most of the rest of the industry. Among the foreign-owned firms, majority-owned firms predominate. The absence of any government policy regulating ownership in the food-processing industry allowed this high degree of foreign ownership to evolve, in contrast to industries where Mexicanization policies have been pursued since World War II.

There is a wide variation in the patterns of foreign affiliates in Mexico. Some parent firms own all of their affiliates and subsidiaries directly, whereas others "pyramid" (having one affiliate own another). Some firms have only food-related affiliates, but others—especially the drug firms that produce infant milk formulas—are diversified in their holdings. Some, such as Campbell's Soup, Carnation, and Gerber, had only one Mexican affiliate; others, like Nestlè, Anderson Clayton, and Beatrice foods, had more than five. Because the 1973 law on foreign investment law was not retroactive and most of the major international firms came into Mexico before that date, during the period of import substitution industrialization, most of the firms were wholly or majority foreign owned.

The first task of the regulators in Mexico was to find out which firms were there. The universe of firms registered in the National Registry on Foreign Investment in Mexico in 1977 consisted of 136 enterprises established in Mexico with foreign participation of at least 20 percent. Twenty-six foreign parent firms with direct investments of at least $1 million each controlled 85 percent of the total direct foreign investment (DFI) in the food industry. Only five of the enterprises in which these parent firms had direct investments showed foreign investment of 49 percent or less. Six had foreign investment between 49 and 50 percent; all the rest were majority owned by foreign investors.

The international enterprises with investments in Mexico included many of the world's largest food-processing firms: Nestlè and Carnation (still separate then), Purina, Kellogg's, Nabisco, Del Monte and International Standard Brands, Kraft, Pillsbury, Gervais Danone (French), and Gerber. Most of these firms have investments around the world.

Conduct

The structure of the food industry in Mexico influences the conduct of the firms. In advertising, research and development, acquisitions, technology transfer, and trademarks, firm behavior reflects the disproportionate importance of marketing for the dominant position of foreign firms in particular product sectors of the food industry.

Advertising, one of the most important aspects of firm conduct, is only now being studied in Mexico. It is known that food firms are among the leading advertisers, as in other countries, but it is not yet possible to compare firm advertising expenditures as a percentage of sales for domestic enterprises and foreign affiliates. Comparative data on research and development are likewise unknown. It is known, however, that foreign food firms register few patents and many trademarks, confirming the marketing emphasis observed in developed-country markets. Only 2.2 percent of all patents in the Fajnzylber and Martínez Tarragó sample of foreign firms (see chap. 5) were in food, whereas 11.4 percent of the trademarks registered to foreigners went to food firms.[21]

Some anecdotal evidence on research and development exists indicating that foreign food firms are primarily interested in the urban middle-class market, with which they are familiar. The Mexican government at one point invited Nestlè to develop an infant milk formula for distribution through the state-owned CONASUPO stores and through health services. Nestlè declined. But when the National Nutrition Institute developed a nutritious formula that it distributes at low cost under the brand name Conlac, the home office of Nestlè reportedly chastised the Mexican subsidiary for the forgone opportunity. A similar situation was reported for the development of a soy-based breakfast food that the government wanted to mass-distribute. Nabisco was invited to produce such a product but declined. The foreign firms have had more success in promoting the products they know to a middle-class market than in making new products suited to a developing country's needs.

Foreign food firms have expanded to Mexico by establishing new subsidiaries or by acquiring local firms. As acquisitions in their home markets by major food processors have increased, foreign acquisitions have increased in Mexico. Most firms affiliated with U.S. companies were formed or acquired after 1965. Affiliates established before 1965 are more likely to have been newly formed than acquired, whereas three quarters of later subsidiaries (1966–73) were acquired.[22] There are too few non-U.S. food firms to generalize for non-U.S. transnationals, but in manufacturing industries as a whole, non-U.S. parent firms seem more likely than U.S. parents to form new subsidiaries. Unpublished data from the Harvard Multinational Enterprise Project shed some additional light on these affiliates: among U.S.-owned firms, almost two thirds of the food subsidiaries were acquired, compared with half of all manufacturing affiliates. Even more striking, more than half of the acquired food subsidiaries were acquired indirectly, through the acquisition of another company. This is a clear example of how changes in concentration in the home country (acquisition of one parent firm by another) lead to changes in concentration in developing host countries. When R. J. Reynolds acquires Del Monte or when Standard Brands and Nabisco merge, concentration in Mexico increases.

Performance

Performance may be measured normatively—in terms of economic criteria such as profits and trade impacts or in terms of national policy goals. The debate revolves around value preferences and the viability of alternatives. Foreign food firms respond to criticism by admitting that their products are luxury items. "We don't aim for the lower end of the market, although we know many poor people buy our products," one manager in a fruit and vegetable firm told me. Another tried to justify purchases of expensive processed food by the poor: "They buy our product to get a shot of good nutrition once in a while." Foreign firms seem best suited to satisfying the demand of that portion of the population able to translate need into purchasing power.

Profits in the U.S. food-processing industry are relatively high; domestic profits in food are comparable to the profits of corporations in other oligopolistic industries, especially for food firms in concentrated and advertising-intensive industries. If transnational food firms in Mexico are members of oligopolistically concentrated sectors of the food-processing industry, then even if the industry as a whole is not concentrated, we would expect firms to earn an "oligopoly rent" comparable to the profits of other concentrated industries. Unfortunately, profit data are not released by the transnationals at the country level, so it is difficult to evaluate profits, let alone to compare advertising-intensive firms with commodity-oriented firms. However, data from the Senate Special Survey of firms in Brazil and Mexico are available. Looking at after-tax earnings as a percentage of equity, reporting affiliates in the food-processing industry in 1972 showed a 9.1 percent return, compared to 13.8 percent for chemicals, 16.1 percent for electrical machinery, and 10.0 percent for the transportation industry.[23] This would seem to contradict the concentration hypothesis. But when "broad earnings" are considered—including royalties, licenses, and technical assistance—the profit levels of the four industries equalize at 19 to 20 percent, compared with a 16.2 percent average for the manufacturing industry as a whole. It is possible to conclude, then, that the food-processing industry is receiving oligopoly rents if international transfer payments are included.

One of Mexico's state goals for foreign investment is that it should make a positive contribution to the balance of payments. In the 1970s, as agricultural production declined in per capita terms and food imports increased, the foreign food processors were net importers as well. Mexico continues to export food, but the exports are not processed foods. Agricultural products have been an important source of Mexican foreign exchange earnings, constituting about 25 percent of total exports and concentrated in cotton, beef, coffee, sugar, and tomatoes. But in Mexico in 1972, a sample of U.S. food-processing affiliates reported in the Senate Special Survey exports of only 2 percent of sales, compared with 4 percent for chemicals, 9 percent for electrical machinery, and 8 percent for transportation, among other leading sectors. Although agricultural exports, especially winter vegetables, have increased, food processors are much less likely than other foreign investors to export. Indeed, when the National Foreign Investment Commission tried to condition expansion of one food processor upon improved export performance, the negotiations were at an impasse until the parties realized that the firm owned a sporting goods subsidiary and was willing to establish an export capacity for those products. This poor export performance for food products is probably due to the fact that processed and convenience foods are already being produced by the transnational firms in their home markets; added transportation costs for these high-weight-to-value products are only partially offset by lower labor costs, and firms have little incentive to export.

Food-processing firms have an impact on agricultural producers because they rely on a steady supply of high-quality agricultural raw materials. In the United States firms have integrated backward into agriculture and have also used production contracts with independent producers. In developing countries such as Mexico, foreign firms are often prohibited from land ownership, so the use of production contracts becomes essential. In a small sample of vegetable processors in Mexico, all eight of the international firms used production contracts. Only ten of the sixteen local firms did so.[24]

Production contracts are most common in perishable products where prompt delivery is necessary for the processor. In the United States, only 10 percent of crops and a third of livestock production were contracted in 1970. But in perishable products, the levels of production contracting are much higher: 98 percent for sugar beets, 55 percent for citrus fruits (30 percent of the fruit is directly produced by the firms); 95 percent for sweet corn and tomatoes; and 85 percent for fruits and vegetables (10 percent of the latter is produced by the firms themselves).[25] Through production contracting, foreign firms often introduce modern techniques and increase the incomes of suppliers. But the increased efficiency for some could mean that others who previously found subsistence work lose their livelihood. In a situation where the foreign processor enjoys a monopsony (sole buyer) position, crops are tailored to the buyer's specifications, and both subsistence crops and hard labor are often replaced.

Foreign investment conditions can be hazardous to firms, especially for firms that fail to adapt to local conditions in dealing with contract farmers. The case of Heinz, which withdrew from Mexico in 1973, is a case in point. Having come to Mexico via the acquisition of several ailing and disorganized fruit and vegetable packing companies, the company tried to implement their standard operating procedures, including contract farming. Their inexperience and poor local management, as well as the condition of the firms they acquired, led to failure; Heinz left Mexico in 1973, leaving its factories to be purchased by the only available buyer, the Mexican government.[26] The president of Del Monte was perhaps making an indirect reference to this failure when he indicated how important it was for a firm with a perishable raw material to build its operations from scratch, thus ensuring a suitable physical plant and local managers familiar with local conditions.[27] Del Monte has been quite successful at introducing contract farming in Mexico.

Public Policy and the Food-Processing Industry in Mexico

The very fact that so much of the food-processing industry in Mexico belongs to Mexican nationals contributes to the popular resentment of the transnationals felt so strongly there. No Mexican competitor objects to the transnational automakers; there are no Mexican competitors. But many Mexican food firms fear the acquisitions and the competition of the transnational food processors. In the late 1960s, this was one of the principal forces encouraging a governmental policy of regulation of foreign investment. It resulted, not in a policy for the food-processing industry but in a set of regulations for foreign investment and for technology transfer that applies to all of manufacturing. What were the results of the regulatory confrontation of the state and the international enterprises in Mexico?

Foreign Investment Regulation

A few cases drawn from the experience of the major food firms in Mexico illustrate the interaction of international corporations and the state following the passage of the law on foreign investment in 1973. Nearly all of the major food firms owned at least one of the four largest plants for the products that they produced. At the extreme is Gerber Products. Included among the four leading producers of canned fruits and vegetables, Gerber was the only producer of canned baby food in Mexico; the law did not change that.

Since processed food products in Mexico are not considered to be a priority industry, new foreign investment in this area is not encouraged. Direct acquisition of Mexican firms was effectively stopped.

But already-existing firms were able to increase their production up to the limit of their existing capacity. Investment could be increased with the permission of the National Foreign Investment Commission, as long as the relative shares of foreign and national capital are not changed. Because the regulation of foreign investment in the manufacturing sector began only after the major international enterprises were already established in the country, it is unlikely that regulation will have significant effect on the structure of oligopoly and the concentration of production for specific food product lines.

In one case, the National Foreign Investment Commission authorized the purchase of the subsidiary of one international enterprise by another, resulting in an increase in concentration of the product in question. The former owner, a 100 percent foreign-owned firm, declared its intention to cease its operations in the breeding and production of chickens. A second firm, a 60 percent foreign-owned firm, offered to buy the subsidiary enterprise, and the proposal was submitted to the National Foreign Investment Commission. The Coordinating Commission for Agriculture, an official dependency of the Ministry of the Presidency, was asked its opinion. The commission explored the possibility of locating a Mexican purchaser for the firm. Although the National Association of Poultry Producers (of which the foreign firms were also members) was contacted, no Mexican investors came forward. Because the enterprise in question was losing money and its original owner threatened to close the operation altogether, a speedy decision was reached. Fifty-one percent of the shares of the enterprise to be transferred were put in a trust fund, which, within seven years, would be sold to Mexican investors. The acquiring transnational enterprise then took over operation of the firm. Mexicanization of the subsidiary would thus eventually be accomplished. After the approval, the Ministry of Agriculture, which had not been consulted, protested the action on the grounds that the acquiring firm would be able to increase its share of the market for chickens and achieve a greater degree of vertical integration by increasing its intrafirm consumption of another product, animal feeds, which it also produced. Although 51 percent of the shares and thus 51 percent of the dividends from this enterprise will eventually go to Mexicans, the position of the international enterprise vis-à-vis domestic Mexican producers of chickens and of animal feeds was strengthened.

In another case, Del Monte, one of the largest producers of canned fruits and vegetables in Mexico, was authorized to open a new establishment with majority foreign ownership—one of the few establishments so authorized under the 1973 law. The firm opened a new plant to produce tomato paste in Culiacán, Sinaloa. The plant was authorized because the majority of the production would be exported, increasing the low levels of processed-food exports from Mexico; in addition, the parent firm argued that new employment would be generated, technical assistance to tomato producers would result in increased yields, and waste would be reduced by using tomatoes for paste that were not suitable for the fresh market.

In both of these cases, decisions were handed down rapidly, and the development of alternatives by national capital or by state-owned enterprises was only briefly explored (in the case of national firms) or was apparently not explored at all (in the case of state-owned firms). In both cases, the structural position of international enterprises in the food-processing industry in Mexico was, if anything, strengthened. But the National Foreign Investment Commission complied with its mission to encourage Mexicanization or to allow exceptions in return for an increase in exports.

In the food industry, the major barrier to the entry of new firms is not the cost of capital investments but rather the ability to promote consumption and consumer loyalty to branded food products identified by trademarks and promoted through heavy advertising. Product differentiation (the production of many similar products with minor variations in color, form, texture, or packaging) is combined with the use of trademarks and advertising to constitute an effective barrier to the entry of new firms.[28] The regulation of foreign investment is clearly not the appropriate instrument to regulate advertising trademarks. Product differentiation, however, could in principle be regulated as part of the regulation of foreign investment. Participants in the drafting of the Law to Promote Mexican Investment and to Regulate Foreign Investment (including the presidential adviser, Miguel Wionczek, and others) indicated to me that they hoped to be able to limit the proliferation of differentiated products by transnational enterprises. Point 4 of article 12 of the law authorized the National Foreign Investment Commission "to decide on the proportion of existing foreign investment in Mexico to be admitted in new fields of economic investment or in new production lines." This regulation, however, only provided the authority to regulate the diversification of foreign-owned firms into products completely different from those they had produced in the past.

For four years after the establishment of the National Foreign Investment Commission, the terms "new fields of economic investment" and "new product lines" were not defined. During this time, foreign-owned food-processing firms seemed to operate under the assumption that any food product fell within their traditional activities. Some firms voluntarily reported new products to the Registry of

Foreign Investment, but others proceeded without either requesting permission or reporting their new activities. One firm expanded from the production of pet foods into the production of accessories, such as dog collars; another introduced pet foods to complement food for humans. A chocolate manufacturer requested and received permission to produce an "instant breakfast" bar. Few expansions into new food product lines were denied. In September 1977, the National Foreign Investment Commission finally issued a lengthy resolution containing an elaborate classification at the four-digit level to define new lines of economic activity and new product lines. Even after the publication of that resolution, however, product differentiation did not fall within the scope of the mandate of the National Foreign Investment Commission. According to commission decisions, a firm that produced breakfast cereals could still introduce new cereals; a firm that produced canned dog food could produce dry dog food; a firm that produced a sugared powdered mix for orange drink could produce powdered mixes for other flavors. All of these products are now produced by firms affiliated with international enterprises in Mexico. Ironically, the diversification into new product lines could increase competition in Mexican industry, whereas product differentiation decreases competition by strengthening the market position of the leading firms. Yet it was diversification, not product differentiation, that the National Foreign Investment Commission was authorized to regulate.

A final example shows how structure constrains Mexico's regulatory capacity. In an effort to reduce the burden of regulation and to speed decisions, Mexico now automatically authorizes majority ownership of decentralized, export-oriented firms. These policy regulations also allow transfers of shares among foreigners. The argument is that one foreigner is as good as another. But this means that mergers and acquisitions at the global level are translated directly into increased concentration in Mexico. The acquisition of Carnation by Nestlè was "just" a transfer of shares among foreigners, but the effect was to eliminate competition among the two major producers of processed milk products in Mexico. The analysis of foreign investment in the food-processing industry in Mexico suggests that the regulations of foreign investment adopted in 1973 were not sufficient to control changes generated at the global level. To preserve competition under such conditions, more foreign investors, not fewer, were needed. Initially developed to combat monopoly, the policy often aided it. The failure of regulation to change structure helps explain the shift to liberalization.

Technology Transfer

An analysis of the contracts registered for the recipient firms in the food-processing industry is revealing both for an analysis of the National Registry on Technology Transfer and for an understanding of the industry itself. Payments for technology imports in the food and beverage industries have been heavily concentrated in foreign-affiliated firms. In one sample, 90 percent of all beverage payments and 93 percent of all food payments were made by foreign firms. Payments were more likely to be made for a package including technology assistance and know-how rather than for trademarks alone. In a 1975 sample of 618 contracts in 20 different industrial sectors, all involving trademark licenses, 32 percent of the contracts were in the food and drink industries. However, of the 198 contracts in these industries, only 38 specified payment amounts, 12 did not contain payment information, and 148 specified that the trademark licenses were free. These figures emphasize the fact that trademarks are important to firms because of the goodwill and the market share they represent, rather than for the extraction of royalty payments.[29]

The following paragraphs summarize data on technology contracts of recipient firms in the food-processing industry for contracts registered in Mexico during the initial registration period of 1973–77. The data submitted by the firms were often incomplete, and the summaries prepared by the staff of the Technology Registry often showed gaping holes. Nevertheless, these data are the best available at the industry level and are the same data with which the registry itself worked. The data cover 170 contracts involving 122 licensee firms. (I also examined about 20 percent of the original contracts.)

Significant differences existed between recipient firms that were majority foreign owned and recipient firms that were predominantly or wholly national. Most striking is the importance of trademarks for foreign-owned licensees. Thirty-six of the 48 majority foreign-owned firms reported contracts including trademark licenses, whereas only 18 of the 55 firms with zero to 24.9 percent foreign ownership reported trademark licenses. Fifty-two of the 77 contracts of majority foreign-owned subsidiaries involved trademarks, whereas only 31 of the 93 majority national recipients did so. Only 13 firms reported patent licenses. Know-how and technical assistance were much more important for both national and foreign-owned licensees. Contracts for administrative services were especially prominent among the contracts between two national firms. With respect to the duration of the contracts, a majority of firms in all categories specified an exact number of years of duration. Among foreign subsidiaries, the average duration was more likely to approach the maximum ten-year limit. Over one third of all firms left the duration of the contract indefinite, however. Contracts of this sort usually specified that the contract would continue until canceled by either party. Among foreign subsidiaries, almost half—38 out of 77—used this indefinite form, but only 26 of the 93 majority national licensees did. This is significant because among firms controlled in their majority by a foreign parent, the cancellation of the contract by the licensee is much less likely to occur. By leaving the duration of the contract open-ended, there is no specific renewal date at which time the contract must be reevaluated.

Of the relatively few contracts that specified payments, 24 out of 69 involved payments (after final negotiations were completed) that exceeded 2 percent. Interestingly enough, these were proportionately more likely among majority national firms than among foreign subsidiaries. More important, the contracts with national recipients were more likely to remain the same after negotiations than contracts with majority foreign-owned firms, which showed decreases in 15 of the 35 reported cases. These data, fragmentary though they are, suggest that majority foreign-owned firms could more easily reduce the level of their payments for technology transfer than national recipient firms. Foreign subsidiaries have alternative avenues for the repatriation of profits.

Conclusion

The establishment of the National Registry on Technology Transfer and the required registration of technology contracts changed the rules of the game for technology in Mexico by permitting state intervention at the negotiation stage of the technology acquisition process. Payments stipulated in the contracts were reduced in many cases and a number of restrictive clauses were eliminated. There were, however, serious limitations on the effectiveness of these regulations. The absence of exchange controls limited the ability to reduce the total foreign remittances by subsidiaries of international enterprises. The use of an indefinite term of duration resulting in an essentially self-perpetuating contract reduced the effectiveness of the ten-year limit on contracts. For firms in the food-processing industry and in other consumer goods industries in which trademarks represent an important element of oligopoly power, these regulations could reduce or eliminate the payment for trademark licenses but could not restrict the use of foreign trademarks by local firms and international subsidiaries.

Neither the regulations of foreign investment nor those of technology were effective in changing industrial structure in the food-processing industry. Instead, the liberal metapreference prevailed. Global competition was the best assurance of competition in Mexico. Opening Mexico to new investment was more likely than regulation to promote competitive behavior.

Eight

The Computer Industry and the Case of IBM

In march 1984, IBM formally asked the Mexican government for permission to establish a wholly owned microcomputer plant in Guadalajara. The planned factory, which would be the largest of its kind in Latin America, would produce some 600,000 personal computers (PCs) during the first five years of operation. IBM planned to export 92 percent of these units to markets in Latin America and Canada, and the company estimated the project would earn over $500 million in export revenues during this period.[1]

Responsibility for deciding on the merits of this proposal fell to Mexico's Ministry of Commerce and Industrial Development. Adolfo Hegewisch, undersecretary in charge of foreign investment, had been personally selected by President Miguel de la Madrid in 1982 to improve the ministry's relations with foreign direct investors while also improving this sector's contribution to the balance of payments. Particularly, Hegewisch was to encourage more actively new direct foreign investment (DFI), especially in high-technology industries and industries that held export potential.

IBM's proposal seemed directed toward these goals. Balance-of-payments concerns had long dominated Mexican economic planning, and a half-billion-dollar export project could alleviate many problems. Yet acceptance of a wholly owned plant in a vital economic sector such as computers would be a departure from traditional Mexican investment policy. IBM's entrance into the Mexican microcomputer market was certain to cause significant changes, not only in the nature of the Mexican computer industry but also in the structure of the industrial economy as a whole. It was initially left to Hegewisch and his ministry to determine whether these changes would work to improve or worsen Mexico's balance-of-payments situation and to recommend a course of action to President de la Madrid.

Mexican planners singled out computers as a sector of primary

194

importance for future Mexican development. The computer industry worldwide and the related technological fields it has spawned were rapidly growing industrial sectors that many saw as the focus of modern industrialization. In terms of specific Mexican development goals as well, the computer industry seemed an area that could provide a great many solutions to Mexico's economic woes.

This case was pivotal for Mexico, marking the shift away from restrictive policies toward foreign investment.

The International Computer Industry

The Structure of the Industry

The international computer industry as a whole was an expanding industrial sector in the mid-1980s. The continued improvement of basic technologies like the microchip, the rapid change in the nature of computing products, and the ever-expanding applications of computing technology kept this industry growing. New markets in related fields such as data communication, software, peripheral equipment, and accessories were also opening every day. All things considered, the computer industry was perhaps the most dynamic sector of modern industry.

Within the industry, however, certain sectors were more developed than others. Internationally, the mainframe computer industry was very mature, with sales concentrated among large producers like IBM, Burroughs, and Honeywell. The enormous capital costs involved in producing in this sector, the complexity of these units, the need for advanced technical expertise, and the limited marketplace made new entry difficult. In fact there had not been a new entrant into the mainframe market in over five years. The advent of smaller computers also reduced demand for these units, and market analysts predicted growth in the mainframe market to be minimal in the coming years.

The minicomputer industry was also a mature market sector, although production was less concentrated than in mainframes. IBM again was the leading producer, with Digital Equipment, Burroughs, and Wang its principal competitors. Smaller computers seemed to be reducing demand for these machines also, and the outlook for further expansion of the minicomputer market was not encouraging.

Microcomputers (PCs) were perhaps the most dynamic sector of the computer industry in the 1980s, with better possibilities for growth than the mainframe and minicomputer industries. The introduction of the IBM PC in 1982, however, added a new element of concentration to what was previously a highly diverse sector. Many analysts predicted IBM to assume market control in PCs just as they had done in every other major field of computing, suggesting that the PC sector was approaching maturation.[2] Furthermore, as the market for PCs expanded, scale economies in production grew increasingly important. Highly capitalized operations were most important in maintaining quality control and were essential for producing high-quality products on a large scale. For example, IBM conducts product testing in an almost fully automated plant. Thus, although small firms had succeeded early in the PC market, future trends seemed to suggest that the large, highly capitalized firms would outperform smaller producers in the years to come.

More dynamic perhaps than the actual production of computers was the variety of related industries the computer industry created. One such industry was peripherals and accessories. This industry included products such as printers, keyboards, terminals, disk drives, and storage disks. The market for these products was just beginning to explode, and with investment costs lower in this sector than in any of the other computer groups, competition was fierce among producers.

A second important industry relating to computers was software. Software had always been an important subsector of the computer market, but with the advent of the PC, the industry developed a new vigor. Developing software for a PC was not the expensive, complex process that it was with larger computing systems. The small size of the computer reduced the scale of development to levels that many could manage. The personalized nature of the PC and the expanding variety of uses it served held enormous potential for highly specialized software that met individual needs. This type of product could best be produced by small firms with low-volume production operations. The fact that one could develop and produce software using the same equipment further encouraged such production.

The feasibility of low-volume production encouraged a third industry, specialized equipment. Specialized equipment comprised products designed to be used with more established, name computers, but which met a specific need not served by the more all-purpose machines. For example, specialized firms produced units to help speed up operations, process greater levels of input, or perhaps make the unit more responsive to individual needs. Such products were tangential to the main firms, with a limited market, but were nonetheless an important subsector of the computer market in the 1980s.

IBM and the Computer Industry

In many ways IBM in the 1980s was an industry unto itself within the computer industry. Its 1983 sales of $35.6 billion were more than those of the next nine competitors combined. It held market share dominance in every important computer sector, and with research and development investments of billions of dollars annually, its stability was second to none. IBM's success was based on a combination of factors.[3]

Coming first helped IBM establish its unshakable reputation as industry leader and its enormous trademark recognition. Computer buyers have been notoriously risk averse, and IBM in the 1980s enjoyed a huge advantage in customer confidence over other firms. The fact that IBM was sure to be around tomorrow was a reassuring fact for most consumers, and it often gave IBM the edge over smaller, less established but perhaps more technically innovative firms.

Another advantage was the full range of products and services offered by IBM. From the firm's point of view, this diversity allowed IBM to spread costs and risks throughout a number of sectors, thus minimizing its dependence on any one sector. This further gave the firm an added flexibility in pricing, since it could underprice producers in one sector while making up for these losses in other sectors. Most of IBM's competitors did not enjoy this flexibility.

For the consumer, IBM's diversity meant a completeness of product line that was second to none. Since industry trends suggested that most consumers preferred staying with one vendor for all their computer needs, the broad range of products and services offered by IBM was a powerful marketing asset. IBM's ability to offer a wide variety of units also made the firm better able to build compatible systems to suit specific customer needs. This was especially important for larger clients in business and industry.

A final advantage was IBM's ability to set standards within the industry. IBM's size, its power in a broad range of markets, and its dominance in the industry as a whole meant that IBM products set de facto standards throughout the industry. Some of the larger firms, such as Burroughs and Honeywell, attempted to compete with IBM outside these standards, but many firms accepted IBM's standards and competed within them. No firm, however, was able to set standards like IBM, and as computer industry analyst William Inmon said, "It allowed IBM to shape the world to meet its needs."[4] For the consumer, it also meant that there was never a shortage of IBM-compatible software, accessories, or equipment.

Computers and Mexico

There was considerable reason for Mexican planners to target the computer industry for greater development. Mexico's computer market was the second largest in Latin America, behind Brazil, and Mexico was one of the twenty largest computer users worldwide.[5] Future prospects for the computer market in Mexico were also encouraging, with analysts estimating 30–50 percent growth in the coming years.[6] Until 1981, virtually all Mexico's computing needs were supplied through foreign imports, and even in 1984 large state-run firms such as PEMEX, CFE, and Sidermex continued to import over 70 percent of their computers.[7] As a result, possibilities for import substitution were also great.

Most generally, however, the main advantage for Mexico in establishing an effective computer sector was to provide a platform for future industrial development. Many observers saw computers and more specifically electronic computer technology as the industry from which future industrialization would grow. To neglect the development of electronics technology, in their view, was to neglect industrial development.

Early experience seemed to show that the greatest success in computer markets was achieved by countries that were able to take advantage of developing products, markets, or technologies in their early stages. India was able to establish a minicomputer industry and Brazil had some success with microcomputers by moving into production of these products at an early stage of their product lives.[8] Entry possibilities such as these were predicated on the existence of an effective national electronics industry with the ability to take advantage of new technological developments. Thus, although immediate returns from developing local computer-manufacturing capabilities might be slight, a commitment to such a program could yield substantial gains in the long run.

Although the potential gains in developing a computer industry in Mexico seemed great, the realities of the Mexican situation placed major obstacles in the way of realizing these rewards. Policymakers, realizing both the importance of the computer industry and Mexico's deficiencies in this area, began concentrating efforts toward the creation of indigenous computing capacities in Mexico.

The 1981 Policy

Before 1981, there was no indigenous computer industry in Mexico. Mexico purchased what computers it needed from established international firms. Some production was undertaken locally, but these plants were mere assembly operations putting together imported foreign parts. In the mid-1970s an attempt was made to promote a national computing sector. Firms were encouraged to promote greater national integration (local content) in their Mexican operations while a quota system restricted import levels. These policies were never aggressively pursued, however, and when the more free-market-oriented López Portillo administration came to power in 1976, they were abandoned.

In 1981, imports of electronics equipment totaled $663 million, with computer equipment accounting for 40 percent of that total. This represented more than 5 percent of Mexico's total imports of manufactured goods.[9] Fearing an excessive reliance on foreign producers in an expanding and increasingly vital industrial area, the Mexican government passed legislation intended to encourage the development of a local computer industry. The specific goals of the program as laid out were (1) to improve the computer industry's contribution to balance of payments and increase international competitiveness through exports, (2) to increase national integration, (3) to develop a component supply industry, and (4) to improve local technological advancement.[10]

The 1981 package had four principal parts. First were equity restrictions for foreign PC producers. Foreign manufacturers were restricted to 49 percent ownership of their Mexican operations. By contrast, producers of minicomputers and mainframe computers were allowed full ownership of their subsidiaries. The Mexican government singled out PCs because they felt the small-computer industry was of greater importance to future Mexican development. Planner José Warman, with the support of Undersecretary of Industry Mauricio de María y Campos, also saw greater possibilities for success by Mexican firms in this sector than in the more technically sophisticated large-computer sector.

The proposal also imposed new import restrictions on computers and component parts. Import quotas were assigned using the following scale of priorities: (1) components for local assembly and/or manufacturing, (2) spare parts for systems already installed, (3) peripherals intended to balance or improve existing systems, and (4) finished products.[11] Actual quotas for individual firms depended on manufacturing levels. Generally speaking, producers were allowed imports equal to four times the level of local purchases in the first two years and an import quota equal to local purchases in the two subsequent years. Mainframe computer production was exempted from the quotas (they would be "calculated individually," according to the proposed legislation) because no domestic production was expected.[12]

A third element of the legislation was export promotion. Specifically, firms seeking authorization to manufacture in Mexico were called on to export an increasing percentage of their local products. Actual export levels were set depending on the product line and ownership structure of the firm.

The final aspect of the new regulations was an increase in local content demands. Detailed and complicated formulas were used to determine the national content restrictions in the various computer sectors. Although the rules were fairly strictly defined, room was left for some flexibility in application. For example, firms were offered a concession on local content if they could show they had generated local research and development expenses. Further concessions were also available to firms who exported products.

In short, the whole nationalist program of ownership restriction, import substitution, and export promotion was replicated in a single industry policy.

Policy Outcomes: Continued Problems

In the mainframe and minicomputer sectors, the result of the policy was a fairly rapid consolidation of the market, with a few major firms controlling production. IBM dominated both these sectors, gaining 45 percent of the mainframe market and 35 percent of minicomputer sales.[13] Imported parts continued to dominate production in these sectors.

In the PC sector, where the government most aggressively pursued greater self-reliance, the structure of the PC industry in Mexico caused many problems in implementing the plan. The most salient feature of Mexico's PC sector was its small size. Apple, which held 40 percent of the Mexican market in 1984, was by far the largest producer in the country. Its operation was based in a single plant that employed fewer than twenty-five people. Hewlett-Packard, producing its HP-150, was the only other foreign producer with a major production facility. The rest of the market was filled by about thirty other firms who ran literally garage-size operations.[14]

The small size of Mexico's PC firms hindered the government's program in several ways. First, the government hoped import restriction would force firms to develop a local supply network for components, but few if any PC firms in Mexico commanded the necessary capital or skills to develop such a network. Most of these firms operated at just above the margin of survival, and they depended on the reliability, cost-efficiency, and quality of tested foreign components to maintain cost-effective production. They could simply not afford the risks or costs involved in testing new components, let alone commit significant resources toward improvements in this sector.

A second problem was the inability of these firms to take advantage of scale economies. An important component of Mexican industrial policy was legislation designed to protect developing domestic firms from elimination by the more established, cost-efficient foreign producers. Although such legislation guaranteed a Mexican presence in domestic PC markets, protectionist policies led to some significant distortions in the structure of the industry. With little incentive to produce at maximum efficiency due to the lack of competition with more efficient foreign producers, Mexican PC operations on the whole were undercapitalized and inefficiently operated. Product quality, as a result, was on average well below international standards, and the average price of a PC in Mexico was some 40 percent above market levels abroad.[15] The market was also excessively fragmented, and protectionist policies, by allowing firms to continue producing inefficiently, provided no incentive for the consolidation of domestic firms into a larger, more efficient operation.

The high prices and poor quality of Mexican computers led to a third problem—smuggling. With the U.S. market so close, it was not difficult to bring units across the border. Black market firms within Mexico also operated illegal assembly operations, breaking down U.S.-made units, smuggling the parts into the country or even importing some legally, and then reassembling the units and stamping them "Made in Mexico." The ease with which a PC can be assembled, given very basic technical knowledge, and the small-scale operation needed to accomplish this task made this a lucrative, and not easily prohibited, business. Many estimate that as many computers were smuggled into Mexico illegally as were sold in open markets.[16]

The absence of modern productive operations and the lack of competition also hindered the introduction of new technologies into Mexico. Mexican PCs were characteristically a generation behind international markets. As an example, Apple continued to produce the Apple II in Mexico while marketing its state-of-the-art Macintosh elsewhere.[17] The problems of firm size and lack of resources that hindered the development of local suppliers also worked against local technological advancement. And with technology well behind international standards, related industries such as peripherals, software, and tangential equipment, which were based on access to state-of-the-art equipment for their development, also lagged behind market standards abroad.

These structural impediments weighed heavily on the Mexican government's attempts to develop a national computer industry through import/export quotas. The import restrictions placed a heavy burden on the small, national firms and even on some of the more established foreign interests. Tandy, for example, simply decided it was no longer cost-efficient to produce PCs in Mexico using local parts and pulled out altogether in 1983.[18] Others found ways to work around import/export quotas by adjusting levels in different production sectors. NCR, for example, produced a diverse range of products locally, but even after exporting 80 percent of its local production in 1983, the firm retained an import/export deficit of $235,000.[19] Few small firms were able to develop significant local supply linkages, and since they did not command the structural diversity of the larger firms, many simply failed or were swallowed up by bigger enterprises. In fact a major criticism of the program was that it worked in favor of large firms and increased industrial concentration within the market.[20]

With the firms that remained protected from internationally competitive products, product quality remained poor, prices remained high, and technological levels remained well behind international levels. These factors coupled with poor customer recognition and increasing protectionism abroad made exports exceedingly difficult. Little, if any, progress had been made by 1984 in the realization of the goals set out by the Mexican government.

Mexico and IBM

It was with the failures of past policy in mind that Hegewisch and his ministry considered IBM's proposal. The Guadalajara plant would involve an initial investment of $6–$8 million. IBM insisted, however, that it maintain full ownership of its new subsidiary. IBM, more than any other firm, had the resources, experience, and expertise necessary to effect major improvements in the performance of the Mexican computer industry in a short period of time, yet Mexico needed to decide whether this particular proposal would allow Mexico to tap this enormous potential.

Development and Computers:
The Cases of India and Brazil

In considering how to respond to IBM's offer, Mexican planners drew upon the experiences of other newly industrializing countries with respect to computer policy. In particular, both India and Brazil had succeeded during the 1970s in fostering locally owned minicomputer and microcomputer industries while contending with powerful firms like IBM. Their example could be useful in assessing Mexican priorities concerning computer policy.

In India, as in Mexico, local ownership was a goal set by state planners when they first established a national computer policy in the late 1960s. By 1977, three foreign firms were important in the Indian market. The British firm ICL, one of the oldest computer manufacturers in India, had agreed to majority Indian ownership in 1975. Likewise, Burroughs, entering the Indian market for the first time in 1977, agreed to share ownership of its production facility equally with an Indian firm.

The third computer firm in India, IBM, indicated that it would rather leave the Indian market than accept minority ownership. Recognizing the seriousness of the Indian position, IBM worked to win an exemption from the ownership requirement by improving its operation in the country. Specifically, the firm proposed increased manufacturing for export, greater technology transfers for its manufacturing activities, and direct technical assistance to India's data-processing programs. Indian managers would not budge on the ownership question, however, and IBM withdrew from India in 1978. Despite this loss, by the mid-1980s India's minicomputer and microcomputer sectors featured significant local production and ownership.

In Brazil, ownership was less of an issue before the mid-1970s, and computer policy was less centralized than it was in India. In 1975 and 1976, following the oil price shock of 1974 and the subsequent foreign exchange crunch, Brazilian planners began to use import controls to discriminate against computer imports while encouraging the use of computers manufactured by the state-owned agency COBRA. In 1976, IBM proposed to begin manufacturing minicomputers in Brazil to compete with COBRA. Rather than confront IBM directly, the Brazilian government announced a broad-reaching "market reserve policy" that was to limit new entrants to the minicomputer market. The government invited local and foreign firms to submit proposals, which would be judged according to established criteria. Preference was to be given to local ownership and high levels of technology transfer.[21]

Bids were received from a number of major computer TNCs, including IBM; however, they all proposed full ownership and limited technology transfer. The offers from three wholly Brazilian owned firms were accepted. The three firms joined COBRA, and after working out technology transfer agreements with Ferranti (a U.K. computer firm) and Sycor (a small U.S. computer firm), they began operations as a government-protected oligopoly. By 1984, the market reserve policy had been extended downward to include the expanding PC market.

Although many saw the Brazilian experience as a success, there were some important problems. One important deficiency was in tech-

nology. The Brazilians had succeeded in obtaining technology transfer agreements, but the actual technology obtained was for the most
part "off the shelf" components and not equal to the best technologies
abroad. Moreover, given the rapid change in computer technology,
relying on transfer agreements hindered the ability of national firms
to keep pace with international product levels and risked missing a
product generation.

A second problem was the low level of research and development
in Brazil. Since Brazilian computer firms relied on foreign producers
to supply needed technology, little local product development was
attempted. What research was conducted within the country was
geared toward copying current technologies used by established foreign firms. This effort was successful to some degree, yet reliance on
copying existing technologies ensured that Brazilian firms would
never be on the leading edge of technological change, and it again
threatened to leave Brazilian producers a step behind in the rapidly
changing small-computer industry.

Such dangers were even more serious given technological trends
within the PC industry. As the storage capacity of the microchip continued to expand, the traditional all-purpose microchip was becoming
a commodity, with the high-value-added business moving to more
advanced "proprietary chips." These chips were different in that in
addition to normal operational functions, they were designed to include functions normally accomplished by software. Machines that
were designed to do only a few tasks (e.g., word processing or data
analysis) and that had the requisite functions for accomplishing these
tasks built right into them seemed to be the future of the small computer. Firms that did not possess the necessary technological capacities
to design their own products would be left behind, and the low levels
of research and development in Brazil suggested that this was a real
danger.

The Advantages for IBM

IBM's interest in Mexico was based on a number of factors. The
company's primary concern was entrance into the PC market both in
Mexico and in Latin America as a whole. As a late entrant into the
PC market in the United States, IBM was late in seeking to take
advantage of the growing demand for PCs south of the border. The
1981 legislation had further shut IBM out of the Mexican PC business.
Since Mexico's computer market was second only to Brazil's in Latin
America in terms of size, a plant in Mexico would provide both entrance into a potentially lucrative market and a foothold for penetration into other regional markets.

The trend toward greater Latin American integration further attracted IBM to Mexico. The Latin American Free Trade Agreement guaranteed preferential treatment for products that originated from member countries. Thus, IBM products exported from Mexico would be subject to better tariff treatment than goods produced outside the Latin American community; they would also be less likely targets for import quotas. Given IBM's goal of penetrating Latin American markets, there were considerable advantages to establishing production facilities within a Latin American common market country like Mexico.[22]

IBM was also interested in providing an alternative in Mexico to the state-controlled computer experiences of Brazil and India. Since many countries were just beginning to formulate computer policies, it was important to show developing countries the advantages of including IBM in national computer development. These considerations were even more important in Latin America because of the apparent success achieved by Brazil without international companies like IBM. IBM, however, felt that it could better provide advanced technology, exports, and expenditures for local research and development, which seemed neglected by the Brazilian approach. IBM hoped its Mexican project would demonstrate the benefits to underdeveloped countries of allowing a less nationally controlled computer industry.

Further considerations made Mexico a more attractive candidate for a Latin American operation than other countries in the region. For one, a local supply network of some 200 firms was already developed as a result of IBM's mainframe and minicomputer operations. This network would need further development, yet the existence of any local supply vendors was a comparative plus for Mexico. Mexico also had legislation guaranteeing royalty payments and protecting the intellectual property of foreign firms. Furthermore, the government imposed relatively lenient restrictions on profit remittances. Finally, Mexico's proximity to IBM's U.S. headquarters and the comparatively high level of political stability in Mexico made the country an attractive spot for the IBM venture.

The Advantages and Disadvantages for Mexico

Accepting IBM's offer held potential for improving Mexico's computer industry, though at the expense of the nationalist project. Since IBM proposed to export its PCs, the program would provide an immediate source of desperately needed foreign exchange. IBM's brand-name recognition and its market prestige would guarantee immediate market penetration, and the new PCs could help improve the reputation of Mexican-made computers, further aiding Mexican firms trying to export.

Since IBM would be producing computers for sale in international markets, the units would be state-of-the-art, high-quality computers. Introduction of these products into Mexico could provide a competitive incentive for local producers to adopt more cost-efficient production methods. However, since IBM's plant would be significantly larger and more highly capitalized than other factories in Mexico and given IBM's name recognition and marketing budget, local producers would probably find it beyond their means to compete with the new IBM products.

The local content restrictions imposed on IBM by the 1981 law could also force IBM to commit resources to developing local supply industries. IBM, more than any other firm, had the resource base to handle a local development project, and its expertise would suggest that the new industry, if created, would be an efficient, modern one.

Access to state-of-the-art IBM PCs within Mexico could also encourage the development of a wider range of related industries, like software or peripherals. Progress in these areas had been hindered in the past by the backwardness of Mexican technology, but IBM's entrance could remedy the situation. Since these newly developed firms would be developing products for use with IBM systems, possibilities for successful entry into international export markets would also be improved.

Many also saw this proposal as a test of Mexico's newly proclaimed flexibility toward DFI. With foreign debt a continuing problem, it was important for Mexican planners to create an environment conducive to attracting needed DFI. Government statements had already suggested that policy was moving toward greater freedom for foreign firms operating in Mexico, yet investors remained skeptical. They needed to see explicit policy actions demonstrating these new directions before they would forget decades of nationalist control.

IBM's prestige among foreign business interests forced Mexican planners to be especially cautious in considering the computer firm's proposal. For many, IBM was a model of excellence among large corporations. It had a reputation as a highly ethical company that produced service and customer satisfaction. Furthermore, the company had a proven record within Mexico. In addition to its mainframe operations, it had been producing its System 36 minicomputer since 1983, using a large percentage of local content and exporting a large share to demanding markets such as Japan. IBM seemed a highly attractive candidate for acceptance under Mexico's more flexible foreign investment policies, and in light of the visibility the IBM proposal was gaining among investors of all sorts, planners needed to consider what effect rejecting IBM would have on the willingness of future investors to consider Mexico.

Questions remained concerning the wisdom of accepting IBM's proposal. Of notable concern was the 100 percent ownership IBM demanded for its new plant. Legislation had previously restricted the PC sector to joint-venture firms that maintained 51 percent Mexican ownership, and Apple and Hewlett-Packard had already entered the market under these terms. Opposition from these producers was strong. As one executive from a U.S. joint-venture firm in Mexico put it, "It's tough enough to compete with IBM on an equal basis, let alone with a handicap." The majority Mexican ownership law was also the Mexican government's primary instrument ensuring that foreign firms conduct themselves in an appropriate manner and make decisions reflecting Mexican needs. To relinquish this control could mean granting a degree of independence to IBM in Mexico that could weaken nationalist development policies in the future.[23]

Another concern was the power IBM could wield in the Mexican PC market should its plant be approved. Although they planned to export 92 percent of the units produced, projections suggested that even the 8 percent sold domestically would give IBM a 40 percent market share in their first year.[24] IBM already held 45 percent of the mainframe market and 30 percent of the minicomputer market. Since the new plant would also be significantly more modern and cost-efficient than existing factories, many observers feared that IBM could increase this share quickly by underpricing and outperforming their competition. IBM could quickly assume dominance in the market, placing itself in a position to set prices and control markets in an oligopolistic fashion. As Frank Flemming of the Microdata Corporation said, "Mexico may be forced to buy from IBM when they don't really want to."[25]

IBM's experience in the U.S. PC market suggested that such fears were well founded. Upon entering the PC market in 1982, some five years behind its other competitors, the IBM PC immediately earned the firm $500 million and placed the company second in sales among all producers. In just one year, IBM had become the leading PC vendor, with sales of $1.5 billion, some $500 million more than Apple, its nearest competitor. Market power such as this could not be ignored, especially by a developing country such as Mexico.

Political considerations were a factor as well. Distressed by the lack of concern Mexican planners seemed to show for small, domestic industries, many nationalists believed this proposal was a classic example of the Mexican government's increased willingness to sacrifice Mexican independence in favor of foreigners. For these observers, prominent in the Mexican press, allowing a wholly owned foreign computer company, especially with the power of IBM, to step in and assume control of a vital and developing industry was in complete contradiction to the revolutionary goals maintained by the government and was a betrayal of Mexico's nationalist history. They viewed acceptance of this proposal as a desperate act at a time of economic crisis, and they did not believe the program was in the long-term best interests of Mexican development. Such complaints were not isolated. Members of national industry, the government bureaucracy, and Mexico's principal political party all voiced opposition to the proposal.

Further pressure was placed on decisionmakers by the fact that IBM was also conducting negotiations with Argentina over a similar proposal. If Mexico rejected IBM's proposal and IBM decided to locate in Argentina, Mexico could be faced with the irony, due to the Latin American Free Trade Agreement, of importing the same computers it had decided not to produce locally.[26]

For Hegewisch, his colleagues, and his president, the choices were clear. Should Mexico pursue self-reliant development with respect to its computer industry, giving up rapid development and immediate returns in exchange for nationalist control? Or should Mexico sacrifice some of its control to rapidly expand and improve this fledgling industry within the country? These decisionmakers needed a plan that would work to the immediate benefit of the Mexican economy and toward the development of an industrial base for future economic growth. Their plan would also need to ensure that Mexican development goals were realized and that growth was in keeping with Mexican needs. Would the plan reflect the liberal vision of cooperation with IBM or the nationalist vision of the plan developed by Warman and De María y Campos?

The Outcome of IBM's Proposal

The negotiations between IBM and the Mexican government concerning the proposed PC plant stretched over more than a year, in four main steps.

1. In March 1984, IBM officially submitted a proposal to build a wholly owned plant in Guadalajara to the Mexican government. The proposed plant would produce 600,000 PCs over the first five years, with 92 percent of these units being exported. The factory would employ over eighty individuals, and the initial investment would approach $7 million. IBM estimated the plant would earn over $500 million in foreign exchange during the first five years. Although agreeing in principle to certain details of the project, including 100 percent ownership by IBM, the Mexican government rejected the proposal in April 1984 because, as one official said, the proposed

plant would use relatively few Mexican parts and do little to advance Mexico's computer industry.

2. Six months later, IBM revised its initial proposal, agreeing to use 65 percent local parts in production at the outset and to increase the amount to 95 percent later. The company further agreed to spend $40 million on financial and technical help for Mexican suppliers of computer parts. IBM also pledged to hold prices 10 to 15 percent above U.S. levels and to manufacture not only its PC and PC Jr. but its high-powered, then state-of-the-art PC-AT.

3. However, in January 1985, the Mexican government rejected IBM's proposal again, citing investment and employment levels as inadequate. However, IBM was encouraged to submit an improved proposal, and many observers saw the rejection as a face-saving measure aimed at placating political opposition to the plan. IBM statements issued after the rejection said that company officials planned to "continue [their] dialogue with the Mexican government, examining alternatives and other proposals that will permit [their] microcomputer products to reach Mexican users." The head of IBM's international division, John Akers, flew to Mexico to meet personally with President de la Madrid.

4. As a direct result of that meeting, in July 1985 IBM was cleared to build its PC plant in Guadalajara. The proposal accepted was much the same as the one rejected earlier in the year. The only significant change was that IBM increased its total investment to $91 million.

Conclusion

IBM announced the start of its investment project in January 1986. The company also announced programs to establish a local dealer network, train and develop local component suppliers, and organize a Mexican semiconductor technology center. IBM released a list of other projects, which included development of (1) an international distribution center to support export operations to over thirty countries, (2) a software center to distribute software to Spanish-speaking Latin America, (3) an international purchasing program to assist local industry in developing products for IBM manufacturing facilities worldwide, (4) partnership programs with Mexican universities and technical schools, and (5) scholarship programs for Mexican scientists to study at IBM plants and laboratories worldwide.

IBM de México Chairman Rodrigo Guerra said that the package "offers opportunities for a large number of Mexican companies and professionals to supply parts and components, software, technical and distributional services for the IBM products. It could create 1,700 high level jobs in the industry within five years." In fact, the final proposal was probably not too different from the initial proposal; IBM repackaged many of the investment, export, and technology "sweeteners" from its other expansion plans in Mexico.

The significance of this case was not so much the concessions that IBM seemed to make as the decision by Mexico finally to pursue a share of the global market, using liberal policies, rather than to protect the domestic market with nationalist policies. By 1988, Mexico was reported to be producing 10 percent of worldwide production of IBM PC components. Hewlett-Packard and other competitors had been approved for 100 percent foreign ownership. The nationalist meta-preference had given way to international liberalization.

Nine

The Automobile Industry

Industrial Structure of the Global Automobile Industry

The automobile industry is an important indicator of industrial growth. As of 1976, nine of the fifty largest firms in the world were motor vehicle manufacturers, located in the United States, Europe, and Japan.[1] Because the manufacture of automobiles requires steel, aluminum, glass, rubber, computer chips, and other technologically advanced components, the auto industry provides many more jobs than those directly related to automobile production.[2] According to Bennett and Sharpe, a recent estimate is that motor vehicle manufacture accounts for 10 percent of all jobs in the United States, Europe, and Japan.[3] In general, the major international auto firms of the developed countries dominate the industry: Chrysler, General Motors, and Ford in the United States; Renault and Peugeot-Citröen in France; Volkswagenwerk and Daimler Benz in Germany; and Toyota and Nissan in Japan.

Since World War II and the resulting shortage of raw production materials, these auto industries have become increasingly international in sales and manufacturing. During the mid-1950s these firms transferred their services to the developing countries: first through exports and then through investments for the local market. In a third stage, foreign firms invested in manufacturing facilities for export. The oil crisis of the early 1970s caused a major structural reorganization of the international auto industry: car designs were downsized, and arrangements were made for components to be sourced in different countries. The goal was to move automobile production to the developing countries to supply the world market.[4] Since the mid-1970s, global firms have been exporting both vehicles and components from developing countries.

The restructuring of the auto industry in "home" countries has created incentives for liberalization by increasing the opportunities for exports from "host" countries such as Mexico.

The Mexican Automobile Industry
and the Initiation of Manufacturing

In the late 1950s and early 1960s, the main characteristics of the auto industry were (1) high and increasing concentration, due to the large economies of scale and considerable risks involved in automobile production, as well as government policies in developed (home) countries that encouraged concentration; (2) the internationalization of production;[5] (3) increasing international competition; (4) the increasing interpenetration of markets and traditional spheres of influence; and (5) nonprice forms of competition, such as proliferation of models and frequent model changes.[6]

In 1958, when López Mateos took office, no manufacturing of automobiles took place in Mexico. Eleven assembly operations imported and assembled "completely knocked down kits" (CKDs). Of these eleven firms, two, Ford and General Motors, were completely foreign owned. Fábricas-Auto-Mex, the third dominant firm in the Mexican auto industry, was jointly owned: one third was owned by Chrysler and two thirds was owned by a wealthy Mexican family. The other firms were assembling under license from other foreign manufacturers. The assembly stage was a point of converging interests between the international firms and the state. Assembly allowed international firms to jump the tariff barrier, lengthen their production runs, and cut transport costs—all of which were necessary in the increasingly competitive international industry.

The convergence of interests between firms and the state began to break down when the auto industry became the prime candidate for deepening import substitution industrialization (ISI). In 1960 an interministerial committee of state *técnicos*, headed by NAFIN and including representatives from the Bank of Mexico, the Ministry of Industry and Commerce, and the Ministry of Finance, presented a set of proposals regarding ownership, structure, and behavior for auto industry policy.

Proposals concerning firm behavior included

1. production of at least 60 percent of the content of vehicles in Mexico (intended to induce local manufacturing and deepen ISI);
2. limitations on the number of acceptable makes and models produced by each firm;
3. limitations on the frequency of model changes;
4. standardization of certain parts (proposals 2 through 4 were suggested to increase efficiency by raising economies of scale in production).

Proposals concerning industry structure included

1. limitation of the number of firms in the terminal industry (which produces finished vehicles) to between three and five firms (to prevent inefficiency caused by market fragmentation);
2. limitation of the terminal firms to motor machining and final assembly (other manufacturing was to be reserved for a supplier or auto parts industry);
3. creation of a central body-stamping plant (to prevent inefficiencies in the production of exterior body parts).

The committee also proposed

1. majority Mexican ownership of firms in the terminal industry;
2. majority Mexican ownership of firms in the supplier industry (intended to preserve room for local business).

The foreign firms were not enthusiastic about local manufacture because it would require investment in a small Mexican market, the sacrifice of economies of scale in their home markets, and sourcing from an underdeveloped Mexican parts industry. The firms, however, agreed to undertake local production. This agreement can be explained by the "oligopolistic reaction" outlined by Knickerbocker (1973). In a tight oligopoly, firms engage in "follow-the-leader" behavior. Because Ford had moved early to comply with the demand for local manufacturing in a bid to capture the market, the other firms had to follow suit in order to maintain their competitive positions and not forfeit a potential market to a competitor.

The foreign enterprises were concerned about the limit on the number of firms. They did not disagree with the concern for efficiency but were concerned about being excluded from the market. This became one of the most contentious issues in the bargaining. The regulation of firm behavior—such as the standardization of parts, freezing of models, and limitations on the number of acceptable makes and models—"challenged entrenched competitive strategies."[7] Finally, Ford and General Motors insisted on fully owning the subsidiaries and did not want to Mexicanize.

In 1962, when the new auto decree was finally announced, it had been significantly modified. It retained the requirement about producing 60 percent of the content of vehicles in Mexico and the limits on vertical integration of terminal firms, but there was no reference to the Mexicanization of those firms. There was no mention of limiting makes and models or standardizing parts, nor was there a reference to limiting the number of terminal firms allowed in the industry.

Bennett and Sharpe believe that the decree was altered because the foreign firms mobilized the political power of their home governments but there is no hard evidence to support this speculation.[8]

Bennett and Sharpe also argue that "organizational constraints" within the state limited the actual exercise of bargaining power. First, there existed interministerial conflict between the Ministry of Industry and Commerce and the Ministry of Finance. This conflict undermined the state's bargaining position because they failed to coordinate with each other in the bargaining process. In addition, conflict existed within the ministries themselves. The ministers and secretaries, because of their heightened sensitivity to political concerns, were apparently partially responsible for taking a more conciliatory stance toward the foreign investors, in contrast to the *técnicos*, whose midlevel jobs encouraged a less global outlook.[9]

Effects of International Industrial Structure

The oligopolistic structure of the international automobile industry produced an oligopolistic reaction or "pattern of defensive investments" by the other auto firms, once Ford agreed to local manufacture. Increasing competition in the global industry magnified the importance of the Mexican market, thereby ensuring the pattern of defensive investments.

The increasing competitiveness of the global automobile industry can be clearly seen from a few figures on global production and trade. In 1950 the U.S. industry dominated the production market with 7.0 million units, compared with 1.1 million units in Western Europe and less than a million units in Japan. By 1970 Western Europe had moved into first place with 10.4 million units, while the United States stabilized at 7.2 and Japan leapt up to 7.0 million units.

The figures for exports tell a similar story. U.S. exports remained minimal at about 100,000 units from 1950 through 1980, while Western European exports climbed from 0.4 million units to a peak of 1.8 in 1970 and stabilized at 1.3 million units by 1980. Japan's export statistics are the most dramatic: Japanese exports skyrocketed from less than a million units in 1950 and 1960 to 0.7 in 1970 and 3.9 in 1980. This intense and growing competition among American, European, and Japanese producers provided the context for Mexican policy.

In Mexico, global competition initially had negative consequences. Global manufacturers established plants and used standard marketing techniques in Mexico to preserve their relative positions, but for Mexico, the results were small-scale, inefficient plants with short runs and high costs, with high reliance on imported components.

The industry must be analyzed in a broader context, as well. President López Mateos had nationalized electric power, Mexicanized mining, and pursued a left nationalist orientation. In this context, an aggressively nationalist policy toward the leading manufacturing industry would have sent a signal that Mexico was hostile to all foreign investment. As will also be evident in the computer industry, the "demonstration effect" of policy in leading industries is a major concern of policymakers.

The 1969 Export Promotion Decree

The 1962 decree did not contribute to a better balance of payments for the auto industry.[10] The Mexican market grew, but was fragmented and inefficient due to the large number of firms, makes, models, and model changes allowed under the 1962 decree. The decree had inadvertently precipitated the denationalization of a series of Mexican-owned firms;[11] many of the assembly firms could not transfer to manufacturing due to the need for large sums of capital and advanced technological capabilities.[12] In general, the Mexican firms were at a disadvantage in competing with the international firms.

Two plans were proposed to resolve these problems. One plan proposed a merger of all existing Mexican-owned firms combined with an increase in local content requirements. This plan would deepen import substitution, ameliorate the deteriorating balance of payments, and increase efficiency by reducing the number of firms in the market. The other plan proposed to promote exports by requiring that firms increasingly compensate for the imported content of their vehicles with exports.

The merger plan was almost approved and implemented, but Ford offered a counterproposal to the Ministry of Finance when it heard about the merger plan. After the export proposal was modified by the state, Ford accepted it, hoping to preempt the merger. Ford knew it could comply with the export promotion plan, despite its drawbacks,[13] and feared the creation of a "Mexican superfirm." The export plan would allow for the retention of traditional marketing and production strategies (such as the proliferation of models and frequent model changes) and the integration of Mexican operations into a global production organization.

Thus two alternative proposals for auto policy came under the president's consideration: the "national champion" or merger plan backed by the Ministry of Finance and the Mexican firm that suggested it, Fábricas-Auto-Mex; and the export promotion plan backed by Ford and the Ministry of Industry and Commerce. In 1969, President Díaz Ordaz (1964–70) chose the export scheme for several reasons. Important state *técnicos* favored the export promotion plan. Apparently, the director of the Bank of Mexico, along with other *técnicos* who entered the government when Díaz Ordaz assumed office, all favored a new emphasis on exports and were sensitized to the new development orthodoxy of export promotion. The merger plan fell apart during the bargaining process.[14]

In this bargaining episode we can observe the influence of oligopolistic structure. Other firms complied with the export scheme once Ford complied. The need for the efficient production of exterior body parts may have been a factor in the formulation of state policy, since Ford's counterproposal arose, in part, out of the fear of higher local content. Local content requirements could hinder efficiency and economies of scale in the production of exterior body parts and thus adversely affect entrenched nonprice forms of competition, such as model proliferation and frequent model changes, which require new bodies for every model. Also the trend toward the international integration of production made the export scheme more inviting to the firms and influenced Ford's counterproposal.

The 1977 Export Promotion Decree

Export performance was not achieved easily or quickly. Compliance with the mandatory export requirements, reaffirmed in 1972, diminished partially as a result of the recession of 1974–75. Denationalization continued, overcrowding and inefficiency persisted, and the balance of payments worsened. In addition, the international firms had monopsony control over the export markets since most of these exports were intrafirm sales, part of the international firms' global integration of production.[15] In response to these problems, a vigorous ISI attempt was reconsidered, but the proposal was dropped when economic and political crises arose at the end of the Echeverría administration.

The 1969 policy failed because the international firms had geographically dispersed production facilities. It was unlikely that new exports would be undertaken to comply with the 1969 decree, because these exports would threaten to displace production in these already existing facilities. This concern on the part of the firms was particularly important during the oil shock of 1973 and the recession of

1974–75. The low levels of demand during this period forced the firms to sacrifice exports from Mexico to maintain the performance of their established production facilities.

Changes in the international automobile industry made the international firms more receptive to automotive exports the next time around. The home country markets were becoming saturated, thereby increasing the importance of less-developed country (LDC) markets. Manufacturing in the LDCs was overcrowded and inefficient, and the oil shock of 1973 had severely reduced demand and forced the companies to consider downsizing to more fuel-efficient cars. Government export policies required the restructuring of the world auto industry, and when the global industry changed, export promotion had a chance.

As a result of changes in the developed markets and increasingly stiff competition among firms from the United States, Europe, and Japan, the international firms became interested in rationalizing production on a global scale, such as worldwide sourcing to increase economies of scale and to exploit the low wages found in the developing countries. Because of competitive pressures in the global industry, the international firms were ready to make some new investments. They hoped to promise compliance with export requirements in return for a reduction in local content levels, which had inhibited the global rationalization of production.

José López Portillo entered office (1976–82), and a new automotive decree was promulgated in 1977. Rather than proposing a renewed attempt at ISI, the López Portillo administration announced a decree that demanded tougher export requirements.[16] The firms were opposed but the state held its ground in the ensuing bargaining process. The new auto decree required the following:

1. Terminal firms would have to fully compensate for all imports (and other foreign payments) with exports. In other words, a firm-specific balance of payments was required.
2. One half of the exports would have to be sourced from the Mexican-owned supplier industry.
3. Special consideration would be given to the two remaining Mexican-owned firms in the terminal industry, due to their special difficulties in developing markets for their exports.
4. ISI would not be wholly abandoned; the terminal firms' local content requirement was raised slightly.
5. The instrument of regulation was changed. Price controls were eliminated, more emphasis was placed on market constraints, and fiscal incentives were offered instead of direct prescriptions for behavior.

TABLE 9.1   The Mexican Automobile Industry (Terminal Firms)

Firm	Ownership	Market Share		
		1970	1975	1980
Chrysler de México	99% foreign	20.9	18.5	23.2
Diesel Nacional (DINA)[a]	100% domestic (Mexican government)	9.7	9.4	4.3
Ford Motor Company	100% foreign	20.1	16.4	18.9
General Motors de México	100% foreign	14.2	11.0	8.4
Nissan Mexicana	100% foreign	8.4	9.1	10.4
Renault de México[a]	40% foreign 60% domestic (Mexican government)	NA	NA	4.7
Vehiculos Automotores Mexicanos	6% foreign 94% domestic (Mexican government)	7.1	6.8	6.0
Volkswagen de México	100% foreign	19.2	28.4	23.8
Others		0.4	0.4	0.4

Total Production 1970: 185,031   1975: 341,419   1980: 456,372

Source: Raul Hinojosa Ojeda and Rebecca Morales, "International Restructuring and Labor Market Interdependence: The Automobile Industry in Mexico and the United States" (paper presented at the Conference on Labor Market Interdependence between the United States and Mexico, El Colegio de México City, September 1986).

Note: Information given for cars and trucks less than 13,500 kg.

[a]Renault de México was created in 1978 by separating the automobile operations from the rest of Diesel Nacional. Diesel Nacional continued as a truck manufacturer.

Bennett and Sharpe note that the decree is technically sophisticated, reflecting both increased knowledge and increased influence of the *técnicos* in the ministries. The changes in the instruments of regulation also reflect the increased sophistication of the *técnicos*. The *técnicos* had moved up the learning curve.[17]

Bargaining over this decree occurred after it was announced. Because the foreign firms were forced by international competition to embark on the global reorganization of production and to make the new investments that this strategy would require, they were not generally resistant to the policy of export promotion this time around. There was no threat to foreign ownership in the terminal industry in the new decree, nor was there any possibility that the number of firms in the terminal industry would be limited (see table 9.1).[18]

Ford, which mounted the major opposition to the policy, deliberated over the following issues:

1. Ford's elimination from the diesel trucks market, which was set aside for Mexican firms in the decree.
2. GM's decision to downsize in response to changes in the world industry (Ford decided to wait longer before deciding on its global strategy, so it was not in a good position to make the necessary investments to comply with the export requirements).
3. The high volume of exports demanded.
4. The short time period in which to generate these exports.
5. The difficulty in sourcing from local suppliers as required by the decree.

Ford did not succeed in having the policy altered and threatened to pull out of Mexico, but GM's compliance with the policy necessitated Ford's compliance as well, a result of the dynamics of oligopolistic reaction, this time with Ford as a "follower." The state successfully used the Mexican market as a bargaining chip.

Bennett and Sharpe suggest that the increased knowledge of the state *técnicos* was the key to the state's success in bargaining. The *técnicos* understood that the influence of oligopolistic reaction would be more powerful precisely because the international firms were not acting in unison.[19] But once again, a cross-industry consideration came into play. Trademarks were extremely important to the automobile industry. Ford was concerned about the linked trademark, and in January 1977, the president of Ford Motor Company came to Mexico to meet with President López Portillo to discuss the issue.[20] At least according to one version of the story, Ford required the indefinite postponement of the trademark link in exchange for its acquiescence to the automobile decree.

The new auto policy and the new export strategy were the results of the failure of import substitution. Trends in the industry and in the economy in general also favored the export promotion scheme over ISI: the international integration of production and worldwide parts sourcing, the need to downsize car production in response to the oil shock of 1973, growing competition due to the increasing interpenetration of home country markets, the performance and expansion of Japanese firms, and the desire on the part of the firms to continue the proliferation of models and frequent model changes. Expanded exports would be possible only if ISI were not reaffirmed with a higher local content requirement.

As in the other bargaining episodes, the dynamics of oligopolistic reaction prevailed. GM led the way, and the other firms complied with the legislation.

In its protection of the two Mexican firms, the legislation responded

Production Units (x 1000)

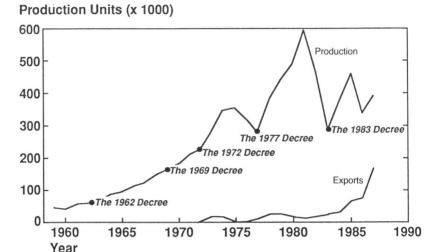

FIGURE 6. Production (1959–1987) and Export (1970–1987) of Motor Vehicles in Mexico

Sources: For 1959–82: Raul Hinojosa Ojeda and Rebecca Morales, "International Restructuring and Labor Market Interdependence: The Automobile Industry in Mexico and the United States" (paper presented at the Conference on Labor Market Interdependence between the United States and Mexico, El Colegio de México, Mexico City, September 1986). For 1983–87: M. Twomey and W. Milberg, *The Debt Crisis and the Transnational Corporations: The Case of the Mexican Automotive Sector,* Economics Working Paper no. 62 (Dearborn: University of Michigan, 1989).

to the disadvantages these firms experienced in competition with the foreign investors. In particular, the foreign firms have a virtual monopoly on exports, since most are intrafirm sales.

Finally, the market constraints and incentives in the new legislation reflect the failure of the 1969 auto policy and the structure of international automobile production (see fig. 6). The international firms would not displace production in well-established facilities without profit incentives. On the other hand, direct prescriptions for behavior were ineffectual during the oil shock and the recession.

The 1983 Decree for the Rationalization
of the Automobile Industry

Fueled by oil revenues, Mexico's domestic auto market experienced a tremendous boom during 1978–81. In 1981 domestic car sales totaled more than 340,000 units.[21] This sales figure was Mexico's highest ever; at the time Mexico ranked tenth among world automakers.[22] Sales of total motor vehicles increased from 287,000 in 1977 to 561,000 in 1981.[23] With the political-economic crisis of 1982, sales dropped precipitously to 462,000 in 1982, 272,000 in 1983,[24] and 218,000 units in 1984.[25]

During the boom the industry had generated a huge trade deficit. To keep pace with the boom, the automobile firms had to import immense quantities of components. Export sales could not counterbalance imports because the 1978–79 oil shock had depressed sales in the industrialized countries and thus reduced exports. In addition, the new export plants took years to begin production, and export prices were often'uncompetitive in international markets.[26] The auto industry's trade deficit was almost one quarter of Mexico's total trade deficit in 1977.[27] By 1980 it was more than one third of the total. In 1981 the industry accounted for more than half of the commercial trade deficit.[28] The total foreign exchange deficit generated by the industry in 1981 was more than 2 billion dollars.[29]

In September 1983 a major new auto decree was promulgated in response to the massive balance-of-payments deficit and the need for foreign exchange. The decree increased the local content requirement from the 50 percent stipulated in the 1977 decree to 55 percent for 1986 and to 60 percent for 1987.[30] Local content requirements for trucks and buses were also increased.[31] Although the decree relied more on local content requirements than on exports to handle the trade deficit, the commitment to export promotion was not weakened: firms were still required to compensate imports with exports (or more precisely, the firms were required to maintain a positive balance of payments, not just a positive balance of trade).[32] The new policy attempted to avoid a repetition of the trade deficit experienced during the 1978–81 boom.[33]

In addition, the decree attempted to increase economies of scale by reducing the number of makes and models.[34] In 1981, the relatively small Mexican market was fragmented by seven manufacturers, nineteen makes, and forty-seven models.[35] Minister of SECOFIN Hector Hernández Cervantes stated that "whereas Japan, the U.S., and the principal European countries produce an average of 13,000 units per line, this year [Mexico] will produce less than 7,000."[36] Efficient scales of production were not feasible given this market fragmentation. Referring to the large number of models in comparison to domestic sales in Mexico, one analyst stated that "you can't have any scale of efficiency with that many models requiring different tooling, engines, and other parts."[37]

The decree required the auto firms to reduce the number of makes and models they produce. For 1984 the firms were not allowed to produce more than three makes and seven models; for 1985 and 1986 the limit was two makes and five models; and for 1987 and thereafter, the firms can only produce one make and five models.[38] A firm can manufacture an additional model if it is self-sufficient in foreign exchange and if one half of the production for the new model is exported.[39]

The reduction in the number of makes and models was intended not only to increase exports (through increases in efficiency) but to allow higher local content levels. "Firms import parts for small-volume models because they cannot be manufactured domestically at competitive costs."[40] Rationalization, through the reduction of makes and models, thus allows for higher local content. Supplier firms were "previously reluctant" to expand due to the proliferation of makes and models.[41] The reduction of models was intended to stimulate expansion of the supplier firms.[42]

The decree also required that "at least 20% of the production in the next model year be 'austere' cars with no 'superfluous accessories.'" This limit increased to 25 percent in 1985.[43] Eight-cylinder engines were banned beginning in November 1984 for cars and November 1985 for trucks. This regulation was adopted because eight-cylinder engines create more pollution and waste gas.[44] Finally, the decree also eliminated government subsidies.[45]

In 1980, when it became clear that several firms would not meet the export requirements set out in the 1977 decree, the Mexican government adopted a system of foreign exchange advances, wherein a firm could receive an "advance" or a "loan" on foreign exchange needed for a particular model year on the condition that they present detailed investment plans showing how, within two years, exports would be generated to "pay back" the foreign exchange.[46] This requirement of "paying back" the government for foreign exchange deficits was continued under the new policy.[47] Thus the automakers were required not only to compensate for imports (and other foreign payments) with exports but to "reimburse" the government for accumulated foreign exchange deficits. As noted earlier, the automakers accumulated a foreign exchange deficit of $2 billion during 1980 and 1981. As a result, the industry has continued to invest in export projects. Most exports have been engines and components, but now even finished vehicles are being exported, particularly to the United States.[48] Low wages and trainable labor, along with a weak peso, and the continuing trend toward globally integrated production have made Mexico an attractive export site. As did the 1977 decree,

TABLE 9.2   Auto Industry Balance of Trade (in Millions of U.S. Dollars)

Year	Auto Industry			Total Balance	Role of Auto Industry
	Imports	Exports	Balance		
1960	124	NA	−124	−351	35.3%
1970	266	34	−232	−888	26.1%
1975	617	78	−539	−3,271	16.5%
1980	1,468	403	−1,065	−2,830	37.6%
1981	2,576	456	−2,120	−4,099	51.7%
1982	1,252	534	−718	6,796	−10.6%
1983	666	1,083	417	13,767	3.0%
1984	773	1,558	785	12,897	6.1%
1985	1,063	1,592	529	8,449	6.3%
1986	839	2,269	1,430	4,577	31.2%
1987	1,332	3,295	1,963	8,450	23.2%
1988	2,137	3,513	1,376	1,755	78.4%

Source: M. Twomey and W. Milberg, *The Debt Crisis and Transnational Corporations: The Case of the Mexican Automotive Sector*, Economics Working Paper no. 62 (Dearborn: University of Michigan, 1989).

through export requirements the 1983 policy successfully forced the international auto firms to give Mexico an important place in their global production schemes.[49]

Most notably, Ford has invested $500 million in a plant at Hermosillo, Sonora, to produce approximately 103,000 finished cars, mostly for the U.S. market.[50] Chrysler (which, like Ford, "owed" approximately $500 million in foreign exchange) generated a foreign exchange surplus of $70 million in 1983. GM balanced its foreign exchange account and moved its production lines of the Chevrolet El Camino and the GMC Caballero pickup trucks to Mexico from Texas. In February 1985 Chrysler announced plans to move production of the "Ram Charger sports utility vehicle" to Mexico City from Michigan. Nissan, too, undertook major new investments.

In this round, global competition resulted in competitive compliance with Mexican policy preferences. The policies could hardly be called noninterventionist. As industrial policy, however, they moved in the direction of a liberal regime in trade and investment rather than in the direction of either a state-owned national champion or an import-substitution strategy based on a protected domestic market.

The results have been dramatic (see table 9.2). Exports have grown every year since 1980. The auto industry has evolved from being the major cause of Mexico's trade deficit to contributing a significant share to a positive balance. The interests of Mexico coincided with the competitive needs of the firms in an internationalized oligopoly. In 1989, modifications of the *maquiladora* regulations made possible the sale on the local market of products worth 50 percent of the value of exports in the previous year. This made possible many major investments for both local and export markets, under maquila rules. This foreshadowed the opening of the Mexican market with a North American Free Trade Agreement.

Conclusion

Industrial structure shaped bargaining outcomes in a number of ways: (1) the oligopolistic structure of the international auto industry and the attendant pattern of defensive investment known as oligopolistic reaction; (2) the need for high efficiency and large economies of scale in the production of exterior body parts to continue the proliferation of models and frequent model change; (3) the international integration of production and worldwide sourcing; (4) downsizing in response to the oil shock; and (5) growing competition as a result of the increasing interpenetration of markets and the saturation of home country markets. The oligopolistic structure pressured all the other firms to comply once the market leaders (Ford or GM) complied. Because of the need for efficient production of exterior body parts, it was difficult for the Mexican state policymakers to raise the local content requirement over 60 percent in an attempt to revive ISI. Instead, export promotion responded to the international integration of production, the oil shock, and increasing competition. This made a renewed attempt at ISI extremely unfavorable for the international firms and may have helped preempt it as a policy option. Over time it appears that these elements of industrial structure ensured a policy shift, initially generated by the worsening balance of payments, from ISI to export promotion and market liberalization.

Part Four

Constraints on Choice

Ten

The Political Economy of Nationalism

THIS BOOK HAS been about the political economy of foreign invest-ment in Mexico. The essence of my argument has been that inter-national constraints have been fundamental to the choices shaping Mexico's political economy. We began by considering leading theories in the field of development, especially dependency, which held that the preferences of international enterprises are likely to prevail in their interactions with the newly developing countries. In contrast, the statist perspective put emphasis on the state and on state action, examining the choices made about the involvement of the state in the economy. As I have presented the issue, both of these perspectives are necessary, but neither is sufficient. Choices are made in the context of structural constraints, both international and domestic.

Because the focus of this work has been on constrained choice, the concept of metapreferences has been especially useful. In contrast to the related concept of metapower, as Krasner used it in *Structural Conflict*, metapreferences do not depend on the outcome. Metapower refers to the ability to change the constraints; that is, to change the rules of the game. Metapreferences, on the other hand, refer to a political vision of a future in which the rules are different. This po-litical vision may or may not be realized; the result will depend upon the constraints on the actors as well as on their political will. This concept is close to the "embedded orientations" that Bennett and Sharpe used to refer to the political preferences of particular min-istries in Mexico in their study of the Mexican automobile industry. However, in my view, the failure to implement a political vision is due more to the interaction of structural constraints with the political choices that actors make than to a failure of the actors' will. My bias is to assume informed choice rather than either irrational change or what Hirschman calls *akrasia*, or weakness of will.

The concept of metapreference as Hirschman used it[1] is useful precisely because it enables us to examine the disjuncture between preference and outcome. Since public choice, just as individual choice, involves the difficulties of choosing among various goals, a meta-preference is in essence a preferred ranking of preferences or desired outcomes. This second-order ranking then provides the basis for future choices necessary to realize the preferred future. If choice and action are always consistent with metapreferences, the notion has little utility. On the other hand, if choice and action never follow the purported metapreference, the metapreference also has little significance. It is useful precisely when there is a debate about changes in direction, in policy, and in action. Competing metapreferences point to different futures, different choices, and therefore different actions. A nationalist metapreference envisions a different future from a liberal metapreference, and it suggests a different plan of policy and action.

The distinction between metapreferences and metapower adds subtlety and complexity to the explanation of outcomes. Although parsimony is usually an advantage in scientific explanations, more complex concepts and arguments may give us a better approximation of reality. In particular, the relationship between metapreferences and policies is important in explaining outcomes in the real world. It is not accurate to attribute outcomes either to choices or to structural determinants. As Hirschman says, "To explain important turns in our lives and societies exclusively in terms of precipitating events would downgrade us to mere playthings of chance; to attribute such turns only to autonomously occurring changes in volitions would on the contrary make us appear as more noble and capable of self-determination than we really are." Precisely because of the disjuncture between metapreference and outcome, we must pay attention to the linkage of preference and power to explain outcomes in times of change. To quote Hirschman again, "Second-order volitions and metapreferences therefore come into their own in periods of actual, if protracted and tormented, transition from one kind of behavior to another."[2]

Three aspects of constrained choice can help us understand the emergence and consolidation of nationalism in Mexico's policies toward direct foreign investment (DFI) in the 1970s and the adoption of more liberal policies in the 1980s: the timing of policies, the effect of crisis, and the complexity of choice under constraint.

These three aspects of change reflect the interaction of the main variables that frame this study: international regimes, industrial organization, and state metapreferences and policy (see fig. 7). International regimes, supportive of nationalism in the 1970s, experienced a worldwide shift toward liberalism in the 1980s and 1990s. Global

International
Industrial
Organization
(crisis)

International
Regimes
(timing)

State Policy Metapreference
(choice under constraint)

FIGURE 7. Relationship between Industrial Organization, Regimes, and Meta-preference

industrial organization, oligopolistic and dominated by the United States in the 1950s and 1960s, was fundamentally transformed by crisis—first in the North by the oil crisis and then in the South by the debt crisis. The effects of these crises, combined with the emergence of Europe and Japan and the relative decline of the United States, was to make global industry more competitive and thus make liberal policies more attractive.

Timing

The emphasis on metapreferences in the context of structural constraint leaves us with a problem of understanding the interaction among constraints on the one hand and between constraint and political choice on the other. In brief, timing matters. Consider the nationalist policies on DFI, technology transfer, and inventions and trademarks adopted during the Echeverría administration (1972–76). Although to a certain extent, particularly in the sectoral differentiation of policies on DFI, these state regulations summarized past practice, to a greater extent they represented a notable increase in state intervention in the economy. Decisions that firms had been able to make freely among themselves, interacting in a market (albeit imperfect), were now subject to the intervention and participation of the state. Entering a new line of business required the permission of the National Foreign Investment Commission if ownership was mostly foreign. So, too, did opening a new establishment. Agreements to license technology were now subject to a registration process, and the payments for such technology were negotiated with state bureaucrats. Protection for intellectual property, admittedly a creation of the state in the first place, was changed by the 1976 law, removing some categories of production from patent protection, changing the terms, and proposing more radical departures from standard international practice.

These policies seemed innovative, even daring, in the context of their times. But in fact, there was ample international precedent, ranging from the Andean Pact to Argentina and India, and including international organizations with heavy Third World participation such as UNCTAD. In the aftermath of the 1973 oil shock, the capacity of developing countries to mobilize and gain greater control over international economic processes seemed part of a growing international trend. Although, as it turned out, relatively stable international regimes continued to exist, there was a strong sense that new regimes, favoring authoritative rather than market-determined decisions, were in the process of formation.[3] The international system provided support in several ways: information was shared by developing countries in their efforts to change the terms of bargains with international corporations. A learning process began, not only from past experience (as Moran had emphasized for bilateral bargaining between states and firms) but also across national boundaries and between states as well. Both the experiences of other developing countries and the support, partial though it was, from international organizations contributed to the legitimation of national efforts (such as Mexico's) to engage in hard bargaining with international enterprises and to change the basis on which foreign investment and foreign technology came into the country.

In the past, prior to the creation of the Registry for Foreign Direct Investment and the Technology Transfer Registry, Mexican officials had only impressionistic, anecdotal information on the foreign investors operating within their country. The existence of even basic information about foreign investment and technology, organized and reviewed by industry and company, increased the ability of the state to take advantage of the competitive structure of industries, even when that competition was oligopolistic. The successful creation of registration requirements and the success of some bargaining experiences fostered an exaggerated sense of potential for the bargaining process. Moreover, it made nationalists realize that the laissez-faire atmosphere of the 1960s was not the only possibility. National goals of balanced external accounts, decentralization from industrially polluted Mexico City, and job creation seemed more within reach through the use of nationalist instruments to confront a competitive international industry.

Domestically, too, the Echeverría years seemed to support the possibilities of the nationalist vision. Young technocrats, lacking experience with economic hard times and flush with the long-term success of the Mexican miracle, felt capable and justified in their efforts to increase the contribution of foreign investors to national development, to reinsert considerations of equity into a development model that had been dominated by growth, and in general to resuscitate the claims of justice that the Mexican Revolution seemed to have lost. These idealists, frustrated by the limits of domestic political transformation in the aftermath of protests in 1968 and 1971 (and the killings of Tlatelolco and of Corpus Cristi), led an increased commitment to reformism vis-à-vis the international economy.

Even the private sector, the most powerful of societal influences on state policies, seemed to acquiesce. The private sector supported new legislation on foreign investment, technology, and patents. Although the manner of implementation became an issue for consultation, debate, and pressure, nevertheless Mexican private capital was comfortable with and benefited from state efforts to protect its interests vis-à-vis international enterprise. On issues closer to their heart, such as tax reform, the traditional alliance of state and private capital prevailed. It was only later, as the nationalist tendencies of the Echeverría administration came to be viewed as statist challenges to the entire private sector (national and foreign), that private capital began to vote with its money. Prior to the devaluation of 1976, the nationalist and statist policies that Mexico pursued seemed controversial, but not enormously costly.

By the 1980s, all of this had changed. The confluence of international and national constraints was much stronger and headed in a different direction. Rapid technological change had an impact at several different levels. The United States, faced with increased competition from European and Japanese enterprises, became more aware of its declining influence as a manufacturing power. To the extent that manufacturing in the United States declined, the United States relied more upon technological advantage, and the protections for intellectual property that established private control over that advantage became more important. Thus, the United States became more and more committed to the explicit defense of the liberal international regime in technology. At the same time, liberal economists from Mexico, often trained in the United States, began to assume positions of power within Mexico.

In industry, technological change had several effects. To some extent, the spread of technology, its division into small manageable pieces, and its rapid diffusion contributed to increased competition in industry, working through the market to make technology rapidly available. But the very pace of change meant that the technological leaders, especially in technology-intensive fields such as pharmaceuticals and computers, could credibly threaten to withhold advanced technology and deprive the national economy in Mexico of access to the most advanced technological developments.

Of course, macroeconomic changes had been dramatic. During the oil boom from 1977 to 1982, Mexico's foreign debt had skyrocketed. De facto, Mexico's policy constituted the "unbundling" of foreign capital from the foreign investment package and the consumption of this delinked capital provided by international banks in massive quantities. During the oil boom, the external debt grew by tens of billions of dollars per year. Then, in August of 1982, the boom went bust (see fig. 8). Gross national product was stagnant. Production per person fell steadily. The real minimum wage dropped every year from 1983 through 1987. On the external account, the terms of trade, based on an index of 1980 equal to 100, had dropped to 77 by 1983 and to 57 by 1987. Interest payments on nearly U.S. $100 billion of debt took more and more export earnings; and at the same time exports were harder to acquire.

The net flow of capital that had until 1981 been in Mexico's favor now turned sharply in the other direction: capital flowed out of Mexico to its creditors at a rapid rate. Financing these flows required cutting back on imports, even imports necessary for continued industrialization, and promoting exports. Given the declining terms of trade for commodities, the promotion of manufactured exports became even more important.

The transformation of Mexico's political economy was dramatic. According to a study by the World Bank, Mexico, Chile, and Uruguay

made more far-reaching changes than any other middle-income countries in the world. . . . Mexico's most far-reaching changes have been made in the size and efficiency of the public sector and external trade. The massive budget deficit in 1982 has been replaced by a non-interest fiscal surplus of close to eight percent of GDP. The adjustment has not been easy, particularly because during the last

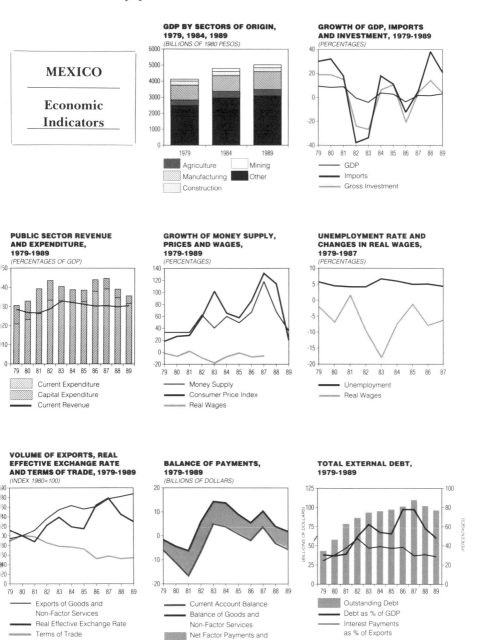

FIGURE 8. Economic Indicators of Crisis and Adjustment, 1979–1989
Source: InterAmerican Development Bank, *Economic and Social Progress in Latin America: 1990 Report* (Washington: IDB, 1990).

four years private creditors refinanced less than twenty percent of Mexico's interest payments to them. To service the remaining portion, the public sector had to resort to inflationary finance and sharp cutbacks in investments. Inflation reached record levels and only now has sharply been reduced. Investment remains low and growth has not yet resumed.[4]

The transformation of the Mexican economy was, to some extent, imposed by the international financial institutions and especially the commercial banks to whom Mexico owed so much. However, the depth of the changes and the unanimous ranking of Mexico as first among the debtor nations in its transformations suggest that there was more to it than dependency and external constraint. That the changes were real and dramatic is beyond dispute.

The Mexican private sector was integral to the effort. The disinvestment of the private sector, combined with the nationalization of the banks in 1982, meant that Mexico no longer faced a choice of favoring local capital over foreign capital; local capital was not interested. The crisis was so severe, and the Mexican private sector so risk averse, that dramatic evidence needed to be provided to stimulate a development process in which the private sector took the lead. In practice, this meant the foreign sector, and particularly foreign direct investors, needed to be wooed first. In other words, the repatriation of flight capital could not be the first step to economic recovery. Rather the sequence was (1) demonstrate good faith with the banks, (2) convince foreign investors of a favorable investment climate in Mexico, and only then (3) convince Mexican investors of a favorable investment climate. Investments by major global firms in the automobile and computer industries in Mexico were important not only in their own terms and as demonstration projects for other foreign investors but also as demonstrations of the viability of investing in Mexico for Mexican investors.

In short, the constraints facing Mexico's policymakers were fundamentally different in the 1980s from those in the 1970s. The effect of this was twofold. First, some policymakers changed their minds. In other words, some adherents to the nationalist vision came to believe that its costs in the 1980s exceeded the probable benefits. Second, another group of political leaders came to power. Those whose liberal economic ideology was more consistent with the requirements of international and domestic constraints increased their power within the state, developing an alternative vision based on their competing rank ordering of policies (their liberal metapreference). These liberal technocrats systematically defeated proposals to increase the interventionist role of the state. They effectively dismantled the protection of the Mexican economy; they reduced the size of the public sector; and they sold off about half of the state enterprises.

Mexico made dramatically different choices in the 1980s than in the 1970s. These choices were influenced by timing, as the relationship of various constraints to each other changed and as the possibilities for translating political visions into political reality changed. If policy is a means for achieving a vision of a possible future, timing affects the possibility of that future.

Crisis and Industrial Development

Change as dramatic as that which Mexico has undertaken does not come easily, even when the opportunity structure shifts to favor the change. Indeed it is probably the case that shifts as dramatic as those observed between 1970 and 1988 can only come as the concomitants of crisis. The evidence given above leaves little doubt about the severity of the crisis that Mexico has suffered since 1982. The crisis has been systemic, influencing every aspect of society and polity. In this sense, the debt crisis has provided the opportunity for new political choices to be made in Mexico. However, here too it is tempting to see the debt crisis as a simplifying single-factor explanation of change. Rather, the debt crisis is a symptom of changes in a variety of structural conditions that have constrained Mexico's development and development policy. It is not as simple as a crisis enabling one group to displace another. The nationalists are still in Mexico, still holding offices within the state, and still envisioning a future with greater autonomy, greater self-reliance, and greater equity and justice. The liberals hold sway at the moment and espouse the same goals but argue for the priority of external adjustment rather than internal development.

The phenomenon of Cuauhtémoc Cárdenas in the 1988 national elections best captures the continued support for the nationalist vision. Cárdenas called for Mexico to challenge its international creditors and give priority to domestic development over external adjustment. The initial success of the Salinas administration weakened the personal following of Cárdenas, but as a political leader, Cárdenas was simply the focal point for broad dissent, primarily within the PRI itself. The disaffection with the regime that became so clear with the opposition votes in the 1988 election has a fundamental sympathy to the nationalist position; it was the nationalist left that grew disproportionately, not the PAN and the right.

If the liberal economic vision is to be viable, it must develop a domestic component capable of addressing the needs of the population that has been deprived as a consequence of the crisis. As the faltering of the nationalist program has shown, the failure to see and understand structural constraints can be as devastating to a political vision as a failure of will or of vision itself. But the economic liberals in power see and understand the external constraints. The limit of their vision is that it is primarily outward looking, oriented toward structural adjustment and insertion into the internationalized global economy. Crisis, the saying goes, represents danger and opportunity. The opportunity resulting from the crisis of the 1980s was for Mexico to become a global player, an intermediate power, in an interdependent world economy. The danger of the liberal vision is the failure to see within, to understand the implications of the liberal program for those marginalized by the crisis. Nationalism can find accommodation with a strategy of insertion into the world economy; national pride can be sustained on the success of Mexican exports. But the domestic side of jobs and justice constitutes the soft underbelly of the liberal alternative to Mexican nationalism. The proposal of a free trade area is a gamble that the Mexican economy will grow with free trade *and* that the Mexican people will support it.

That a liberal foreign economic policy has displaced the nationalist policy should not be taken as the static replacement of one program by another. Rather, the very nature of economic liberalism and nationalism changes over time. It might even be possible to argue that with the internationalization of the world economy, the old distinctions between development strategies are losing their utility. In particular, it is no longer obvious that nationalism, understood as a meta-preference for the advancement of the nation-state, necessarily requires state ownership of industry, extensive protection of the domestic economy, import substitution, or across-the-board limits on DFI. Changes in the world economy have forced changes in the developed countries, and this in turn has meant changes in national strategies of industrialization among the new industrial countries.

The patterns of state intervention and bargaining that characterize the nationalist strategy have survived in modified form under southern liberalism. State-owned enterprises or national champions can succeed in a few concentrated niches, at the same time as foreign investment is encouraged in other sectors. Although Mexico has reduced the number of its state enterprises from more than 1,000 to about 500, this is still five times the number of enterprises that existed in the state sector in 1970. There is little evidence of a state retreat from its role as primary producer of raw materials and basic services.

In the manufacturing sector the private sector is dominant. DFI is still essential, though not in every industry. State regulation provides a better bargain for foreign investors than before, but bargaining is still required. Approval may come quickly, but the requirements of exports, decentralization, technology, and jobs are still the conditions for majority ownership. In manufactured exports, global firms will find state promotional efforts by Mexico just as by other newly industrializing countries, by small export platform states, and by numerous states and regions within the United States and other advanced industrial countries. It is possible that the combined effects of computer-assisted manufacturing and robotization may bring back to the core countries some production that has migrated to low-wage countries. But it is more likely that special export-processing zones are here to stay.

In technology, the shift to liberal policies reflects the weakness of Mexico's technological base and of the state as innovator. As a World Bank report noted in a study of five countries, Mexico's technological exports such as capital goods are mostly by multinational firms—though state regulatory bargaining may serve as a stimulus.[5] However, exports do change. The labor component may become smaller as advanced, capital-intensive techniques are adopted to maintain global competitiveness. New products and services may be produced for export as the service sector that makes up most of the economy in the industrial states finds productivity and cost gains from internationalization, just as manufacturing has done. But this is likely to be in partnership with foreign firms. In Mexico, the mixed economy, with the state at times owner, at times regulator, and at times promoter, has survived the shift in ideology. The role of the state as innovator has become one of stimulating the absorption of foreign technology. The state as financier has become a state struggling to balance its budget and stimulate exports. In short, Mexico shares the problems of many countries in adjusting to a more integrated and competitive world economy.

The organization of industry on a global scale is proceeding apace. Industrial competition is increasingly internationalized. As part of this process the scale of industrial organization is shifting upward, accelerated by the recent wave of mergers and acquisitions within and among the home countries. The largest global producers in many industries will both maintain a presence in all major world markets and produce in a broad variety of product lines within their principal line of business. This process of concentration among the leading global firms will be accompanied by the spread of opportunities in the secondary firms servicing the industry leaders. Firms will face the choice of attempting to compete with the leaders of a global oligopoly or of integrating and servicing that oligopoly. For the newly industrializing countries, often this will mean that the protectionist infant industry strategy will be supplanted by an apprenticeship strategy such as Mexico has adopted in the computer and automobile industries.

Southern Liberalism

Mexico has become a leader in advocating and implementing southern liberalism. This has meant accepting a mixed economy and an active state industrial policy while still fostering an expansion of international trade with relatively free markets. To be sure, Mexico has benefited from the exceptions to pure free trade, such as the Generalized System of Preferences (GSP). After the four Asian tigers[6] were excluded from the GSP by the United States at the end of 1988, Mexico became the leading beneficiary of this special tariff preference for developing countries. But as the United States continues its own adjustment to an internationalized economy, pressures for renewed protection are likely to be asserted with frequency in the United States, and Mexico will be a strong ally of economic liberals in the United States attempting to maintain relatively open markets. As Mexico makes the shift to a more open and export-oriented economy, the rapid pace of technological change will create opportunity for small and medium enterprises and for locally owned Mexican enterprises. This is already evident in the Maquiladora Program, in which some 500 out of 1,200 firms are predominantly owned by local Mexican enterprises.[7] These domestically owned exporters will become important allies of southern liberalism.

Because of the high cost of manufacturing production, the export strategy may become divorced from an employment strategy. Increasingly, export industries will be high value-added, whether or not they are labor intensive. Techniques for export production (to ensure internationally competitive price and quality) can be mobilized for domestic consumption as well. So consumers of international products may also become allies of southern liberalism. However, to the extent that export and employment strategies diverge, the success of the export strategy may rely on the development of a complementary employment strategy to expand and develop the domestic market.

Domestically, the patterns of ownership of industry and incorporation of labor can vary widely while still responding to an internationalized economy. National business has responded to the crisis by modernizing and adjusting, becoming more professional and streamlined. But if this modern attitude on the part of Mexican business is to succeed, it must include a more professional relationship to the state as well. In particular, fiscal responsibility is crucial to industrial success. The state must generate the revenues to pay its way as it goes, and the private sector must foot that bill, directly or indirectly.

Perhaps the toughest challenge for southern liberalism in Mexico will be the integration of this new vision within a political structure that has tended to favor those whose metapreferences ran toward revolutionary nationalism. The Salinas administration placed economic liberals in all of the key economic ministries and put political hard-liners in the traditional social sectors. The government formally espoused modernization in political as well as economic terms. But it was the nationalists under Cárdenas who grabbed the banner of democratization away from the regime in the 1988 elections. It may well be that in a dialectical way rather than in any necessary conjunction, pressure for political liberalization is the concomitant of southern economic liberalism. Southern economic liberals will have to find a way to make peace with their nationalist colleagues, and that may be hard to do in the midst of a struggle for democratization.

Complexity and Choice

It would be comforting, perhaps, to assure ourselves that Mexico's political vision in the 1970s was simply a mistaken choice or that corruption and inefficiency, together with a risk-averse private sector, explained Mexico's failures or, on the other hand, that dependency and the power of transnational institutions forced Mexico to make certain decisions. Indeed, any such simplifying argument ends up reductionist and unsatisfactory. Only a nuanced analysis of choice under conditions of complex constraint can achieve a reasonable explanation of failure in the past, or indeed of success in the future. Neither *akrasia* nor fate, neither the failure of will nor the force of powers beyond our control, can in themselves explain the outcomes of individual and collective choices.

Nevertheless I see a common theme, and a nonintuitive one at that, in the operation of the constraints of international regime and industrial organization on state policy. Perhaps the most remarkable outcome of this analysis is that the very internationalization of the global economy, so much commented upon in the debates about U.S. industrial policy, had the curious effect of promoting southern liberalism. By this I mean to suggest that the failure of the nationalist project and the imposition of liberal policies, consistent with a liberal market metapreference by the policy elite in Mexico, responded to a global process of internationalization that has had systemic influences on each of the structural constraints we have been considering. To some extent I have already suggested this above, but let me summarize the argument explicitly.

The internationalization of the world economy, with increasing competitive pressure on the United States, and the general increase in the interdependence of industries and economies have shifted constraints in the direction of more liberal policies. First, international regimes are defended more vigorously, at least in some cases, by the United States. This has been especially true for the regimes on intellectual property, as I have argued. Simultaneously, however, the United States has been moving toward more protectionist policies in trade. This comes at a time when a major requirement of the Mexican economy is access to markets for the manufactured goods that it is finally producing in export quality and quantity. Thus, the curious effect of internationalization is not only that the once-hegemonic power fights harder to defend an open regime that is in its interests, it is also that newly industrializing countries such as Mexico have become active proponents of the preservation of a liberal international economic system that gives them access to their major markets. Now that Mexico has gone through so much pain to open its economy, it has a strong vested interest in an international system that allows it to reap the benefits of its export orientation. It is no coincidence that the 1990 proposal for free trade talks was initiated by Mexico. Free trade with the United States, which threatened Mexico's autonomy a decade ago, is now in Mexico's interest—even if nationalists in the United States object.

The same point can be made with respect to industrial structure. The reorganization of industry on a global scale has had multiple effects, including the dismantling of Fordist assembly-line procedures for the organization of production in the advanced industrial countries. Mexico and other developing countries first found an opportunity to join the real "new international economic order" by producing the labor-intensive parts of complex products. The rapid and continued growth of Mexico's *Maquiladora* Program, expanding without halt right through the crisis of the 1980s, reflects the shifting of production from north to south. However, the process does not stop there. Mexico will be able to maintain its expansion of industrial exports only by expanding its use of the most advanced technologies, including robotics, computer-aided manufacture, and just-in-time techniques. There is every reason to expect Mexico to do this. Therefore, although the labor share of manufactured products is declining, Mexico has now become an integral part of the internationalization of production. Internationalization has changed the nature of structural constraints, moving them toward greater benefits of liberalism to newly industrializing producers.

Internationalization has shifted domestic constraints as well. This can be seen most markedly in the contrast between the 1980 rejection of Mexico's adhesion to the General Agreement on Tariffs and Trade (GATT) and its subsequent joining of that international agreement. By the time Mexico finally joined GATT, the Mexican private sector in its most influential form had largely come to back the liberal position in favor of GATT. Although there were still divisions between large capital and small, liberalization of Mexico's economy had, on the whole, come to be in the interests of Mexican business. It can easily be argued that the opening of the Mexican economy will be in the long-run interest of Mexican consumers as well, as dropping import quotas and lowering tariffs result in lower prices. During the oil boom, Mexico's middle class became accustomed to having sufficient resources to consume internationally available manufactured commodities. The 1982 crisis brought that to a sharp halt. The recovery of oil prices may offer hopes of a new boom, but the cyclical nature of commodity markets suggests that a more diversified integration of Mexico's economy is more likely to sustain growth in incomes. Through lowered prices and more competitive local production, the growth of a middle-class market can begin again. The middle-class consumer and the large producer have disproportionate political power in Mexico, and to this extent the internationalization of the economy has increased the power of the domestic coalition favoring liberalization.

Even within the state, the internationalization of the world economy has changed the pattern of constraints in a way that has favored the political influence of those with a liberal vision. This can be seen most dramatically in the composition of the Mexican political elite. The quintessential political leader no longer is a lawyer trained at the National Autonomous University of Mexico but is an economist trained at Harvard, Yale, or Chicago. Political and economic elites are more internationalized. It was Carlos Salinas who brought a free trade proposal to the U.S. The liberal prescription matches the structure of constraints much better than do nationalist policies.

Internationalization, with its effect on economies in the center and in the periphery, has tended to shift the constraints of international regime and industrial structure on state policy in the direction of liberalism and away from nationalism. Choice under constraint requires the analyst to acknowledge the complexity of explanation. Some unexpected patterns may emerge out of that analysis. The influence of internationalization on the emergence of southern liberalism is one such unexpected outcome.

Appendix One

Excerpts from Article 27
of the 1917 Constitution

Ownership of all lands and waters comprised within the boundaries of the national territory is vested originally in the Nation. The Nation has had, and has, the right to convey title thereof to private persons, so establishing private property.

Expropriations shall be effected only for reasons of public utility and through indemnification.

The Nation shall have at all times the right to impose on private property such modalities as the public interest dictates, and the right to regulate the use and exploitation of all natural resources susceptible of appropriation, in order to preserve, and to effect an equitable distribution of, the public wealth . . .

In the Nation is vested the direct ownership of all mineral or other substances which in veins, layers, masses or beds form deposits . . . mineral or organic deposits of matters which may be used for fertilizers; solid mineral fuels; petroleum, and all hydrocarbons whether solid, liquid or gaseous.

In the Nation is likewise vested the ownership of the waters of territorial seas to the extent and in the terms fixed by the Law of Nations . . .

In the cases to which the two preceding paragraphs refer, the ownership of the Nation is inalienable and shall not be liable to loss by prescription; concessions may be granted by the Federal Government to private parties, or to civil or commercial corporations organized under Mexican law, on condition that said resources be regularly exploited through duly established works and that all legal provisions be observed.

Legal capacity to acquire ownership of lands and waters of the Nation shall be governed by the following provisions:

I. Only Mexicans by birth or naturalization, and Mexican concerns, have the right to acquire ownership of lands, waters and their appurtenances, or to obtain concessions for the exploitation of mines, waters or mineral fuels in the Republic of Mexico. The State may grant the same right to aliens provided they agree before the Department of Foreign Affairs to be considered as Mexicans in respect to such property and, accordingly, not to invoke the protection of their own Governments in respect to the same, under penalty, in case of breach of that agreement, or forfeiture to the Nation of the property so acquired. Within a zone of 100 kilometers from the sea coast no alien shall under any conditions acquire direct ownership of lands and waters . . .

Source: Gilberto Bosques, *The National Revolutionary Party of Mexico and the Six-Year Plan* (Mexico City, 1937), as reprinted in Robert Freeman Smith, *The United States and Revolutionary Nationalism in Mexico, 1916–1932* (1972), pp. 267–70.

Appendix Two

Excerpts from the 1973 Law to Promote Mexican Investment and to Regulate Foreign Investment

Article 3rd

Foreigners who acquire property of any kind within the Mexican Republic by so doing agree to be treated as Mexican nationals regarding the said property and not to invoke the protection of their own Government in this respect, under penalty in case of default, of losing to the Mexican Nation the property they may have acquired.

Article 4th

The following activities are reserved exclusively for the State:

a) Petroleum and other hydrocarbons
b) Basic petrochemicals
c) Exploitation of radioactive minerals and the generation of nuclear energy
d) Mining in those cases to which the law on that subject refers
e) Electricity
f) Railways
g) Telegraphic and radiotelegraphic communications
h) All others as established by specific laws

The following activities are reserved exclusively for Mexicans or for Mexican companies which exclude foreigners:

a) Radio and television
b) Automotive transportation, whether urban, interurban, or on Federal highways
c) National air and sea transportation

245

d) Forestry exploitation

e) Gas distribution

f) All others as set out by the specific laws or by rules issued by the Federal Executive

Article 5th

In the following activities or companies, foreign investment in the capital will be permitted in the proportions indicated:

a) Exploitation and utilization of mineral substances: Concessions may not be granted or assigned to foreign individuals or companies. In companies devoted to this activity, foreign investment may take part up to a maximum of 49% where the exploitation and utilization of substances subject to ordinary concessions are concerned and up to a maximum of 34% where special concessions for the exploitation of national mineral reserves are concerned.

b) By-products of the petrochemical industry: 40%

c) The manufacture of components for automotive vehicles: 40%

d) Those indicated by specific law or rules issued by the Federal Executive

In cases where the legal dispositions or rules do not stipulate a certain percentage, foreign investment may participate in a proportion not exceeding 49% of the companies' capital, provided that foreigners do not have the right in any capacity to manage the company.

The National Foreign Investment Commission may pass decisions on the increase or reduction of the percentage to which the preceding paragraph refers, when in their opinion it is advantageous for the economy of this country, and they may set the conditions according to which foreign capital will be admitted, in specific cases.

The participation of foreign investment in the administration agencies of the company may not exceed its participation in the capital.

Where there are laws or legal rules in existence for a certain line of activity, foreign investment must be adjusted to the percentage and conditions indicated in the said laws or rules.

Article 13th

In order to decide on the advantage of authorizing foreign investment and to determine the percentage and conditions under which it will be admitted, the Commission will take into consideration the following criteria and characteristics of the investment:

I. If it is complementary to national investment.

II. If it does not displace national companies and if it is not directed to fields of activity adequately covered by them.

III. If its effects on the balance of payments will be positive and in particular on the increase in exports.

IV. Its effects on employment, the level of employment it will generate, and how much the laborers will be paid.

V. The employment and training of Mexican technicians and administrative personnel.

VI. The utilization of Mexican products and parts in the manufacture of its products.

VII. The proportion in which its operations are financed with resources from abroad.

VIII. The diversification of investment sources and the need to stimulate regional and subregional integration in the Latin American area.

IX. Its contribution to the progress of zones and regions of relatively slower economic development.

X. If it will not occupy a monopolist position in the national market.

XI. The capital structure of the field of economic activity under consideration.

XII. Its technological contribution and its share in the research and technological development of this country.

XIII. Its effects on price levels and production quality.

XIV. If it will maintain the social and cultural values of this country.

XV. The importance of the activity under consideration within the national economy.

XVI. The foreign investor's identification with the interest of this country and his connections with countries of economic decision abroad.

XVII. The extent to which, in general, it contributes to the achievement of and supports the policy of national development.

A Comparison of Selected Provisions of the 1973 Law on the Transfer of Technology and the Use and Exploitation of Patents and Trademarks and the 1982 Law on the Control and Registration of the Transfer of Technology and the Use and Exploitation of Patents and Trademarks*

(REPLACED IN ITS ENTIRETY JUNE 28, 1991.)

Purpose

Article 1. This law is of public order and of social interest and will be applied by the Federal Executive through the Ministry of Patrimony and Industrial Development. *Its purpose is to control and direct the transfer of technology, as well as the development of national technological resources.*

Coverage

Article 2. For the purpose of this law: all agreements, contracts and all other acts that are contained in documents that will have effect in Mexico in connection with the following must be registered in the National Registry of the Transfer of Technology:

a) Licenses for the use or authorization of exploitation of trademarks.

b) Licenses on patents of invention of improvements, *and on Certificates of Invention.*

c) Licenses on industrial models or drawings.

d) *Trademark assignments.*

e) *Patent assignments.*

f) *Tradename or service mark licenses.*

g) Transfer of technical knowledge (know-how) through plans, diagrams, models, instruction manuals, formulas, specifications, educating and training of personnel, and other means.

h) Technical assistance, however provided.

i) Supply of basic or detail engineering.

j) Operation or administrative services for enterprises.

k) *Advisory, consulting and supervisory services, when rendered by foreign individuals or corporations or their subsidiaries regardless of their domicile.*

l) *Copyright licenses that imply industrial exploitation.*

m) *Computer programs.*

On the Causes for Refusal of Registration

Article 15. The Ministry of Patrimony and Industrial Development shall not register the acts, agreements, or contracts referred to in Article Two of this Law, in the following cases:

I. When they include clauses according to which the supplier is allowed to regulate or intervene directly or indirectly in the administration of the acquirer of the technology.

II. When they establish the obligation to turn over to the technology supplier, on onerous terms or free of charge, the patents, trademarks, innovations or improvements obtained by the acquiring company, except in those cases in which there should exist reciprocity or benefit for the acquiring company in the exchange of information.

III. When they impose limitations on research or technology development by the purchasing company.

IV. When they establish the obligation to purchase equipment, tools, parts, or raw materials, from a specific origin exclusively, when other sources exist in the national and international market.

V. When the export of the purchasers's goods or services is forbidden in a manner contrary to the interests of Mexico.

VI. When the use of complementary technologies is forbidden.

VII. When the obligation is set forth to sell the goods produced by the purchaser to an exclusive customer.

VIII. When the purchaser is under the obligation to use, permanently, personnel appointed by the supplier of the technology.

IX. When production volumes are limited or if selling or reselling prices are imposed for the national production or for the exports of the purchasers.

X. When the purchaser is under the obligation to execute sale or exclusive representation contracts with the supplier of the technology, unless exports are involved, and the acquirer accepts and it is proven to the satisfaction of the Ministry of Patrimony and Industrial Development that the supplier has proper distribution outlets of the commercial standing necessary to sell the products in better conditions than the acquirer.

XI. When the purchaser is under the obligation to keep secret the technical information given by the supplier, beyond the term of the acts, agreements or contracts or beyond the times established by the applicable laws.

XII. When it is not expressly established that the supplier shall be liable for the infringement of industrial property rights of third parties.

XIII. When the supplier does not guarantee the quality and results of the contracted technology.

Article 16. The acts, agreements or contracts referred to in the Second Article will not be registered either in the following cases:

I. When their purpose is the transfer of technology from abroad which is already available in Mexico.

II. When the price or counterservice is out of proportion to the acquired technology or constitutes an unwarranted or excessive burden for the national economy or for the acquiring company.

III. When the excessive terms are established; in no case such terms may exceed ten years, obligatory for the purchaser.

IV. When the knowledge or the resolution [that] may arise in connection with the interpretation or fulfillment of the acts, agreements or contracts is submitted to foreign courts (except in cases of exportation of Mexican technology or of express submission to private international arbitration, provided that the arbiter applies Mexican Law substantively to the controversy, in accordance with the international agreements on the subject signed by Mexico).

Exceptions

Article 17. In the cases provided for in the two preceding articles, the Ministry of Patrimony and Industrial Development, through the National Registry of Transfer of Technology, shall determine in accordance with its judgement those exceptional cases regarding benefits for the country.

*This document gives the text of the 1982 law. Changes introduced in the 1982 law, compared with the 1973 law, are italicized.

Source: For the 1973 law, Banco Nacional de Comercio Exterior, English translation of the law published in *Diario Oficial*, December 30, 1972, effective January 29, 1973. For the 1982 law, *Diario Oficial*, January 11, 1982, effective February 10, 1982. The bill to the Congress was signed December 20, 1981.

Excerpts from the 1976 Law on Inventions and Trademarks

(REPLACED IN ITS ENTIRETY JUNE 28, 1991.)

Preliminary Provisions

Article 1. The Law regulates the grant of patents of invention and of improvements; of certificates of invention; the registration of models and industrial designs; the registration of trademarks; the denominations of origin and the commercial slogans and names; as well as the repression of unfair competition in relation to the rights granted by the same.

. . .

Article 9. For the purposes of this Law, the following are not inventions:

I. Theoretical or scientific principles and mathematical methods.

II. A discovery which consists simply of revealing, making evident or visible something which already existed in nature, even though previously unknown to man.

III. Commercial, accounting, financial, educational and advertising systems and plans; typographical characters; rules of games; presentation of information and computer programs.

IV. Artistic or literary creations.

V. Methods of surgical or therapeutic treatment of the human body and those methods relating to animals or plants as well as the methods of diagnosis in these fields.

Article 10. The following are not patentable:

I. Plant varieties and animal breeds as well as biological processes for obtaining the same.

II. Alloys.

III. Chemical products, with the exception of new industrial processes for obtaining the same and their new uses of an industrial nature.

IV. Chemical-pharmaceutical products and their mixtures, medicines, beverages and foods for human or animal use, fertilizers, pesticides, herbicides, fungicides.

V. Processes for obtaining mixtures of chemical products, industrial processes for obtaining alloys and industrial processes for obtaining, modifying or applying products and mixtures to which the preceding paragraph refers.

VI. Inventions pertaining to nuclear energy and security.

VII. Anti-pollution apparatus and equipment or the processes for manufacture, modification or application thereof.

. . .

Chapter III, Rights granted by the patent.

Article 37. With the limitations set forth in this Law, the patent confers upon its owner the right to exploit the invention in an exclusive manner, either by himself or by other persons with his consent.

The patent does not grant the right to import the patented product or a product manufactured with the patented process.

. . .

Article 40. The term of the patents shall be ten years, non-extendible, counted from the date of issuance of the Letters Patent; however, the day and hour of filing the application shall be considered as its legal date.

Chapter IV, Exploitation of patents.

Article 41. The grant of the patent implies the obligation to exploit it in national territory.

The exploitation must be initiated within a term of three years, from the date of grant of the patent.

. . .

Article 48. The patent shall lapse if, after the expiration of the term referred to in Article 41, more than one year elapses without the owner of the patent initiating the exploitation, and if no obligatory licenses have been requested within this latter period of time.

. . .

Chapter V, Compulsory and public benefit issues.

Article 50. After the expiration of the term referred to in Article 41, any person may apply before the Department of Industry and Commerce for the grant of a compulsory license to exploit a patent in the following cases:

I. When the patented invention has not been exploited.

II. If the exploitation of the patent has been suspended for more than six consecutive months.

III. When the exploitation of the patent does not satisfy the national market.

IV. When there are export markets which are not covered by the exploitation of the patent and some person declares his interest in using the patent for export purposes.

In the cases of Sections III and IV, before granting the license, the owner of the patent will be given an opportunity to correct the insufficient exploitation of the patent and he will be granted a preferential right to broaden his exploitation so as to adequately cover the national consumption or the international demand.

. . .

Title Second, of the Certificates of Invention. Sole Chapter.

Article 65. The inventions referred to in Sections V, VI and VII of Article 10 of this Law may be subject to registration, which shall be established by means of the issuance of a certificate of invention. Said certificate shall confer the rights established in this Chapter.

Such inventions shall be registrable if they comply, to the extent applicable, with the requisites established in Articles 4, 5, 6 and 7 of this Law, unless their publication or exploitation are contrary to the Law, to the public order, to health, to public security, to morals or to good customs.

. . .

Article 67. The effects of the registration referred to in Article 65 shall last ten years, counted from the date of grant.

During said term, the owner of the certificate of invention shall be entitled to receive a royalty from every interested party that exploits his invention, during the life of the registration.

Article 68. Any interested party may exploit an invention which is subject to this registration after reaching an agreement with the owner of the certificate of invention on the payment of royalties and on the other conditions inherent in the exploitation of the invention.

In order to be effective, said agreement must be approved and recorded by the National Registry of Transfer of Technology.

Article 69. If the owner of the certificate of invention and the person interested in the exploitation do not reach an agreement in respect to the payment of royalties and the other pertinent conditions, the General Bureau of Inventions and Trademarks, at the request of the interested person, shall invite them to a conciliatory hearing.

If the parties do not reach an agreement or if the owner of the certificate of invention does not appear, the matter will be forwarded to the General Bureau of the National Registry of Transfer of Technology which, after a hearing of parties, may authorize the exploitation and establish the payment of royalties and the other applicable conditions. If the owner of the certificate of invention does not appear, it will resolve the matter with the elements which are available. If the party who does not appear is the interested party, his application will be considered as withdrawn.

The resolution of the General Bureau of the National Registry of Transfer of Technology shall have the effect of an authorization to exploit the invention involved and the term referred to in the second paragraph of Article 67 will begin as of its date.

The parties shall be notified of said resolution with a copy to the General Bureau of Inventions and Trademarks so that it may take note of the same.

Article 70. The contracts and the authorizations of exploitation referred to in the preceding Articles shall not be exclusive. They shall be non-transferable unless otherwise provided or if, in the absence of an agreement, the transfer is authorized by the General Bureau of the National Registry of Transfer of Technology, following to the extent applicable the procedure established in the preceding Article.

Article 71. The owner of the certificate of invention may exploit the invention himself.

Article 72. In order to establish the payment of royalties for the exploitation of a registered invention, the circumstance that the owner of the certificate of invention undertakes to furnish the necessary technical assistance and the duration and scope of the same shall be taken into account.

Article 73. The owner of the certificate of invention must furnish in every case the information necessary for the exploitation of his invention. Non-compliance with this obligation shall result in the cancellation of the certificate and of the corresponding registration at the National Registration of Transfer of Technology.

Article 74. The object of the contracts and the authorizations to exploit may be the rights arising from an application for registration. In these cases, such contracts and authorizations shall be considered subject to a resolutory condition. In view of the foregoing, if the application for registration is rejected or abandoned, the contracts or the authorizations shall remain without effect and the payments made as a result of the exploitation of the invention referred to in the rejected or abandoned application must be returned.

Article 75. At the expiration of the term established in the first paragraph of Article 67 or if the registration is declared null and void or is cancelled, its effects shall cease and the inventions to which it refers may be exploited freely without the obligation to make any payment whatsoever.

Article 76. The registration shall be null and void and shall not produce any effect whatsoever if the invention which is subject of the same is not registrable, the provisions that regulate the nullity of patents being applicable to the extent pertinent.

Article 77. When a third party exploits an invention registered pursuant to this Title without having reached an agreement with the owner of the certificate of invention or having obtained the authorization referred to in Article 69, said owner shall have the rights granted by this Law to the owner of a patent arising from an infringement of his rights.

. . .

Chapter IV, Use of the trademarks.

Article 117. The owner of a trademark must prove to the satisfaction of the Department of Industry and Commerce the effective use of the same, at least in one of the classes in which it is registered, within three years following its registration. If he does not prove said use, the corresponding registration shall be considered as extinguished by operation of Law.

. . .

Article 125. The Department of Industry and Commerce may declare, for reasons of public interest, the registration and obligatory use of trademarks on any product or service.

Also for reasons of public interest and after first hearing the organisms representative of the interested sectors, the said Department may prohibit the use of trademarks, registered or not, on particular products of any field whatsoever of economic activity.

The corresponding declaration shall be published in the *Diario Oficial* of the Federation and the persons subject to the same must comply with its provisions within the term and in accordance with the rules indicated in said declaration. Failure to comply shall give rise to the corresponding sanctions.

Source: *Diario Oficial*, February 10, 1976; effective February 11, 1976.

Notes

Introduction to Part I. The Role of the State in Foreign Investment

1. Stephen Krasner argued presciently in a review essay that the state "will once again become a major concern of scholarly discourse." He suggested that more attention would be devoted to political institutions: the "attention of scholars will turn from behavior within a given set of institutional constraints to constraints themselves" ("Approaches to the State" [1984], pp. 243–44). I argue that both the choices and the constraints must be present in a satisfactory explanation.

2. Bertrand Russell, *Dictionary of the Social Sciences*, s.v., "power."

3. Hirschman, *Shifting Involvements: Private Interest and Public Action* (1982), p. 70.

Chapter One. State Policy and the Question of Choice

1. "The emphasis on sovereignty may tend to direct attention from the very real limits that constrain the decision of even the most powerful nations" (Deutsch, *The Nerves of Government* [1966], p. 213).

2. Elster, *Explaining Technical Change* (1983); Von Wright, *Explanation and Understanding* (1971); Bunge, *Causality* (1959).

3. Simon, "Rationality," in his *Models of Bounded Rationality* (1982), p. 405.

4. The word *development* refers to a process of change (usually within a state or national economy) resulting in a greater capacity to satisfy the needs of its citizens. This definition leaves open the question of whether needs are defined according to some objective standard or are the self-defined needs of the people. However, it does avoid the problems of defining development in terms of simple economic growth, which is tied to effective demand rather than to need satisfaction. A seminal work on development in Latin America is Albert O. Hirschman's "Ideologies of Economic Development in Latin America," in his book *A Bias for Hope* (1971), pp. 270–311. The term has been controversial in political science, and the phrase *political development* was dropped even by some of its earlier proponents, including Samuel P. Huntington; see his article "The Change to Change" (1971), pp. 283–322.

5. The analysis of individual and collective choice was an important element in theories of modernization. For this point in a discussion of development and modernization literature, see Almond's "Approaches to Developmental Causation" (1973), pp. 17–19. However, choices are treated in an uncritical causalist way, on which I say more below. See also Almond's review

essay "Corporatism, Pluralism, and Professional Memory" (1983). For a discussion of the modernization literature from a statist perspective, see Stepan, *The State and Society* (1978), chap. 1. Gary Gereffi gives an extended comparison of the modernization and dependency literatures in *The Pharmaceutical Industry and Dependency in the Third World* (1983), chap. 1.

6. Most stage theories were teleological in the sense that later stages were preferable to earlier ones. For a recent example of a stage argument using an analogy from biology, see Krasner's discussion of the evolution of the state as a case of "punctuated equilibrium" ("Approaches to the State" [1984]). For a general discussion of functionalism as the characteristic mode of analysis in biology, see Elster, *Explaining Technical Change* (1983).

7. On systems theory, see Von Bertalanffy, *General Systems Theory* (1968), which reviews the evolution of the systems approach. For the continued use of systems theory in behavioral science, see Deutsch, *The Nerves of Government* (1966) and his review, "Major Changes in Political Science, 1952–77" (1978). On modernization theories, see Huntington, "The Change to Change" (1971), pp. 283–322. Gabriel Almond's recent essay is a critical review by a "founding father" of the modernization school, stressing the shortness of institutional memory regarding the advances and the diversity of the modernization theorists (Almond, "Corporatism, Pluralism, and Professional Memory" [1983]).

8. Summarized in Von Bertalanffy, *General Systems Theory* (1968).

9. Parsons, *The Social System* (1951).

10. Bendix et al., *State and Society* (1968).

11. As Stepan has pointed out, the functionalists and systems analysts writing in the 1950s and 1960s were not the first U.S. political scientists to attack the concept of the state (The State and Society [1978], p. 12n.) Arthur Bentley, in *The Process of Government* (1908), allowed that the "idea of the state" was too unimportant to figure in his study.

12. Easton, *The Political System* (1952), p. 106.

13. This reform was no simplification: "The political system is that system of interactions to be found in all independent societies which performs the functions of integration and adaptation (both internally and vis-à-vis other societies) by means of the employment, or threat of employment, of force or less legitimate physical compulsion" (Almond and Coleman, eds., *The Politics of Developing Areas* [1960], pp. 4–7). This varies from a Weberian definition of the state primarily in its functionalism: instead of a system of interaction performing several functions, Weber saw the State as a relationship of domination that has no special function except to elicit obedience to the rulers. (See my discussion in chap. 2.)

14. Huntington and Domínguez, "Political Development" (1975), pp. 5–10.

15. Deutsch, "Social Mobilization and Political Development" (1961), pp. 493–514; and idem, *The Nerves of Government* (1966), passim.

16. Cardoso and Faletto, *Dependency and Development in Latin America* (1979, first published in Spanish in 1969). Although dependency analysis had its origins in Latin America, critiques of modernization were widespread within U.S. social sciences as well. For example, Joseph Gusfield argued that rather

than modernity representing the polar opposite of tradition, there was substantial syncretism between traditional and modern patterns of belief and behavior; he concluded, "Nationalism is deeply committed to both horns of the dilemma of tradition and modernity" ("Tradition and Modernity" [1967], pp. 351–62).

17. See Evans, *Dependent Development* (1979). Dependency theory's prominence is reflected in the now voluminous writings on dependency; in addition to Cardoso and Faletto and Evans cited above, see Jaguaribe et al., *La dependencia político-económica de América Latina* (1970); Bodenheimer, "Dependency and Imperialism" (1971); Cardoso, "The Consumption of Dependency Theory in the United States" (1977); Cockcroft, Frank, and Johnson, *Dependence and Underdevelopment* (1972, first published in Spanish, 1970); *Latin American Perspectives* (Beverly Hills, Calif.), various numbers; Dos Santos, "The Structure of Dependence" (1970); Cardoso, "Associated-Dependent Development" (1973); Frank, *Latin America* (1969); Frank, *Capitalism and Underdevelopment in Latin America* (1967); Chilcote and Edelstein, eds., *Latin America* (1974); Rosen and Kurth, eds., *Testing Theories of Economic Imperialism* (1974); Furtado, *Economic Development of Latin America* (1970); Fagen, "Studying Latin American Politics" (1977); Caporaso, ed., *Dependence and Dependency in the Global System* (1978); Sunkel, "Big Business and 'Dependencia' " (1972); Gereffi, *The Pharmaceutical Industry and Dependency in the Third World* (1983); Amin, *Accumulation on a World Scale* (1974); Bonilla and Girling, eds., *Structures of Dependency* (1973); D. Senghaas, "Multinational Corporations and the Third World" (1975).

18. Though diffusion was a major factor in the spread of modernity, for example, the mechanisms were of less concern than the effects. At the same time, the specialization within U.S. political science·had led scholars of international relations to examine the international system without much attention to its effects on domestic society. A corrective in this direction is Gourevitch, "The Second Image Reversed" (1978).

19. In an interview with Fernando Henrique Cardoso conducted at the University of California, Berkeley, in 1981, he elaborated on his broad sociological training in Brazil, which was more within the European tradition, including Marx and other German scholars, than within the North American tradition. (The interview is recorded and is available from the author.)

20. Actually at ILPES, a research institute associated with CEPAL.

21. Although the decline in Latin American terms of trade is indisputable for the 1980s, contributing to the extended recession, the long-term postwar trends seem to be indeterminate. High volatility clearly characterizes commodity prices and, by extension, terms of trade; secular decline is more difficult to establish.

22. For an early essay showing the linkage of direct investment to policies of import substitution, see Hirschman, "The Political Economy of Import Substituting Industrialization."

23. Cardoso and Faletto were writing at about the same time as Debray was composing his *Revolution in the Revolution* (New York: Monthly Review Press, 1967) and Carlos Marighela was writing his more pragmatic how-to

primer, "Minimanual for the Urban Guerrilla" (included in his *For the Liberation of Brazil* [1971]).

24. Frank, *Latin America: Underdevelopment or Revolution?* Also see Carnoy, *The State and Political Theory* (1984), chap. 7.

25. Cardoso, "Associated-Dependent Development" (1973).

26. Sanjaya Lall makes a good critique of "dependence" that is compatible with my argument; he suggests that many of the ills attributed to dependence are in fact due to capitalism. (Contrast this with Ray Vernon's argument in *Storm over the Multinationals* [1977] that the ills attributed to foreign corporations are due to industrialization.) Lall suggests an analysis oriented to the kind of national change one desires: a more equitable capitalism or socialism. He concludes, "Neither is furthered by dependency theories" ("Is 'Dependence' a Useful Concept in Analyzing Underdevelopment?" p. 806). Robert Packenham has leveled the harshest criticisms at dependency theory, on the grounds of utility, measurement, and nonfalsifiability ("Trends in Brazilian National Dependency since 1964" [1976], a moderate version of what later became an extended polemic). In the Marxist tradition, dependency has also been criticized by David Becker for underestimating local capitalism, for "populist" nationalism, for elitism (inattention to the working class), and for failing to identify a test for nondependency (*The New Bourgeoisie and the Limits of Dependency* [1983], especially pp. 10–11).

27. Gereffi, *The Pharmaceutical Industry and Dependency in the Third World* (1983), p. 15.

28. The distinction between dependency and dependence is elaborated by Caporaso, *Dependence and Dependency in the Global System* (1978).

29. Gereffi, *The Pharmaceutical Industry and Dependency in the Third World* (1983), p. 43.

30. Cardoso and Faletto, *Dependency and Development in Latin America* (1979), pp. ix–x.

31. See, e.g., ibid., p. 209, for a discussion of the inequities of "dependent development." Also p. xxiv, where Cardoso and Faletto suggested that "it is not realistic to imagine that capitalist development will solve basic problems for the majority of the population. In the end, what has to be discussed as an alternative is not the consolidation of the state and the fulfillment of 'autonomous capitalism,' but how to supersede them. The important question, then, is how to construct paths toward socialism."

32. Ibid., p. xiv.

33. With regard to the expanded role of the state, see, e.g., ibid., pp. 199–200. Although Cardoso and Faletto explicitly espoused the search for ways "to construct paths to socialism," there is a certain ambiguity in their work that suggests a willingness to act to improve national development without necessarily rejecting capitalism, at least in the short and medium run. For a discussion of the issues of "nondependency" and dependency reversal, see Gereffi, *The Pharmaceutical Industry and Dependency in the Third World* (1983), pp. 21–36; Robert Packenham, 1982, "Plus ça change" (1982). Cardoso's recent involvement in political party leadership in Brazil is testimony to his pragmatism.

34. *El desarollo en el banquillo* (1979), p. 35.

35. Karl Deutsch raised a similar question in terms of the "emancipatory potential" of developing countries in his article "Imperialism and Neocolonialism" (1974).

36. Vernon, *Sovereignty at Bay* (1971), pp. 45–51.

37. Perhaps this shortcoming was in part because many of the leaders of the modernization school, such as Almond, Apter, Coleman, and Weiner, had done their original research on the new nations of Africa and Asia, where foreign investment was not yet as important an issue as it was in Latin America. In any case, international economic forces were not central to their work.

38. See Aharoni, *The Foreign Investment Decision Process* (1966).

39. Wilkins, *The Emergence of Multinational Enterprise* (1970); and idem, *The Maturing of Multinational Enterprise* (1974).

40. See Servan-Schreiber, *The American Challenge* (1969).

41. Vernon, *Sovereignty at Bay* (1971). A few authors later became concerned with the impact of U.S. foreign investment on the United States itself, especially the impact on U.S. labor; see Gilpin, *U.S. Power and the Multinational Corporations* (1975); Barnet and Müller, *Global Reach* (1974); also cf. Bergsten, Horst, and Moran, *American Multinationals and American Interests* (1978).

42. Vernon, *Sovereignty at Bay* (1971), p. 204.

43. Ibid., p. 197.

44. Harry Johnson attributed "psychic income" rather than economic benefits to Third World countries following nationalist policies.

45. Casanova, "The Ideology of the United States Concerning Foreign Investments" (1966), p. 244.

46. Wionczek, "La industria eléctrica en México, 1900–60," and "La explotación del azufre, 1910–66," in *El nacionalismo Mexicano y la inversión extranjera* (1967).

47. Moran, *Multinational Corporations and the Politics of Dependence* (1974).

48. Ibid., p. 164.

49. "Multinational Corporations and Dependency" (1978), pp. 80–93.

50. See, e.g., Cardoso and Faletto, *Dependency and Development in Latin America* (1979), pp. 160–71 and post-scriptum. Biersteker gives a more extended analysis of dependency along lines similar to those of Moran (*"Distortion or Development?"* [1978], chaps. 1 and 2).

51. Cardoso and Faletto, *Dependency and Development in Latin America* (1979), pp. ix–x.

52. Ibid., p. x.

53. Ibid., pp. 199ff. See also Hamilton, *The Limits of State Autonomy* (1982), and Gereffi, *The Pharmaceutical Industry and Dependency in the Third World* (1983), for two other dependency authors who considered the state explicitly. Bennett and Sharpe, in *Transnational Corporations versus the State* (1985), put state policy more explicitly at the center of their research agenda and thus moved beyond the traditional focus of dependency studies.

54. For example, one ordering was used by Keohane and Nye in *Power and Interdependence* (1977) to suggest which variable (or "model") to look at first in seeking an explanation for international regime change: economic

process, overall power structure, issue structure, and international organization models.

55. Keohane and Nye, "Power and Interdependence Revisited" (1987).

56. Krasner, *Structure Conflict: The Third World against Global Liberalism* (1985).

Chapter Two. Mexico: Dependence and State Strength

1. Under conditions of congruence, constraints may or may not constitute limits on state action; see Nordlinger, *On the Autonomy of the Democratic State* (1981).

2. Krasner, *Structural Conflict* (1985), relies heavily on this issue.

3. See, e.g., Kobrin, "Testing the Bargaining Hypothesis" (1987). Citing Keohane and Nye, Klaus Knorr, and others at the general level on bargaining and Bennett and Sharpe, Moran, Vernon, Gereffi, Newfarmer, and others for the foreign investment issue, Kobrin finds quite mixed results about bargaining in manufacturing and uncertainty about the operation of constraints and concludes with a call for more case studies.

4. Caporaso, *Dependence, Dependency, and Power in the Global System* (1978).

5. To create an index of dependence, first calculate the relative share of trade of each country (A and B):

$$a = \frac{\text{A's trade with B}}{\text{A's trade with world}}$$

$$b = \frac{\text{B's trade with A}}{\text{B's trade with world}}$$

A good index of dependence should range from 0 to 1 and should represent the relationship of how dependent each country is on the other. If they are truly interdependent, this should be reflected as well. Set the dependence index X:

$$X_{ab} = \frac{a}{a+b}$$

It should be clear that this will range from 0 (if A has no trade with B) to almost unity (if A has almost all its trade with B but B is so much bigger that almost none of its trade is with A).

X_{ab} may approach unity at its limit because

$$X_{ab} + X_{ba} = 1$$

Finally, perfect interdependence will equal 0.5. This will hold whenever the shares of total trade are equal and is true whatever the shares of total trade may be.

6. Approximately 17 percent of these exports were manufactured goods.

7. International Bank for Reconstruction and Development (World Bank), *World Development Report, 1988* (New York: Oxford University Press, 1988), pp. 244–45.

8. International Bank for Reconstruction and Development (World Bank), *World Development Report, 1982*. (New York: Oxford University Press, 1982).

9. The population for West Germany was 61.2 million in 1984. The population of Mexico was 76.8 million in 1984 (International Bank for Reconstruction and Development [World Bank], *World Development Report, 1986*).

10. Measures of GNP, of course, do not indicate how these goods and services are actually distributed.

11. UNCTAD, *The Capital Goods Sector in Developing Countries* (1985), p. 26, gives 71 percent. This statistic is somewhat misleading, because transport equipment, defined as a capital good, includes consumer durables such as passenger cars and because machinery, also defined as a capital good, includes electrical appliances. The accurate statistic is thus probably considerably lower, and this point is important since Mexico is highly dependent on capital goods imports to bridge the gap between domestic supply and demand. Nevertheless, the purpose at hand is to demonstrate the highly developed nature of Mexico's capital goods sector with respect to other developing countries. In this regard, Mexico and the other countries within the top six are far ahead of other developing countries.

12. Wionczek, "Electric Power: The Uneasy Partnership" (1964).

13. NAFINSA, *Statistics on the Mexican Economy, 1977* (1977); idem, *La economía Mexicana en cifras* (1981).

14. Data are from the International Bank for Reconstruction and Development (World Bank), *World Development Report*, various years, unless otherwise noted.

15. "Stock" figures refer to the accumulated value of foreign investment in a country; "flows" refer to annual increments of capital. Each year, positive flows of capital add incrementally to the stock.

16. UN Statistical Office, Department of Economic and Social Affairs, *Statistical Yearbook* (1971); ibid. (1981).

17. James Wilkie and Adam Perkal, eds., *Statistical Abstract of Latin America*, vol. 24 (Los Angeles: UCLA Latin American Center Publications, 1985), table 661, p. 100.

18. Ibid., table 1308.

19. Hernández Laos and Córdova Chavez, "Estructura de la distribución del ingreso en México" (1979).

20. Similarly, differences arise in the figures for Gini coefficients (a measure of inequality that describes the area between a Lorenz curve and a line of perfect equality). For example, the Gini coefficient for 1963 elicited three separate statistics from four sources: de Navarette (1970) and Wouter von Ginneken, *Socioeconomic Groups and Income Distribution in Mexico* (New York: St. Martin's Press, 1978), arrived at .55; the World Bank (1979) arrived at .526; and Hernández Laos and Córdova Chavez, "Estructura de la distribución del ingreso en México," arrived at .527.

21. Bernal Sahagún, *El impacto del las empresas multinacionales en el empleo y los ingresos* (1976).

22. Bernal Sahagún, *Anatomía de la publicidad en México* (1974), pp. 126–33.

23. International Bank for Reconstruction and Development (World Bank), *World Development Report* (1988), Statistical Appendix.

24. Linz, "Totalitarian and Authoritarian Regimes" (1975), p. 264.

25. The technocratic policy elite is a frequent, but not necessary, concomitant of authoritarian rule (Robert R. Kaufman, "Industrial Change and Authoritarian Rule" [1979], p. 187). For an argument from a Marxist perspective that stresses similar points, though with more emphasis on the dominance of business in the business-state alliance, see Hamilton, *The Limits of State Autonomy* (1982), especially chap. 1. For a related study of the politics of stabilization in the 1980s, see Kaufman, *The Politics of Debt in Argentina, Brazil, and Mexico* (1988).

26. Note that these balances between corporatism and pluralism are not the same as institutional checks and balances among executive, judicial, and legislative branches.

27. Tilly, "Western State-Making and Theories of Political Transformation" (1975), pp. 18–19.

28. It should be clear that it is not the individuals per se but the offices and roles they occupy that are important. The change in individual occupants of offices is irrelevant to the state. If all the individuals in office were to change, we would be likely to refer to a change of government. If the offices and roles changed, we would speak of a regime change. Only if the authority relationship itself were to break down (e.g., due to foreign occupation or revolutionary insurgency) would we be likely to speak of the breakdown of the state. Nordlinger uses a narrow and peculiar definition of the state in *On the Autonomy of the Democratic State* (1981), limiting the state to individuals holding office. Although it is obvious that the state includes individual officeholders, there is no reason to limit the definition to this simple level of analysis. Indeed there is good reason not to do so. The state is a good example of a concept that requires embedded levels of analysis. If we are concerned with individual officeholders legitimately making authoritative decisions, must we not be concerned with the selection procedures for the individuals, the institutions that define the offices, the process of decision-making, and the sources of legitimacy? And since authority requires a relationship, the state at the most abstract level must include those over whom authority is exercised. In international relations, the state is a sovereign territorial unit. There is no reason for a different definition of the state for domestic and international politics.

29. Note that a given individual may have several roles, with the "power to command" in one role and the "duty to obey" in another. Whether or not the citizens constitute a single nation is a complex question. Karl Deutsch has defined a nation as "a people in possession of a state" in his essay "Nation and World" (1967) and in *Nationalism and Social Communication* (1966a). Historically, the nation-state has existed (by definition) where the two coincide: "When a significant part of the members of a people desires to gain political power for its ethnic or linguistic group, we may call it a nationality. When such power is acquired, usually through controlling the machinery of the

state, we call it a nation" (Deutsch, "Nation and World" [1967], pp. 207–8). See also Deutsch, *The Nerves of Government* (1966b, first published 1963), pp. 17–28.

30. See Almond and Powell, *Comparative Politics* (1966); Easton, *A Systems Analysis of Political Life* (1965); and idem, *The Political System* (1952).

31. Krasner, *Defending the National Interest* (1978), pp. 55–57; Nordlinger, *On the Autonomy of the Democratic State* (1981).

32. Nordlinger, *On the Autonomy of the Democratic State* (1981), pp. 29–30. Type III poses no conflict. In types I and II, in which there is conflict, Nordlinger refers to the "inherent powers" of the state, without explaining why they are inherent.

33. Huntington, *Political Order in Changing Societies* (1968), p. 12.

34. Meyer, "The Historical Roots of the Authoritarian State in Mexico" (1977). Meyer points out that the president was powerful both before and after the revolution, but prerevolutionary Mexico lacked a succession mechanism.

35. In Chile at the end of the nineteenth century, the dominant class in society was a powerful oligarchy, as in Mexico. When the emerging middle classes and discontented workers and peasants challenged that hegemony, the personal rule of Porfirio Díaz in Mexico and the parliamentary republic in Chile were thrown into crisis. The challenge of a new ideology mobilized workers and peasants in Chile in the 1960s. The challenge to the existing hegemony again resulted in a crisis of the institutionalized democratic regime. Mexico has not faced a serious threat to the authority of the state since the revolution.

36. Hansen, *The Politics of Mexican Development* (1974, first published 1971), chap. 6.

37. Ibid., p. 171.

38. Only about 6 percent of the Mexican population were monolingual Indians at the start of the 1970s. In contrast to Peru or Bolivia, where Indians are a large portion of the population, Mexico is a thoroughly mestizo nation. Although Mexico was the site of one of the great Indian civilizations, the Indians were decimated by diseases brought by the Europeans; this has been documented by Woodrow Borah and his associates, who have estimated that the Indian population in Mexico fell from 25 million to 2 million in one century (Borah and Cook, "Why Population Estimates Are Important in the Interpretation of Mexican History" [1974], p. 119). The magnitude of the figures has generated much debate among historians, but the fact of a massive decline is not in doubt. The remaining Indians have been subjected to repeated efforts to teach them Spanish and incorporate them (Heath, *Telling Tongues* [1972]).

39. Purcell and Purcell, "State and Society in Mexico" (1980).

40. For a discussion of the political "rules of the game," see Smith, *Labyrinths of Power* (1979).

41. Raymond Vernon has commented on these factors of scale of investment and externality of benefits in *The Dilemma of Mexico's Development* (1963) and *Public Policy and Private Enterprise in Mexico* (1964).

42. Wionczek, "Electric Power: The Uneasy Partnership" (1964).

43. Bennett and Sharpe, "The State as Banker and Entrepreneur" (1980).
44. Huntington, *Political Order in Changing Societies* (1968), pp. 14–17.
45. Weber, *From Max Weber* (1946), p. 229.
46. Those who argue this position include Purcell, *The Mexican Profit-Sharing Decision* (1975); Purcell and Purcell, "State and Society in Mexico" (1980), pp. 194–227; and Weinert, "The State and Foreign Capital" (1977), pp. 109–28.
47. Recent examples of differentiation of organizations include the creation of special bureaus for science and technology, technology transfer, and regulation of foreign investment, discussed below. As a more general example, the administrative reform of the López Portillo administration combined all responsibility for industry—national, foreign, and state-owned—under a single ministry. The De la Madrid administration also reorganized the bureaucracy. Notable early examples include the formation of the national development bank, NAFINSA, and the state-owned petroleum company, PEMEX. Once established as separate institutions, both of these agencies sought—rather successfully—to expand the scope of their operations.
48. Malloy, "Politics, Fiscal Crisis, and Social Security Reform in Brazil" (1985).
49. Note that "state variables" in this context refer to factors descriptive of the current condition or "state" of the system (Hollings, "Resilience and Stability in Ecological Systems" [1985], pp. 177–78).
50. See Cornelius, "The Political Economy of Mexico under De la Madrid" (1985), p. 86; Schmidt, "The Mexican Foreign Debt and the Sexennial Transition from López Portillo to De la Madrid" (1985), p. 254; Sanderson, "Presidential Succession and Political Rationality in Mexico" (1983), p. 318.
51. Cardoso, "The Characterization of Authoritarian Regimes" (1979a), p. 38.
52. Manuel Villa, "History and Structure of the State as a Strategic Constraint," in Van Whiting, ed., *Overcoming Constraints on Mexican Development*, forthcoming.
53. The national confederations are the Confederación Nacional Campesina, the Confederación de Trabajadores Mexicanos, and the Confederación Nacional de Organizaciones Populares. These are the three traditional "pillars of the PRI."
54. Ronfeldt, "The Modern Mexican Military" (1985). Ronfeldt identifies three bases of the regime: the PRI, state-owned enterprises, and the army.
55. Collier and Collier, "Inducements versus Constraints" (1979).
56. NAFINSA, *La economía Mexicana en cifras* (1981), pp. 351–65; and Aspe and Sigmund, *The Political Economy of Income Distribution in Mexico* (1984).
57. See, e.g., Stevens, *Protest and Response in Mexico* (1974).
58. Ronfeldt, "The Modern Mexican Military" (1985).
59. Juan J. Linz, "Crisis, Breakdown, and Reequilibration," in *Breakdown of Democratic Regimes,* vol. 1, edited by Juan J. Linz and Alfred Stepan (Baltimore: Johns Hopkins University Press, 1978).
60. I have returned to the established distinction between elite and mass because it captures better the coincidence of social, economic, and political

power in a "social stratum" that is nonetheless not homogeneous in class or functional terms.

61. Huntington, *Political Order in Changing Societies* (1968), pp. 78, 80.

62. Ibid., p. 91.

63. Huntington and Domínguez, "Political Development" (1975), pp. 40–43.

64. Seymour Martin Lipset, *Political Man: The Social Bases of Politics* (Garden City, N.Y.: Doubleday, Anchor Books).

65. On the political reform, see Middlebrook, "Political Liberalization in an Authoritarian Regime" (1986), pp. 123–47.

66. A revealing anecdote shows the importance of turnout in comparison to party participation: a municipal vote-counter in a congressional election explained with some pride that when it was necessary to stuff the ballot boxes in order to bring the turnout rate over the 50 percent mark, the additional "votes" were allocated to all the parties in the same proportion as the actual votes cast! (The fraud failed in any event; reported abstention was 50.67 percent.)

67. Roderic A. Camp, *The Role of Economists in Policymaking* (1977), p. 53.

68. Hansen, *Politics of Mexican Development,* (1974), p. 107.

Chapter Three. The Nationalist Tradition

1. See Bennett and Sharpe, "The State as Banker and Entrepreneur" (1980); see also Gereffi and Newfarmer, "The State and International Oligopolies" (1985).

2. This usage of metapreference for collective second-order preferences is consistent with Hirschman's usage (though he is concerned with the meta-preferences of individuals). Note that by this definition, some action must be taken, but that action need not be successful. Plans, proposals, meetings, and draft laws may all be evidence of a metapreference. If the plans succeed, so much the better. If we compare this to the economists' notion of "revealed preference," we might say that a purchase is not necessary to reveal a preference, but window-shopping (or some other action) is necessary.

3. The *situ classicus* of countervailing power is the discussion by Galbraith in *American Capitalism* (1952).

4. The broader Marxist debate on theories of the state is ably captured in Carnoy, *The State and Political Theory* (1984). A specific application of the structural Marxist approach to Mexico is Hamilton, *The Limits of State Autonomy* (1982). Also see the discussions in Nordlinger, *On the Autonomy of the Democratic State* (1981), and in Krasner, *Defending the National Interest* (1978).

5. Evans and Gereffi, "Foreign Investment and Dependent Development" (1979).

6. Vernon, *Sovereignty at Bay* (1971); and idem, *Storm over the Multinationals* (1977).

7. Rueschemeyer and Evans, "The State and Economic Transformation" (1985).

8. Villarreal, "The Policy of Import-Substituting Industrialization, 1925–1975" (1977), p. 68.

9. John Womack, Jr., has reevaluated the economic impact of the Mexican Revolution, suggesting that modern capitalism, with an active foreign participation in a variety of sectors, predated the revolution and continued after it. See Womack, "The Mexican Economy during the Revolution, 1910–1920" (1978), pp. 96ff. Womack's table 2, p. 95, gives the available, scanty data on the value of foreign investment for an assortment of years between 1880 and 1940. He also reproduces Raymond Vernon's pair of tables on pre- and postrevolutionary levels of production, showing that although growth stopped, production in most sectors was at about the same level in 1921 as in 1910, except for mining (which had recovered by 1924). See Vernon, *The Dilemma of Mexico's Development* (1963), p. 83.

10. Villarreal, "The Policy of Import-Substituting Industrialization 1925–1975" (1977), p. 68.

11. In order to accommodate foreign firms, Díaz had let lapse the traditional Latin jurisprudence granting the nation control of subsoil rights.

12. Though the phrasing may be construed broadly to include all private property, the logic of the argument is that natural resources belong to the nation, the nation gives them out, and the nation can take them back. According to this reasoning, wealth accumulated from labor rather than natural resources may not be subject to the same limitations.

13. Quoted in Smith, *The United States and Revolutionary Nationalism in Mexico, 1916–1932* (1972), p. 138. One of the more curious tutelary exercises cited by Smith was the establishment for a time of a football (American football) team in Mexico by a group of Yale alumni convinced that team spirit would help build the character of the country that had just fought a revolution.

14. Womack, "The Mexican Economy during the Revolution, 1910–1920" (1978); and Smith, *The United States and Revolutionary Nationalism in Mexico, 1916–1932* (1972).

15. Smith, *The United States and Revolutionary Nationalism in Mexico, 1916–1932* (1972), p. 149.

16. Wionczek, "Electric Power" (1964).

17. *Industrial Property* will be defined and discussed below; the expression refers to rights related to nontangible assets such as inventions and trade names.

18. Calles may have been a personal scoundrel and politically ambitious. He was certainly a political enemy of Cárdenas, the most popular of Mexico's presidents. But Calles steered Mexico through a critical period of history, including the establishment of the party and the institutionalization of the regime.

19. Clark Reynold's figure of comparative growth rates (reproduced by Womack, "The Mexican Economy during the Revolution, 1910–1920" [1978], p. 100) shows this well.

20. King, *Mexico* (1970), pp. 10–11, 22; Reynolds, *The Mexican Economy* (1970); Villarreal, "The Policy of Import-Substituting Industrialization,

1925–1975" (1977), pp. 68–71.

21. Cárdenas, *Ideario político* (1972), p. 188. This is a collection of Cárdenas's speeches and writings; the quote is from the 1930s.

22. Cárdenas also laid the foundation for removing the military from the regular exercise of political power. Under Cárdenas the military became just one of four sections of the national party (later the PRI), and in the 1940s it lost even that status.

23. Polanyi, *The Great Transformation* (1966, first published 1944), p. 251.

24. Smith, *The United States and Revolutionary Nationalism in Mexico, 1916–1932* (1972), p. 9.

25. Wionczek, "Electric Power" (1964); and "La industria eléctrica en México," in idem, *El nacionalismo mexicano y la inversión extranjera* (1967).

26. In this distribution, Mexico was fairly representative of Latin America. To take sales rather than investment as a measure, chemicals and food products ranked first and second in sales of U.S. manufacturing affiliates in Latin America in 1968. Food products accounted for almost 1.5 billion dollars in sales, or 18 percent of total affiliate sales in Latin America. Food sales were 17 percent of all manufacturing affiliate sales in Mexico at about the same time. Figures on food sales in Latin America are from Vernon, *The Economic and Political Consequences of Multinational Enterprise* (1972), p. 3. For Mexico, the figures come from Newfarmer and Mueller, *Multinational Corporations in Brazil and Mexico* (1975), p. 195.

27. Total direct investment is the sum of new investment plus reinvested profits, less acquisitions. Some Mexican sources no longer include reinvested profits, because they are not considered to be new capital; but since parent companies have the option of repatriating and exercise that option at variable rates, reinvested profits represent capital the availability of which is determined abroad and hence should be considered in the total of all foreign investment. Table 3.2 also gives remittances on foreign investment, to which reference will be made later; these remittance figures do not include reinvested profits. (In national accounts, if reinvested profits are counted as foreign investment, they would first be added to remittances to show their source and then added to investments.) Net long-term capital inflows are shown in the first column. This is the net total of direct and indirect investments, including net securities transactions and new loans to government and to public and private enterprise, less amortization of principal.

28. ECLA/NAFINSA, *La política industrial en el desarrollo económico de México* (1971), p. 367.

29. Manufacturing accounted for less than one quarter of the GDP; in 1965 it was just under 21 percent.

30. Since law and policy in this period have been the subject of an extensive study in English by Harry Wright as well as numerous studies in Spanish, a brief review should suffice to set the stage for examining the policy initiatives of the 1970s in the next chapter. See Wright, *Foreign Enterprise in Mexico* (1971); and Ramos Garza, *México ante la inversión extranjera: legislación, políticas, y prácticas* (1974).

31. Wright, *Foreign Enterprise in Mexico* (1971), p. 102.

32. Ibid., p. 107.

33. Ibid., p. 348.

34. It is relevant to note that although Miguel Alemán extended the intervention of the state in the economy, he is widely accepted as having laid the foundation for the growth of the domestic private economy, not state enterprise. In Cinta's survey of Mexican entrepreneurs, 57 percent named Alemán as the president that most favored industrialization and the business sector (Cinta G., "El empresario industrial y el desarrollo económico de México" [1972b]).

35. Reynolds, *The Mexican Economy* (1970); and Bennett and Sharpe, *Transnational Corporations versus the State* (1985).

36. Hansen, *The Politics of Mexican Development* (1974), p. 169.

37. Mexican administrations run through November, with new presidents taking office on December 1. López Mateos thus took office on December 1, 1958.

38. Wionczek, "La industria eléctrica en México," in idem, *El nacionalismo mexicano y la inversión extranjera* (1967), pp. 147–49.

39. Ibid., pp. 140–41.

40. Wionczek, "La explotación del azufre, 1910–66," in idem, *El nacionalismo mexicano y la inversión extranjera* (1967), pp. 237–51.

41. Wright, *Foreign Enterprise in Mexico* (1971), pp. 122, 137–39, 140ff.

42. Bennett and Sharpe, *Transnational Corporations versus the State* (1985); and idem, "Agenda Setting and Bargaining Power" (1979), pp. 57–89.

43. Wright, *Foreign Enterprise in Mexico* (1971), p. 106.

44. The *amparo* is a uniquely Mexican legal form by which judicial authorities are asked to protect or relieve a private party from legislative or executive decisions. Though only applicable in a single case, a series of five *amparos* on the same issue and with the same result can establish legal precedent. The *amparo* is discussed by ibid., pp. 28–30; and more extensively by Karst and Rosenn, *Law and Development in Latin America* (1975), pp. 127–59. They also discuss the Química Industrial case and emphasize the independence of the Mexican judiciary on pp. 148ff.

45. Note the jump in new investments in 1965 shown in table 3.2. Though the Ministry of Foreign Relations began to deny requests by foreign firms to acquire majority interests in existing Mexican companies in 1966, the holding-company option made this difficult to enforce.

46. Wright, *Foreign Enterprise in Mexico* (1971), pp. 145–49.

47. Wionczek, *El nacionalismo mexicano y la inversión extranjera*, p. 270.

48. The case is described in detail by Miguel Wionczek in ibid. and in "Foreign-Owned Export-Oriented Enclaves in a Rapidly Industrializing Economy" (1971a).

49. Wright, *Foreign Enterprise in Mexico* (1971), p. 149.

50. Ibid., p. 110.

51. Even before 1967, Ministry of Industry and Commerce was using its power over import licenses to require Mexicanization in many industries not on the restricted list.

Chapter Four. Nationalist Regulation of Foreign Investment in the 1970s

1. In 1965, the secretary of the Ministry of Industry and Commerce stated official policy on foreign investment to the American Chamber of Commerce.

The government (the Treasury Department, the Department of Industry and Commerce, and the Bank of Mexico) generally asks that 51 percent of the capital be Mexican when companies seek the additional benefits of the Law on New and Necessary Industries. It also asks for 51 percent national capital when a foreign company wishes to enter a field in which other national or mixed-capital companies already exist and manufacture the products with reasonable quality and price, or when there are existing national or combined companies with adequate resources and technical knowledge, which are also seeking to produce the article concerned. Companies which are not included in the above cases are urged to associate with national capital, although they do so or not, as they wish; and when they do so, they decide on the composition of the capital in free negotiation with private Mexican interests. Numerous cases exist in which it is decided to establish these companies with 100 percent foreign capital.

The transcripts of these comments by the secretary, Octaviano Campos Salas, were distributed to companies by the accounting firm Price Waterhouse and Company, which provided the translation.

2. Newfarmer and Mueller, *Multinational Corporations in Brazil and Mexico* (1975).

3. A similar study was conducted by the Stanford Research Institute on contract to the American Chamber of Commerce in Mexico: Robinson and Smith, *The Impact of Foreign Private Investment on the Mexican Economy* (1976). That study examined whether (but not when) firms had been acquired. Over 33 percent of their total sample had been acquired. The responses to their survey were incomplete, however, and did not include many of the major firms in Mexico. The data from the U.S. Senate and the Harvard studies indicate that their figures on acquisitions are much too low.

4. In food processing, for example, the two-digit classification 20 indicates all food processing: the three-digit classification 202 indicates dairy products; and the four-digit classification 2023 corresponds to condensed and evaporated milk, according to the U.S. standard industrial code. Mexican codes use similar classifications, with some variation from the U.S. code.

5. Fajnzylber and Martínez Tarragó, *Las empresas transnacionales* (1976).

6. The identity of the top plants is not disclosed either in the census or in the Fajnzylber and Martínez Tarragó study, but I was able to gain access to the unpublished list.

7. Newfarmer and Mueller, *Multinational Corporations in Brazil and Mexico* (1975), p. 61. The citation refers to 238 separate "industries."

8. Robinson and Smith, *The Impact of Foreign Private Investment on the Mexican Economy* (1976), p. 73; Newfarmer and Mueller, *Multinational Corporations in Brazil and Mexico* (1975), p. 73.

9. NAFINSA and CEPAL, *La política industrial en el desarrollo económico de México* (1971), p. 93.

10. Ibid.

11. Tourism of Mexicans abroad contributed but was more than offset by tourism within Mexico. Border transactions likewise showed a net positive effect on the balance of payments.

12. If a similar analysis is made for merchandise trade alone, comparing the balance of trade to merchandise exports, in only five years from 1939 to 1965 was that ratio less than or equal to − 0.50. In only one year from 1965 to 1976 was it greater than − 0.50.

13. Navarrete, *México* (1971), pp. 418–19.

14. NAFINSA and CEPAL, *La política industrial en el desarrollo económico de México* (1971) p. 223.

15. Wionczek, Bueno, and Navarrete, *La transferencia internacional de tecnología* (1974), p. 70.

16. Fajnzylber and Martínez Tarragó, *Las empresas transnacionales* (1976), pp. 286–315.

17. This analysis of the balance-of-payments effects of foreign investment has left aside the question of the effect of transnational enterprises on merchandise imports. Although the share of imports attributable to foreign-owned firms exceeded their share of production, and their share of capital goods was even higher, it could well be argued that national firms would have required the same imports. Though most emphasis was placed on remitted funds, imports were also a concern, however. For 1970–72, imports by transnational subsidiaries in the Fajnzylber and Martínez Tarragó sample grew faster than all industry imports (9.2 percent and 7.8 percent respectively), growing from U.S. $662.9 million to $777.8 million. Subsidiary imports grew in that three-year period from 36.6 percent to 38.9 percent of all private industry imports, and from 47.8 percent to 51.5 percent of imports of capital goods by private industry (ibid., p. 288).

18. Ibid., p. 312.

19. NAFINSA and CEPAL, *La política industrial en el desarrollo económico de México* (1971), p. 232.

20. Domínguez, "The Implications of Mexico's Internal Affairs for Its International Relations" (1980), p. 20.

21. NAFINSA and CEPAL, *La política industrial en el desarrollo económico de México* (1971), p. 232.

22. As cited in a working document of the National Registry of Foreign Investment in Mexico.

23. DeRossi, *The Mexican Entrepreneur* (1971), pp. 281–83.

24. Cinta G., "El empresario industrial y el desarrollo económico de México" (1972).

25. The Bilateral Businessman's Committee is a private U.S.-Mexico group established in the 1950s. The quote is from a document of the group provided by Fausto R. Miranda.

26. Miranda, 1973, p. 1221.

27. Siqueiros, 1967, p. 107.

28. The text of the inaugural address is given in Navarrete, *México: La política económica del nuevo gobierno* (1971).

29. Miranda, 1973, pp. 1222–23.

30. Indeed, his devotion to a fixed rate of exchange contributed to overvaluation and the subsequent need for a maxi-devaluation in 1976.

31. Siqueiros, 1967, p. 107.

32. COPARMEX, *Franco diálogo entre gobierno y empresarios* (1971), p. 11.

33. Ibid., p. 3.

34. Ibid., pp. 77–87. All quotations in the text are from this document.

35. The comments of both Ambassador McBride and Undersecretary Campillo Sáinz are reproduced in ANADE, *Inversión extranjera y transferencia de tecnología en México* (1973).

36. Ibid., p. 72.

37. Ibid., p. 66.

38. Ibid., p. 77. The comments of the undersecretary echo those of the president. For the president's speech to UNCTAD in Santiago, as well as for details on the Mexican participation in that meeting, see Jorge Castañeda et al., *Derecho económica internacional* (1976).

39. The ministries of National Property and of Industry and Commerce became the Ministry of National Property and Industrial Development and the Ministry of Commerce, respectively, in 1977. Later, the original division was restored. Note that the secretary of labor was included in the commission, though that ministry had not been a member of the commission that functioned from 1947 to 1953. This does not reflect the power of the labor sector but does show that job creation was thought to be an important function of foreign investment.

40. Bennett and Sharpe, *Transnational Corporation versus the State* (1985); Biersteker, *Distortion or Development?* (1978).

41. In the most recent regulations of the law, small investors should receive automatic approval, even for full foreign ownership. This should reduce the recourse to *prestanombres*.

42. Data are from the Bank of Mexico and the Secretariat of Tourism.

Chapter Five. Technology Regimes, Patents, and Trademarks

1. National Academy of Sciences (1978), p. 11.

2. Sábato, "El cambio tecnológico necesario y posible en América Latina" (1976), p. 545.

3. Ladas, *Patents, Trademarks, and Related Rights* (1975), p. 1128.

4. Ibid., p. 1307.

5. Belgium, Brazil, France, Guatemala, Italy, the Netherlands, Portugal, Serbia, Spain, Salvador, and Switzerland.

6. The text of the convention allowed for revision through amendment. After all the states present at the first Conference of Revision at Rome in 1886 failed to ratify it, the Union decided that "restricted unions" might be formed between states agreeing on certain improvements. As a result, different configurations of states have signed various revisions and agreements.

7. Ladas, *Patents, Trademarks, and Related Rights*, p. 90.

8. WIPO brochure, pp. 9, 37.

9. UNCTAD, "The Role of the Patent System in the Transfer of Technology to Developing Countries" (1975), p. 2.

10. Ladas, *Patents, Trademarks, and Related Rights*, p. 172; UNCTAD, 1972, p. 9.

11. UNCTAD, 1975c, p. 3.

12. UNCTAD, 1975c, pp. 37, 21.

13. UNCTAD, 1975c, p. 63.

14. UNCTAD, 1975a, p. 47.

15. UNCTAD, 1979, p. 29.

16. UNCTAD, 1979, pp. 38, 42. "The aim of any policy should be to diminish the market power created by the enterprises through product differentiation activities in which trademarks play a prominent role" (p. 46).

17. UNCTAD, "The Role of Trademarks in Developing Countries" (1979), p. 14. The largest number were in pharmaceuticals (p. 26).

18. UNCTAD, "Report of the Intergovernmental Group of Experts on a Code of Conduct on Transfer of Technology" (1975b), annex 1, p. 1; annex 2, p. 1.

19. UN Department of Development and International Economic Cooperation, "Towards the New International Economic Order" (1982), p. 40.

20. The only published work of importance prior to 1970 was Miguel S. Wionczek, *Disposiciones para la transmisión de tecnología práctica a los países en desarrollo* (1968). Important unpublished but widely circulated works included De María y Campos, "Transferencia de tecnología, dependencia del exterior y desarrollo económico." (1968); and Herman von Bertrab, "The Transfer of Technology: A Case Study of European Private Enterprises Having Operations in Latin America, with Special Emphasis on Mexico" (Ph.D. diss., University of Texas at Austin, 1968).

21. The literature on technology is extensive. For a complete bibliography on scientific and technological policy in Latin America through 1976, see the listing by Dilmus D. James in *Latin America Research Review* 12 (3) (1977), reproduced in the Mexican journal *Comercio Exterior* 28 (12) (1978). *Comercio Exterior* is an indispensable reference, with frequent articles on technology and technology transfer. Special numbers dedicated to the topic include the just-cited issue for 1978; see also the issue for November 1976. For Mexico, the basic reference is Wionczek, Bueno, and Navarrete, *La transferencia internacional de tecnología* (1974), which is the result of the study proposed by Wionczek in his 1968 ECOSOC study, *Disposiciones para la transmisión de tecnología práctica a los países en desarrollo*. Wionczek has published widely on technology transfer, participated in debates within Latin America, advised the Andean Pact, and was the principal adviser and architect of Mexico's policies. On Mexico, see Nadal Egea, *Instrumentos de política científica y tecnológica en México* (1977). An annotated bibliography is Sábato, *Transferencia de tecnología* (1978). A thorough economic study with data primarily from Argentina is Katz, *Importación de tecnología, aprendizaje, e industrialización dependiente* (1976). In English, consult Goulet, *The Uncertain Promise* (1977); Street and James, eds., *Technological Progress in Latin America* (1979); and the four-

volume study commissioned by the U.S. Department of State in preparation for the UN Conference on Science and Technology for Development: Fund for Multinational Management Education et al., *Public Policy and Technology Transfer: Viewpoints of U.S. Business* (New York, 1978), which contains a number of instructive case studies.

22. Fajnzylber and Martínez Tarragó, *Las empresas transnacionales* (1976), p. 351.

23. Ladas, *Patents, Trademarks, and Related Rights*, pp. 446–49.

24. The INIC evaluation is quoted in Wionczek, Bueno, and Navarrete, *La transferencia internacional de tecnología* (1974), p. 15, n. 5. The history of INIC, CONACYT, and the 1973 law on technology transfer is given on pp. 13–25.

25. According to a personal communication to me from Echeverría's adviser, the late Miguel Wionczek, dated January 15, 1980.

26. All technology contracts must be registered, regardless of the nationality of the supplier.

27. A grant-back refers to the obligation to "grant back" to the original supplier of technology all rights to any modifications or improvements.

28. See the studies by Miguel Wionczek cited above, and the statement of the undersecretary of industry and commerce, José Campillo Sáinz, in ANADE, *Inversión extranjera y transferencia de tecnología en México* (1973).

29. The cases discussed here were actual registry files examined with a guarantee of confidentiality.

30. I.e., upon expiration of the ten-year term.

31. Business International, *Mexico* (1978); and Conference Board, *Mexico 1980* (1980).

32. My translation of the "Exposición de Motivos" of the law (Mexico City: Registry on Foreign Investment and Technology Transfer, 1982).

33. For example, some contracts contain certain prohibitions on exports to some countries or regions but not to others; according to registry officials, prohibitions such as these were frequently interpreted to be "in the country's interest." Similarly, in at least one case, payment in kind rather than in cash or in a percentage of sales was allowed, contrary to stated rules. Although submission of claims to private international arbitration was not specifically forbidden or allowed in the first technology transfer law, it was informally permitted under the first law and explicitly approved in the revised 1982 law.

34. Like the law on technology transfer, which was approved on December 28, 1972, this law was passed as part of the *dicembrazo*, the year-end rush during which much pending legislation is approved.

35. The new law referred to "inventions" and trademarks rather than to patents and trademarks, since the law introduced the Certificate of Invention (discussed below) as well as the patent to protect inventions.

36. Though never implemented, it was this provision that attracted most attention in UNCTAD, in other LOCs, and in the U.S.

37. From the unpublished transcript of the secretary's statement to the Senate.

38. A law office document from 1977 indicated 3,023 applications were

submitted from January 1 to September 15 of that year, for an annual rate of 3,818 for 1977. Since then, the rate of patent applications has continued to fluctuate, with 5,472 applications in 1980 and 4,048 in 1985; nonetheless, the sharp reduction in 1976 seems to have been temporary.

39. Campillo Sáinz, "Fundamentación de la nueva ley de invenciones y marcas" (1976).

40. James and Lister, "Galbraith Revisited" (1980), p. 88.

41. The Malinchista mentality alludes to Malinche, the Indian translator and lover of Spanish conquerors.

42. Smuggling to avoid duties had reached sufficient proportions that it was necessary for Mexico to adopt a publicity campaign with the slogan "Contraband is against Mexico."

Chapter Six. The Limits of Nationalism

1. Vernon, *Sovereignty at Bay* (1971), and Moran, *Multinational Corporations and the Politics of Dependence* (1974), explore the learning curve. Tugwell, *The Politics of Oil in Venezuela* (1975), develops a similar argument; see also Moran, "Multinational Corporations and Dependency" (1978). On Mexican nationalization of oil, see Lorenzo Meyer, *México y los Estados Unidos en el conflicto petrolero (1917–1942)* (Mexico: El Colegio de México, 1972; also published in English by University of Texas Press). Wionczek's *El nacionalismo mexicano y la inversión extranjera* (1967) explores the takeover by the state of the electric power and sulphur industries in Mexico.

2. Merrie G. Klapp makes the argument that state power is likely to increase in the oil industry in developing countries, in "The State: Landlord or Entrepreneur?" (1982).

3. World Bank, *World Development Report, 1989*, p. 11.

4. Vernon, *Sovereignty at Bay* (1971), p. 66. He maintained the thesis with respect to manufacturing firms in his *Storm over the Multinationals* (1977). And for "Vernon on Vernon," claiming the obsolescing bargain as one of the most enduring insights of his earlier book, see "Sovereignty at Bay: Ten Years After" (1981).

5. Arguments supporting the renewable bargain thesis include Gereffi and Newfarmer, "The State and International Oligopolies" (1985); Bennett and Sharpe, "Agenda Setting and Bargaining Power" (1979); Whiting, "Transnational Enterprise and the State in Mexico" (1981); Mytelka, *Regional Development in a Global Economy* (1979); Biersteker, "The Illusion of State Power" (1980). For arguments against, see Vernon, *Storm over the Multinationals* (1977), and Grieco, "Between Dependency and Autonomy" (1979); Vernon's argument seems to fly in the face of the evidence unless a much restricted definition of the obsolescing bargain is adopted, stopping far short of state ownership. Grieco's argument applied the bargaining approach to computers in India. He pointed to substantial gains for the Indians, but the gains were hardly comparable to those from the takeovers of oil and railroads. Thus, it is appropriate to consider entry and participation in an industry as an intermediate stage between high and low bargaining power. Compatible with the emphasis

on structural characteristics, Grieco pointed out that India's bargaining power came largely from changes in the structure of the international industry. He also acknowledged the importance of India's size; the attractiveness of the Indian market increased India's leverage. The renewable bargain implies that bargaining takes place but stops short of fade-out. Encarnation's book on India, *Dislodging Multinationals* (1989), came to my attention after this book was finished. Although he argues correctly that India replaced most multinationals, some did find a way to stay even there.

6. See my article, "The International Food Processing Industry" (1985) and chap. 7 of this book.

7. Bennett and Sharpe, "Agenda Setting and Bargaining Power" (1979), p. 87.

8. For an expanded discussion of technology transfer policy in Mexico, see Whiting, "The Politics of Technology Transfer in Mexico" (1983) and chap. 5 of this book.

9. Following the administrative reform adopted at the beginning of the López Portillo administration, SEPAFIN, the Ministry of National Property and Industrial Development, was formed by splitting the Ministry of Industry and Commerce and fusing industry to the previously separate Ministry of National Property. Thus, one ministry was responsible for commerce, and another, SEPAFIN, was responsible for all industry, whether state, foreign, or national. The De la Madrid administration again joined industry and commerce in a single ministry, known as SECOFI. Examples of the background publications of the Ministry of Commerce are *Aspectos jurídicos del comercio exterior de México* and the information handbook *México: Hechos, cifras, tendencias*, both published by the Banco Nacional de Comercio Exterior.

10. For one of the earliest full descriptions of the border program, see Baerresen, *The Border Industrialization Program in Mexico* (1973). For case material and critiques see Baird and McCaughan, *Beyond the Border* (1979); debate and conflicting perspectives can be found in Whiting, ed., *Proceedings, Workshop on Mexico's Border Industrialization Program* (1982). See also Manuel Martínez de Campo, "Ventajas e inconvenientes de la actividad maquiladora en México," *Comercio Exterior* 33(2) (1983); also Laurie Kassman García, "Border Industries: Something for Everyone" (1982). The Reagan administration's Caribbean Basin Initiative encouraged foreign investment in off-shore processing industries. For a debate on the initiative see the various authors in the section entitled "Caribbean Basin Initiative" in *Foreign Policy* 47 (Summer 1982): 114–38. For an earlier article by one who later went on to serve as undersecretary of commerce under De la Madrid, see René Villarreal, "The Policy of Import-Substituting Industrialization" (1977).

11. Most of these are still women, though the proportion of men in these factories has been slowly rising. By 1988 men held about 30 percent of the maquila jobs (*El Mercado de Valores* 49 [9] [May 1, 1989], 25).

12. See the presentation by Richard Bolin, one of the founders of the Maquiladora Program in Mexico, summarized in Whiting, ed., *Proceedings, Workshop on Mexico's Border Industrialization Program*, (1982), especially pp. 6–9.

13. For example, in 1987, of the total value-added under the program,

labor was 46.4 percent; raw materials 5.4 percent; profits 19.7 percent; and miscellaneous expenses 28.5 percent (*El Mercado de Valores* 49 [9] [May 1, 1989].

14. Sábato, *Ciencia, tecnología, desarrollo y dependencia* (1971), pp. 6–10; Wionczek, "Industrialización, capital extranjero, y transferencia de tecnología" (1986), p. 12.

15. CONACYT, *Plan nacional indicativo de ciencia y tecnología* (Mexico City: CONACYT, 1976), tables 12 and 13.

16. Dan Levy has published an excellent study of the autonomy of UNAM, arguing that it has enjoyed much greater autonomy from state control than is usually believed. In fact, the study calls into question the unqualified characterization of the Mexican regime as authoritarian. See "University Autonomy in Mexico" (1979).

17. For the National Commission on Foreign Investment, see *Diario Oficial*, March 9, 1973; for the National Commission on Industrial Development, see ibid., March 19, 1979; for the National Commission on Agroindustrial Development, see ibid., August 21, 1979. The president is empowered to form interministerial commissions by the Law on Secretariats and Departments of State (December 23, 1958). This law is discussed in the context of a more general evaluation of the administrative reform by Jorge M. Aguirre Hernández in *Jurídica* 10 (1) (1978): 225.

18. The Sistema Nacional de Información (within the Ministry of Programming and Budget) publishes a monthly "Gaceta Informativa" reporting on available statistical publications.

19. Founded in 1934, NAFINSA has been rapidly expanding into many areas. When López Portillo was still secretary of the treasury, NAFINSA was authorized to become a multiservice bank, merging with the Grupo Financiera Internacional in 1975. NAFINSA now owns capital in seventy-one firms, making it one of the largest economic groups in Mexico. On this rapid growth, see *El Mercado de Valores* 39 (28) (July 1979): 569–75.

20. See "Informe de Banca SOMEX," speech of the president and director general of SOMEX, Lic. Mario Ramón Beteta, in ibid., 39 (39) (September 1979): 818–22.

21. A brief description of these trust funds is given in CONACYT, *Plan nacional indicativo de ciencia y tecnología* (Mexico City: CONACYT, 1976), pp. 268–70; a more detailed description is in Nadal Egea, *Instrumentos de política científica y tecnológica en México* (1977), pp. 264–75; current reports on each of them can be found in various issues of *El Mercado de Valores*.

22. Sábato, *Ciencia, tecnología, desarrollo y dependencia* (1971), pp. 6–10.

23. Ibid., p. 57.

24. Morgan Guaranty Trust Company, *World Financial Markets*, December 30, 1988.

25. Purcell and Purcell, "State and Society in Mexico" (1980), p. 215.

26. As numerous authors have pointed out, information on decisions made at high levels of government is difficult and often impossible to obtain. Information on nondecisions is even scarcer. Morton Halperin noted in *Bureaucratic Politics and Foreign Policy* (1974) that research on bureaucratic politics

is difficult in a closed decision-making system: there are fewer "shared images" than in foreign policy, less agreement over "mission," and a less easily defined "essence" (p. 4). In addition, he acknowledged that it is necessary in analyzing economic policy to take into account the actions and interests of the private sector.

27. Campillo Sáinz's former fellows in the private sector lamented his conversion; and after 1972 he remained in the government, becoming secretary of industry and commerce during the latter years of the Echeverría administration and heading the workers' housing fund (INFONAVIT) during the López Portillo administration.

28. The analysis was published as a working paper by the International Labour Office.

29. It is possible that Campillo Sáinz privately opposed the tax reform, but if so, it is likely that he would have argued against it in the meetings reported by Solís.

30. Arriola, "Los grupos empresariales frente al estado, 1973–75" (1976), p. 339.

31. This section draws on research by Andrés Lederman, with data from Mexico's Ministry of Finance. In debt-equity swaps, the bank sells Mexican debt in a secondary market to another bank or any other investor, perhaps a multinational corporation, at a discount. The prices in the secondary market of Mexican debt were quoted at 80 percent of face value in 1985, 54 percent in 1986, and 51 percent in 1987. Then, Mexico buys back its debt in local currency at a discount, usually no more than 10 percent of the face value. For Mexico, the discount was 12 percent for most of the period in which the swap program was carried out. Only toward the end when the price in the secondary market suffered considerable losses did Mexico increase its discount to 20 percent.

Introduction to Part III: International Industrial Structure and State Policy: Three Case Studies

1. See Newfarmer, ed., *Profits, Progress, and Poverty* (1985); Bain, *Industrial Organization* (1968); F. M. Scherer, *Industrial Market Structure and Economic Performance* (Chicago: Rand McNally, 1980); Bennett and Sharpe, *Transnational Corporations versus the State* (1985).

Chapter Seven. The Food-Processing Industry

1. In essence, this constitutes a test of the obsolescing bargain thesis, as put forward by Vernon in *Sovereignty at Bay* in 1971 (p. 66) and *Storm over the Multinationals* in 1977 (p. 151). In a test of that thesis, Stephen Kobrin found that "obsolescence does not appear to be structurally inherent in manufacturing." He does find, however, that states that attempt regulation do have an impact on the level of ownership of firms, especially in food and

consumer product subsidiaries ("Testing the Bargaining Hypothesis in Manufacturing Sector in Developing Countries" [Autumn 1987], pp. 609–38).

2. UN-CTC, *Transnational Corporations in Food and Beverage Processing* (1980), pp. 6–8.

3. Ibid.

4. At the other extreme, Iowa Beef Processors and Associated Milk Producers both rank in the top thirty firms but are involved in only one commodity: meat and dairy products, respectively. Except in these commodities, however, the trend has been for the largest firms to be diversified across many food sectors.

5. Alperts, *The Good Provider* (1973), p. 41. See also Derry and Williams, *A Short History of Technology from the Earliest Times to A.D. 1900* (1961), pp. 66–67.

6. Mintz, "Choice and Occasion" (1980).

7. John Heer, *World Events 1866–1966: The First Hundred Years of Nestlè* (Switzerland: Chateau de Glerolles-Rivaz, 1966), p. 43.

8. Horst, *At Home Abroad* (1974), especially p. 25.

9. *Food Engineering*, June 1988.

10. Horst, *At Home Abroad* (1974), 66; Buzzell and Nourse (1967), p. 94.

11. Buzzell and Nourse, *Production Innovation in Food Processing, 1954–1964* (1967).

12. *Wall Street Journal*, August 26, 1978.

13. Connor, *Competition and the Role of the Largest Firms in the U.S. Food and Tobacco Industries* (1979), p. 25.

14. Horst, *At Home Abroad* (1974), p. 115.

15. Ibid., p. 111.

16. Albrecht and Locker, eds., *CDE—Stock Ownership Directory: No. 2.* (1979), p. 23.

17. Lall, *Private Foreign Investment and the Transfer of Technology in Food Processing* (1977), p. 5.

18. Horst, *At Home Abroad* (1974), pp. 120–21.

19. Sepúlveda and Chumacero, *La inversión extranjera en México* (1973).

20. Ibid., appendix, tables 15 and 17.

21. Fajnzylber and Martínez Tarragó, *Las empresas transnacionales* (1976), pp. 348–49.

22. Newfarmer and Mueller, *Multinational Corporations in Brazil and Mexico* (1975), pp. 187–88.

23. Newfarmer and Mueller, *Multinational Corporations in Brazil and Mexico* (1975), p. 90.

24. Morrissy, *Agriculture Modernization through Production Contracting* (1974).

25. Albrecht and Locker, eds., *CDE—Stock Ownership Directory: No. 2* (1979), pp. 17, 24.

26. Williams and Miller, *Credit Systems for Small-Scale Farmers* (1973); also a confidential interview with a former manager with Heinz in Mexico.

27. Eames and Landis, *The Business of Feeding People* (1974).

28. Domike and Rodríguez, "Agroindustria en México" (1977); Horst, *At*

Home Abroad (1974); UN-CTC, *Transnational Corporations in Food and Beverage Processing* (1980).

29. Soberanis, *La regulación de las invenciones y marcas y de la transferencia de tecnología* (1979), pp. 22–25.

Chapter Eight. The Computer Industry and the Case of IBM

1. This case has been prepared from interviews in the United States and Mexico, supplemented by newspaper and magazine accounts of the negotiations between IBM and the Mexican government. The sections on the structure of the international computer industry are drawn from William H. Inmon's book *Technomics* (1986). The material on Mexico's early computer industry comes from a report prepared by Paulo Bastos Tigre for UNIDO entitled "The Mexican Professional Electronics Industry and Technology" (15 November 1983) and from "Mexican Small Computer Markets," written by Creative Strategies Research International (CSRI) (March 1983); both studies reflected the structure of the industry at the time Mexico was making its decision on IBM. Most of the press sources cited below are from an IBM press clipping book and are used to confirm points made in confidential interviews.

2. Inmon, *Technomics*, pp. 75–79.

3. Ibid., chap. 4.

4. Ibid., p. 140.

5. Bastos Tigre, "The Mexican Professional Electronics Industry" (1983), p. 13.

6. Steve Frazier, "Mexico Lures Personal-Computer Makers, but IBM Tries to Change Rules of the Game," *Wall Street Journal*, August 21, 1984, p. 33; and idem, "Mexican Small Computer Markets," ibid., pp. 69–81.

7. Bastos Tigre, "The Mexican Professional Electronics Industry" (1983), p. 31.

8. Grieco, "Between Dependency and Autonomy" (1979).

9. Bastos Tigre, "The Mexican Professional Electronics Industry" (1983), pp. 1–2.

10. Ibid.

11. Ibid.

12. CSRI, "Mexican Small Computer Markets" (1983), p. 41.

13. Alejandro Junco, "Computer-Hungry Mexicans vs. Power-Hungry Bureaucrats," *Wall Street Journal*, March 22, 1985, p. 25.

14. Frazier, "Mexico Lures Personal-Computer Makers," *Wall Street Journal*, August 21, 1984, p. 33.

15. Creative Strategies Research International reported in 1982 that a Radio Shack computer valued at $6,000 in the United States was selling for the equivalent of $20,000 in Mexico. They similarly reported a $3,000 Apple IIe selling for more than $10,000 in Mexico. See also Steve Frazier, "Mexico to Decide Soon on Whether to Allow Computer Venture 100%-Owned by IBM," *Wall Street Journal*, October 29, 1984, p. 37.

16. Junco, "Computer-Hungry Mexicans," *Wall Street Journal*, March 22, 1985, p. 25.

17. Frazier, "Mexico Lures Personal Computer Makers," *Wall Street Journal*, August 21, 1984, p. 33.

18. Bastos Tigre, "The Mexican Professional Electronics Industry," p. 39.

19. Ibid., p. 14.

20. See Lawrence Rout, "Mexico Puts Limits on U.S. Makers of Computers," *Wall Street Journal*, January 26, 1982, p. 31.

21. Evans, *Dependent Development* (1979); Evans, "The Brazilian Computer Case" (1985); Adler, *The Power of Ideology* (1987).

22. There appears to be a trend toward specific cooperation on data processing as well between Mexico, Brazil, Colombia, Uruguay, and Argentina.

23. It should be mentioned that it has been a long-standing policy of IBM to maintain complete ownership of their subsidiaries. IBM in fact has never given in on this issue. The firm maintains full ownership of its plant in the People's Republic of China.

24. Frazier, "Mexico Lures Personal Computer Makers," p. 61.

25. Rout, "Mexico Puts Limits on U.S. Makers of Computers," p. 31.

26. Junco, "Computer-Hungry Mexicans," p. 25. For political reasons, Argentina did not represent a credible alternative to Mexico, however.

Chapter Nine. The Automobile Industry

1. For a good overall discussion of the international auto industry see Douglas Bennett and Kenneth Sharpe, "The World Automobile Industry and Its Implications," in Newfarmer, ed., *Profits, Progress, and Poverty* (Notre Dame: University of Notre Dame, 1985).

2. Albert O. Hirschman discusses the forward and backward links of the auto industry in chapter 3 of *Rival Views of Market Society* (1986).

3. Bennett and Sharpe in Newfarmer, ed., *Profits, Progress, and Poverty* (1985), p. 193.

4. Robert B. Cohen calls this the fourth phase of developed-country investment in developing countries ("La reorganización internacional de la producción en la industria automotriz," *Trimestre Económico* 48 [2] [1981]).

5. The phrase *internationalization of production* refers to the shift to "global sourcing" of the labor-intensive components of a finished product. Under internationalization, components of a car or a computer can come from five or even ten countries.

6. Jenkins, *Dependent Industrialization in Latin America* (1977); Bennett and Sharpe, "Agenda Setting and Bargaining Power" (1979).

7. Bennett and Sharpe, "Agenda Setting and Bargaining Power" (1979), pp. 202–7.

8. Jenkins, *Dependent Industrialization in Latin America* (1977), p. 58.

9. Bennett and Sharpe, "Agenda Setting and Bargaining Power" (1979), pp. 218–20.

10. Bennett and Sharpe, *Transnational Corporations versus the State"* (1985), chap. 7, p. 17.

11. *Denationalization* refers to the purchase of locally owned firms by foreign investors. Production quotas, instituted soon after the 1962 decree, resulted in fewer denationalizations than occurred in Argentina or Brazil. *Dependent Industrialization in Latin America* (Jenkins, [1977], pp. 150–51).

12. At the time of this bargaining episode, four of the eight firms in the industry were wholly owned subsidiaries.

13. The drawbacks for Ford included displacement of home country production, smaller production capacities, and higher material costs.

14. See Bennett and Sharpe, *Transnational Corporations versus the State* (1985), chap. 8, pp. 7, 19.

15. Ibid., chap. 9, p. 1.

16. Ibid., p. 30.

17. Theodore Moran, *Multinational Corporations and the Politics of Dependence* (1974).

18. The firms involved were Ford, GM, Chrysler, Nissan, Volkswagen, DINA, and VAM. Also at this time oil and gas discoveries increased the attractiveness of investment in Mexico.

19. Bennett and Sharpe, *Transnational Corporations versus the State* (1985), chap. 10, pp. 22–25, 33–35, 38–39.

20. Confidential interviews, Dirección General de Inversiones Extranjeras.

21. Sources disagree on the exact figure. *Wall Street Journal*, September 16, 1983: 351,000. Ibid., January 11, 1984: 343,000. *Business Week*, March 18, 1985: 340,363. *Los Angeles Times*, December 3, 1983: 340,000.

22. *Los Angeles Times*, October 6, 1983.

23. Bennett and Sharpe, *Transnational Corporations versus the State* (1985), p. 273.

24. Ibid.

25. *Business Week*, March 18, 1985.

26. Bennett and Sharpe, *Transnational Corporations versus the State* (1985), pp. 238, 240–41, 274; *New York Times*, September 15, 1983.

27. Bennett and Sharpe, *Transnational Corporations versus the State* (1985), p. 349.

28. Ibid., p. 274.

29. *Business Week*, January 30, 1984.

30. Bennett and Sharpe, *Transnational Corporations versus the State* (1985), p. 274.

31. Ibid.

32. *New York Times*, September 15, 1983; Bennett and Sharpe, *Transnational Corporations versus the State* (1985), p. 204.

33. According to SECOFIN Minister Hernández Cervantes, the "industry was ill prepared for this (boom) in terms of capacity" (*New York Times*, September 15, 1983).

34. SECOFIN defined a "car type" as autos with the same drivetrain, front end, and chassis. The ministry defined models as variations in the body design (*Los Angeles Times*, October 6, 1983).

35. Bennett and Sharpe, *Transnational Corporations versus the State* (1985), p. 274; *New York Times*, September 15, 1983.

36. *New York Times*, September 15, 1983.

37. *Wall Street Journal*, September 16, 1983.

38. Bennett and Sharpe, *Transnational Corporations versus the State* (1985), p. 274; *Wall Street Journal*, September 16, 1983. As of yet I have not seen any information that suggests that these limits were only selectively implemented.

39. Bennett and Sharpe, *Transnational Corporations versus the State* (1985), p. 274; *Wall Street Journal*, September 16, 1983.

40. Bennett and Sharpe, *Transnational Corporations versus the State* (1985), p. 274.

41. *Wall Street Journal*, September 16, 1983.

42. *Wall Street Journal*, September 16, 1983. Some companies were better prepared than others for the reductions in the number of makes and models. When the policy was announced, Chrysler already produced only one line/make of cars (*New York Times*, September 15, 1983). Renault, on the other hand, produced three types (*Wall Street Journal*, September 16, 1983).

43. *New York Times*, September 15, 1983.

44. Ibid.

45. *Los Angeles Times*, October 6, 1983.

46. Bennett and Sharpe, *Transnational Corporations versus the State* (1985), p. 240.

47. *Business Week*, January 30, 1984.

48. Ibid., March 18, 1985.

49. *Wall Street Journal*, January 11, 1984; Bennett and Sharpe, *Transnational Corporations versus the State* (1985).

50. *Business Week*, January 30, 1984.

Chapter Ten. The Political Economy of Nationalism

1. Hirschman, *Shifting Involvements* (1982), pp. 70–74.

2. Ibid., pp. 71–72.

3. Krasner of course identified this trend with Third World preferences in *Structural Conflict* (1985).

4. Quotation from Vice-President for Latin America and Caribbean of the World Bank S. Shahid Husain, "Reviving Growth in Latin America," *Finance and Development*, June 1989, p. 4.

5. Dahlman and Sercovich, "Local Development and Exports of Technology" (1984).

6. Taiwan, Singapore, Hong Kong, and South Korea.

7. Foreign and domestically owned firms alike can profit from the tariff benefits that guide the Maquiladora Program. Although foreign firms get an automatic blanket exception to Mexicanization rules under the program, they do not have an exclusive opportunity to participate in the program, and Mexican business has grown along with foreign business as the program has expanded.

Bibliography

Adler, Emanuel. 1987. *The Power of Ideology: The Quest for Technological Autonomy in Argentina and Brazil*. Berkeley: University of California Press.

Aharoni, Yair. 1966. *The Foreign Investment Decision Process*. Boston: Division of Research, Harvard University Graduate School of Business Administration.

Albrecht, Stephen, and Michael Locker, eds. 1979. *CDE-Stock Ownership Directory: No. 2*. New York: Corporate Data Exchange.

Almond, Gabriel A. 1973. "Approaches to Developmental Causation." In *Crisis, Choice, and Change: Historical Studies of Political Development*, edited by Gabriel Almond, Scott C. Flanagan, and Robert J. Mundt. Boston: Little, Brown.

———. 1983. "Corporatism, Pluralism, and Professional Memory." *World Politics* 35 (1).

Almond, Gabriel A., and James Coleman, eds. 1960. *The Politics of Developing Areas*. Princeton: Princeton University Press.

Almond, Gabriel A., and G. Bingham Powell, Jr. 1966. *Comparative Politics: A Developmental Approach*. Boston: Little, Brown.

Alperts, Robert C. 1973. *The Good Provider: H. J. Heinz and His 57 Varieties*. Boston: Houghton Mifflin.

Alvarez Soberanis, Jaime. 1979. *La regulación de las invenciones y marcas y la transferencia de tecnología*. Mexico City: Editorial Porrua.

Amin, Samir. 1974. *Accumulation on a World Scale: A Critique of the Theory of Underdevelopment*. 2 vols. New York: Monthly Review Press.

ANADE (Asociación Nacional de Abogados de Empresas). 1973. *Inversión extranjera y transferencia de tecnología en México*. Mexico City: Editorial Tecnos.

Arriola, Carlos. 1976. "Los grupos empresariales frente al estado, 1973–75." *Foro Internacional* 16 (4): 336.

Aspe, Pedro, and Paul E. Sigmund. 1984. *The Political Economy of Income Distribution in Mexico*. Philadelphia: Holmes and Meier.

Baerresen, Donald W. 1973. *The Border Industrialization Program in Mexico*. Lexington, Mass.: D. C. Heath.

Bain, Joe S. 1968. *Industrial Organization*. New York: Wiley.

Baird, Peter, and Ed McCaughan. 1979. *Beyond the Border: Mexico and the U.S. Today*. New York: North American Congress on Latin America.

Barnet, R. S., and R. E. Müller. 1974. *Global Reach: The Power of Multinational Corporations*. New York: Simon and Schuster.

Bauer, Raymond, Ithiel de Sola Pool, and Lewis Anthony Dexter. 1963. *American Business and Public Policy*. New York: Atherton.

Becker, David. 1983. *The New Bourgeoisie and the Limits of Dependency: Mining, Class, and Power in "Revolutionary" Peru*. Princeton: Princeton University Press.

Bendix, Reinhard, et al. 1968. *State and Society: A Reader in Comparative Political Sociology*. Berkeley and Los Angeles: University of California Press.

Bennett, Douglas, and Kenneth Sharpe. 1979. "Agenda Setting and Bargaining Power: The Mexican State versus Transnational Automobile Corporations." *World Politics* 32 (1): 57–89.

———. 1980. "The State as Banker and Entrepreneur: The Last Resort Character of the Mexican State's Economic Intervention, 1917–1976." *Comparative Politics* 12 (2).

———. 1985. *Transnational Corporations versus the State: The Political Economy of the Mexican Auto Industry*. Princeton: Princeton University Press.

Bentley, Arthur. 1908. *The Process of Government: A Study of Social Pressures*. Chicago: University of Chicago Press.

Bergsten, C. Fred, Thomas Horst, and Theodore Moran. 1978. *American Multinationals and American Interests*. Washington, D.C.: Brookings Institution.

Bergsten, C. Fred, and Lawrence B. Krause, eds. 1975. *World Politics and International Economics*. Washington, D.C.: Brookings Institution.

Bernal Sahagún, Victor M. 1974. *Anatomía de la publicidad en México: Monopolios, enajenación y desperdicio*. Mexico City: Editorial Nuestro Tiempo.

———. 1976. *El impacto de las empresas multinacionales en el empleo y los ingresos: El caso de México*. WEP 2-28/WP 13. Geneva: International Labour Office.

Bernstein, Marvin D., ed. 1966. *Foreign Investment in Latin America: Cases and Attitudes*. New York: Alfred A. Knopf.

Biersteker, Thomas J. 1978. *Distortion or Development? Contending Perspectives on the Multinational Corporation*. Cambridge: MIT Press.

———. 1980. "The Illusion of State Power: Transnational Corporations and the Neutralization of Host-Country Legislation." *Journal of Peace Research* 27.

Bodenheimer, Susanne J. 1971. "Dependency and Imperialism: The Roots of Latin American Underdevelopment." In *Readings in U.S. Imperialism*, edited by K. T. Fann and D. C. Hodges. Boston: Porter Sargent.

Bonilla, Frank, and Robert Girling, eds. 1973. *Structures of Dependency*. East Palo Alto, Calif.: Nairobi.

Borah, Woodrow, and Sherbourne F. Cook. 1974. "Why Population Estimates Are Important in the Interpretation of Mexican History." In *Latin America: A Historical Reader*, edited by Lewis Hanke. Boston: Little, Brown.

Bunge, Mario Augusto. 1959. *Causality*. Cambridge: Harvard University Press.

Business International. 1978. *Mexico: New Look at a Maturing Market*. New York: Business International.

Business Latin America. New York.

Buzzell, Robert D., and Robert E. Nourse. 1967. *Production Innovation in Food Processing, 1954–1964*. Boston: Harvard University Graduate School of Business Administration.

Camp, Roderic A. 1977. *The Role of Economists in Policymaking: A Comparative Case Study of Mexico and the United States.* Tucson: University of Arizona Press.

―――. 1985. "The Political Technocrat in Mexico and the Survival of the Political System." *Latin American Research Review* 20 (1).

Camp, Roderic A., and Miguel Basáñez E. 1983. "The Nationalization of the Banks and Mexican Public Opinion." Unpublished manuscript.

Campillo Sáinz, José. 1976. "Fundamentación de la nueva ley de invenciones y marcas." *Comercio Exterior* 26 (8): 962–67.

Caporaso, James A., ed. 1978. *Dependence and Dependency in the Global System.* Special issue of *International Organization* 32 (1): 1–43.

Cárdenas, Lázaro. 1972. *Ideario político.* Mexico City: Ediciones Era.

Cardoso, Fernando Henrique. 1973. "Associated-Dependent Development: Theoretical and Practical Implications." In *Authoritarian Brazil: Origins, Policies, and Future,* edited by Alfred Stepan. New Haven: Yale University Press.

―――. 1977. "The Consumption of Dependency Theory in the United States." *Latin American Research Review* 12 (3): 7–24.

―――. 1979a. "The Characterization of Authoritarian Regimes." In *The New Authoritarianism in Latin America,* edited by David Collier. Princeton: Princeton University Press.

―――. 1979b. *El desarrollo en el banquillo.* DEE/D24/e. Mexico City: Instituto Latinoamericano de Estudios Transnacionales.

Cardoso, Fernando Henrique, and Enzo Faletto. 1979. *Dependency and Development in Latin America.* Translated by Marjory Mattingly Urquidi. Berkeley and Los Angeles: University of California Press. First published 1969.

Carnoy, Martin, 1984. *The State and Political Theory.* Princeton: Princeton University Press.

Casanova, Pablo González, 1966. "The Ideology of the United States concerning Foreign Investments." In *Foreign Investments in Latin America: Cases and Attitudes,* edited by Marvin D. Bernstein. New York: Alfred A. Knopf.

CEESP. 1971. *La legislación mexicana en materia de inversiones extranjeras.* 3d ed. Mexico City: Centro de Estudios Económicos del Sector Privado.

CEPAL/CET. 1978. "Tendencias y cambios en la inversión de las empresas internacionales." Working Paper no. 12. Santiago de Chile: Economic Commission on Latin America.

Chalmers, Douglas A. 1970. "Developing the Periphery: External Factors in Latin American Politics." In *Linkage Politics: Essays on the Convergence of National and International Systems,* edited by James Rosenau. New York: Free Press.

Chilcote, Ronald H., and Joel C. Edelstein, eds. 1974. *Latin America: The Struggle with Dependency and Beyond.* Cambridge, Mass.: Schenkman.

Cinta G., Ricardo. 1972a. "Burguesía nacional y desarrollo." In *El Pérfil de México en 1980,* edited by Martínez Ríos et al. Mexico City: Siglo XXI Editores.

———. 1972b. "El empresario industrial y el desarrollo ecónomico de México." Unpublished survey results of joint project of CEPAL (ECLA) and El Colegio de México.

Cline, William R. 1982–83. "Mexico's Crisis, the World's Peril." *Foreign Policy* 49:107–18.

Cockroft, James D., Andre Gunder Frank, and Dale L. Johnson. 1972. *Dependence and Underdevelopment: Latin America's Political Economy.* Garden City, N.Y.: Doubleday, Anchor Books. First published in Spanish, 1970.

Cohen, Robert B. 1981. "La reorganización internacional de la industria automotriz." *El Trimestre Económico* 48 (2).

Collier, David, and Ruth Berins Collier. 1977. "Who Does What, to Whom, and How: Toward a Comparative Analysis of Latin American Corporatism." In *Authoritarianism and Corporatism in Latin America*, edited by James M. Malloy. Pittsburgh: Pittsburgh University Press.

Collier, Ruth Berins, and David Collier. 1979. "Inducements versus Constraints: Disaggregating Corporatism." *American Political Science Review* 73 (4).

Collins, Randall. 1968. "A Comparative Approach to Political Sociology." In *State and Society: A Reader in Comparative Political Sociology*, edited by Reinhard Bendix. Boston: Little, Brown.

Comité Bilateral de Hombres de Negocios México-Estados Unidos—Sección Mexicana. 1971. *Inversiones extranjeras privadas directas en México.* Mexico City: Comité Bilateral de Hombres de Negocios México–Estados Unidos—Sección Mexicana.

Conference Board. 1980. *Mexico 1980*, by Joseph LaPalombara. New York: Conference Board.

Connor, John M. 1979. "Competition and the Role of the Largest Firms in the U.S. Food and Tobacco Industries." Economics, Statistics and Cooperatives Service of the USDA and the Food Systems Research Group of North Central Regional Project NC-117. Preliminary draft.

Connor, John M., and Willard F. Mueller. 1977. *Market Power and Profitability of Multinational Corporations in Brazil and Mexico.* Report prepared for the Subcommittee on Foreign Economic Policy of the Senate Committee on Foreign Relations. Washington, D.C.: U.S. Government Printing Office.

COPARMEX. 1971. *Franco diálogo entre gobierno y empresarios.* Mexico City: Confederación Patronal de la República Mexicana.

Cordero, Salvador, and Rafael Santín. 1977. *Los grupos industriales: Una nueva organización económica en México.* Mexico City: El Colegio de México, Cuadernos del CES #23.

Cornelius, Wayne, 1985. "The Political Economy of Mexico under De la Madrid." *Mexican Studies/Estudios Mexicanos.*

Dahl, Robert A. 1975. "Governments and Political Oppositions." In *Handbook of Political Science*, vol. 3, edited by F. Greenstein and N. Polsby. Reading, Mass.: Addison-Wesley.

Dahlman, Carl J., and Francisco C. Sercovich. 1984. "Local Development and Exports of Technology." World Bank Staff Working Paper no. 667. Washington, D.C.: World Bank.

De María y Campos, Mauricio. 1968. "Transferencia de tecnología, dependencia del exterior y desarrollo económico." Professional thesis, National Autonomous University of Mexico, Mexico City.

———. 1977. "La industria farmacéutica." *Comercio Exterior.*

DeRossi, Flavia. 1971. *The Mexican Entrepreneur.* Paris: Development Center of the Organization for Economic Cooperation and Development.

Derry, T. K., and Trevor I. Williams. 1961. *A Short History of Technology from the Earliest Times to A.D. 1900.* New York: Oxford University Press.

Deutsch, Karl W. 1961. "Social Mobilization and Political Development." *American Political Science Review* 55 (3): 493–514.

———. 1966a. *Nationalism and Social Communication: An Inquiry into the Foundations of Nationality.* Cambridge: MIT Press. First published 1953.

———. 1966b. *The Nerves of Government: Models of Political Communication and Control.* New York: Free Press. First published 1963.

———. 1967. "Nation and World." In *Contemporary Political Science: Toward Empirical Theory,* edited by Ithiel de Sola Pool. New York: McGraw-Hill.

———. 1974. "Imperialism and Neocolonialism." In *Testing Theories of Imperialism,* edited by Steven J. Rosen and James R. Kurth. Lexington, Mass.: D. C. Heath.

———. 1978. "Major Changes in Political Science, 1952–1977." *Político* 43 (2): 193–220.

Deutsch, Karl W., Bruno Fritsch, Helio Jaguaribe, and Andrei S. Markovits. 1977. *Problems of World Modeling: Political and Social Implications.* Cambridge, Mass.: Ballinger.

Dexter, Lewis Anthony. 1970. *Elite and Specialized Interviewing.* Evanston, Ill.: Northwestern University Press.

El Día. Mexico City.

Diario Oficial. Mexico City.

Díaz-Alejandro, Carlos F. 1975. "North-South Relations: The Economic Component." *International Organization* 29:214–41.

Dirección General de Inversiones Extranjeras y Transferencia de Tecnología, 1981–89. *Anuario estadístico.* Mexico City.

Domike, Arthur, and Gonzalo Rodríguez. 1977. "Agroindustria en México: Estructura de los sistemas y oportunidades para empresas capesinas." 2 vols. Unpublished manuscript. CIDE, Mexico City.

Domínguez, Jorge I. 1978. "Consensus and Divergence: The State of the Literature on Inter-American Relations in the 1970s." *Latin American Research Review* 13 (1): 87–126.

———, ed. 1980. "The Implications of Mexico's Internal Affairs for Its International Relations." Unpublished manuscript prepared for a conference sponsored by the U.S. Department at State of Harvard University Center for International Affairs.

Dos Santos, Theotonio. 1968. "The Changing Structure of Foreign Investments in Latin America." In *Latin America: Reform or Revolution?* edited by James Petras and Maurice Zeitlin. Greenwich, Conn.: Fawcett Publications.

———. 1970. "The Structure of Dependence." *American Economic Review* 60 (5): 231–46.

Eames, Alfred W., Jr., and Richard G. Landis. 1974. *The Business of Feeding People: The Story of Del Monte Corporation*. New York: Newcomen Society in North America.

Easton, David. 1952. *The Political System: An Inquiry into the State of Political Science*. New York: Knopf.

———. 1965. *A Systems Analysis of Political Life*. New York: John Wiley and Sons.

Eckstein, Susan. 1977. *The Poverty of Revolution: The State and the Urban Poor in Mexico*. Princeton: Princeton University Press.

ECLA/NAFINSA. 1971. *La política industrial en el desarrollo económico de Mexico*. Mexico City: Nacional Financiera.

Eisenstadt, S. N., ed. 1973. *Building States and Nations*. Beverly Hills: Sage Publications.

Elster, Jon. 1983. *Explaining Technical Change: A Case Study in the Philosophy of Science*. New York: Cambridge University Press.

Encarnation, Dennis J. 1989. *Dislodging Multinationals: India's Strategy in Comparative Perspective*. Ithaca: Cornell University Press.

Engels, Frederick. 1972. *The Origin of the Family, Private Property, and the State*. New York: International Publishers.

Erb, Guy F., and Valeriana Kallab, eds. 1975. *Beyond Dependency: The Developing World Speaks Out*. Washington, D.C.: Overseas Development Council.

Evans, Peter. 1985. "State, Capital, and the Transformation of Dependence: The Brazilian Computer Case." *Working Papers on Comparative Development*. Providence: Brown University Center for the Comparative Study of Development.

Evans, Peter B. 1971. "National Autonomy and Economic Development: Critical Perspectives on Multinational Corporations in Poor Countries." In *Transnational Relations and World Politics*, edited by Robert O. Keohane and Joseph S. Nye, Jr. Cambridge: Harvard University Press.

———. 1979. *Dependent Development: The Alliance of Multinational, State, and Local Capital in Brazil*. Princeton: Princeton University Press.

Evans, Peter, and Gary Gereffi. 1979. "Foreign Investment and Dependent Development: Comparing Brazil and Mexico." In *Brazil and Mexico: Pattern of Dependent Development*, edited by Sylvia Ann Hewlett and Richard S. Weinert. Philadelphia: Institute for the Study of Human Issues.

Excelsior. Mexico City.

Fagen, Richard R. 1977. "Studying Latin American Politics: Some Implications of a Dependency Approach." *Latin American Research Review* 12 (2): 3–26.

Fajnzylber, Fernando, and Trinidad Martínez Tarragó. 1976. *Las empresas transnacionales: Expansión a nivel mundial y proyección en la industria Mexicana*. Mexico City: Fondo de Cultura Económica.

Fishlow, Albert, et al. 1977. *Rich and Poor Nations in the World Economy*. New York: McGraw-Hill.

Fitzgerald, E. V. K. 1978. "The State and Capital Accumulation in Mexico." *Journal of Latin American Studies* 10 (2): 263–82.

Flamm, Kenneth. 1979. "Technology, Employment, and Direct Foreign Investment." Ph.D. dissertation, Massachusetts Institute of Technology.

FMME (Fund for Multinational Management Education) et al. 1978. *Public Policy and Technology Transfer: Viewpoints of U.S. Business.* New York: Council of the Americas.

Foley, John. 1972. *The Food Makers: A History of General Foods Ltd.* Banbury, Oxon, England: General Foods.

Frank, Andrew Gunder. 1969. *Latin America: Underdevelopment or Revolution.* New York: Monthly Review Press.

———. 1976. *Capitalism and Underdevelopment in Latin America: Historical Studies of Chile and Brazil.* New York: Monthly Review Press.

Furtado, Celso. 1970. *Economic Development of Latin America: Historical Background and Contemporary Problems.* 2d ed. Cambridge: Cambridge University Press.

Galbraith, John Kenneth. 1952. *American Capitalism: The Concept of Countervailing Power.* Boston: Houghton Mifflin.

García, Laurie Kassman. 1982. "Border Industries: Something for Everyone." *Comercio Exterior* 33 (2): 146–51.

Garza, Oscar Ramos. 1971. *México ante la inversión extranjera: Legislación, políticas, y prácticas.* 3d ed. Mexico City: Docal Editores.

Gereffi, Gary. 1983. *The Pharmaceutical Industry and Dependency in the Third World.* Princeton: Princeton University Press.

———. 1985. "The Global Pharmaceutical Industry and Its Impact on Latin America." In *Profits, Progress, and Poverty: Case Studies of International Industries in Latin America,* edited by Richard Newfarmer. Notre Dame: University of Notre Dame Press.

Gereffi, Gary, and Richard N. Newfarmer. 1985. "The State and International Oligopolies: Some Patterns of Response to Uneven Development in Latin America." In *Profits, Progress and Poverty: Case Studies of International Industries in Latin America,* edited by Richard Newfarmer. Notre Dame: University of Notre Dame Press.

Gerschenkron, Alexander. 1962. *Economic Backwardness in Historical Perspective.* Cambridge: Harvard University Press.

Gilpin, Robert, 1975. *U.S. Power and the Multinational Corporation.* New York: Basic Books.

Glade, William P., Jr. 1963. "Revolution and Economic Development: A Mexican Reprise." In *The Political Economy of Mexico,* by William P. Glade, Jr., and Charles W. Anderson. Madison: University of Wisconsin Press.

Gold, David A., Clarence Y. H. Lo, and Erik Olin Wright. 1975. "Recent Developments in Marxist Theories of the Capitalist State." *Monthly Review* 27 (October-November).

González Casanova, Pablo, and Enrique Florescano, eds. 1979. *México Hoy.* Mexico City: Siglo XXI Editores.

Goodman, Louis Wolf. 1980. "Horizons for Research on International Business in Developing Nations." *Latin American Research Review* 15 (2): 225–40.

Goulet, Denis. 1977. *The Uncertain Promise: Value Conflicts in Technology Trans-*

fer. New York: IDOC/North America, in cooperation with the Overseas Development Council.

Gourevitch, Peter. 1978. "The Second Image Reversed: International Sources of Domestic Politics." *International Organization* 32 (Autumn): 881–912.

Grieco, Joseph M. 1979. "Between Dependency and Autonomy: India's Experience with the International Computer Industry." *International Organization* 36 (1): 57–89.

Grindle, Merilee, ed. 1980. *Politics and Policy Implementation in the Third World.* Princeton: Princeton University Press.

Gusfield, Joseph R. 1967. "Tradition and Modernity: Misplaced Polarities in the Study of Social Change." *American Journal of Sociology* 72 (4): 351–62.

Haas, Ernst B. 1964. *Beyond the Nation-State: Functionalism and International Organization.* Stanford: Stanford University Press.

Halperin, Morton H. 1974. *Bureaucratic Politics and Foreign Policy.* Washington, D.C.: Brookings Institution.

Hamilton, Nora. 1982. *The Limits of State Autonomy: Post-Revolutionary Mexico.* Princeton: Princeton University Press.

Hansen, Roger D. 1974. *The Politics of Mexican Development.* Baltimore: Johns Hopkins University Press. First published 1971.

Heath, Shirley Brice. 1972. *Telling Tongues: Language Policy in Mexico: Colony to Nation.* New York: Teachers College Press, Columbia University.

Heer, John. 1966. *World Events 1866–1966: The First Hundred Years of Nestlè.* Switzerland: Chateau de Glerolles-Rivaz.

Helleiner, G. K. 1975. "Transnational Enterprises in the Manufacturing Sector of the Less Developed Countries." *World Development* 3 (9): 641–50.

Hernández, Jorge M. Aquirre. 1978. *Jurídica.*

Hernández Laos, Enrique, and Jorge Córdova Chavez. 1979. "Estructura de la distribución del ingreso en México." *Comercio Exterior* 29 (5): 505–20.

Hirschman, Albert O. 1968. "The Political Economy of Import Substitution Industrialization." *Quarterly Journal of Economics* 82:1–32.

———. 1971. *A Bias for Hope: Essays on Development and Latin America.* New Haven: Yale University Press.

———. 1978. "Beyond Asymmetry: Critical Notes on Myself as a Young Man and on Some Other Old Friends." *International Organization* 32 (1): 45–50.

———. 1982. *Shifting Involvements: Private Interests.* Princeton: Princeton University Press.

———. 1986. *Rival Views of Market Society.* New York: Viking.

Hollings, Crawford S. 1985. "Resilience and Stability in Ecological Systems." Annual Review of Ecology and Systematics 4, in Charles Muses *Destiny and Control in Human Systems.* Boston: Kluwer-Nijhoff.

Horst, Thomas. 1974. *At Home Abroad: American Corporations and the Food Industry.* Cambridge, Mass.: Ballinger.

Huntington, Samuel P. 1968. *Political Order in Changing Societies.* New Haven: Yale University Press.

——. 1971. "The Change to Change: Modernization, Development, Politics." *Comparative Politics* 3 (2): 283–322.

——. 1973. "Transnational Organizations in World Politics." *World Politics* 25 (3): 333–68.

Huntington, Samuel P., and Jorge F. Domínguez. 1975. "Political Development." In *Handbook of Political Science*, vol. 3, edited by F. Greenstein and N. Polsby. Reading, Mass.: Addison-Wesley.

Hymer, Stephen H. 1976. *The International Operations of National Firms: A Study of Direct Foreign Investment.* Cambridge: MIT Press.

Inmon, William H. 1986. *Technomics: The Economics of the Computer Industry.* Homewood, Ill.: Dow Jones Irwin.

International Bank of Reconstruction and Development (World Bank). 1953. *The Economic Development of Mexico: Report of the Combined Mexican Working Party*, by Raul Ortiz Mena, Victor L. Urquidi, Albert Waterston, and Jonal H. Haralz. Baltimore: Johns Hopkins University Press.

——. *World Development Report.* Various annual editions.

Jaguaribe, Helio, et al. 1969. *La dependencia político-económica de América Latina.* Mexico City: Siglo XXI Editores.

James, Dilmus D. 1978. "Bibliographía sobra política científica y tecnológica en América Latina." *Comercio Exterior* 28 (12): 1477–93. (First published in *Latin American Research Review* 12 [1977]: 71–101.)

James, Jeffrey, and Stephen Lister. 1980. "Galbraith Revisited: Advertising in Non-Affluent Societies." *World Development* 8:87–96.

Jenkins, Rhys O. 1977. *Dependent Industrialization in Latin America: The Automotive Industry in Argentina, Chile, and Mexico.* Praeger Special Studies in International Economics and Development. New York: Praeger.

Johnson, Harry G. 1967. *Economic Nationalism in Old and New States.* Chicago: University of Chicago Press.

Kahl, Joseph A. 1968. *The Measurement of Modernism: A Study of Values in Brazil and Mexico.* Austin: University of Texas Press for the Institute of Latin American Studies.

Karst, Kenneth L., and Keith S. Rosenn. 1975. *Law and Development in Latin America: A Case Book.* Berkeley and Los Angeles: University of California Press.

Katz, Jorge M. 1976. *Importación de tecnología, aprendizaje, e industrialización dependiente.* Mexico City: Fondo de Cultura Económica.

Katzenstein, Peter J. 1978. "Introduction: Domestic and International Forces and Strategies of Foreign Economic Policy" and "Conclusion: Domestic Structures and Strategies of Foreign Economic Policy." In *Between Power and Plenty: Foreign Economic Policies of Advanced Industrial States*, edited by Peter J. Katzenstein. Madison: University of Wisconsin Press.

Kaufman, Robert R. 1979. "Industrial Change and Authoritarian Rule." In *The New Authoritarianism in Latin America*, edited by David Collier. Princeton: Princeton University Press.

——. 1988. *The Politics of Debt in Argentina, Brazil and Mexico: Economic Stabilization in the 1980s.* Berkeley: Institute of International Studies, University of California, Berkeley.

Keohane, Robert O., and Joseph S. Nye, Jr. 1977. *Power and Interdependence: World Politics in Transition*. Boston: Little, Brown.

———. 1987. "Power and Interdependence Revisited." *International Organization* 41 (4): 725–53.

———, eds. 1971. *Transnational Relations and World Politics*. Cambridge: Harvard University Press.

King, Timothy. 1970. *Mexico: Industrialization and Trade Policies since 1940*. New York: Oxford University Press.

Klapp, Merrie G. 1982. "The State: Landlord or Entrepreneur?" *International Organization* 36 (3): 575–608.

Knickerbocker, Frederick T. 1973. *Oligopolistic Reaction and Multinational Enterprise*. Boston: Harvard University Graduate School of Business Administration, Division of Research.

Kobrin, Stephen J. 1987. "Testing the Bargaining Hypothesis." *International Organization* 41 (4): 609–38.

Kojima, Kiyoshi, and Miguel S. Wionczek. 1975. *Technology Transfer in Pacific Economic Development*. Japan Economic Research Center Paper no. 25. Tokyo.

Krasner, Stephen. 1978. *Defending the National Interest*. Princeton: Princeton University Press.

———. 1984. "Approaches to the State: Alternative Conceptions and Historical Dynamics." *Comparative Politics* 16 (2): 243–44.

———. 1985. *Structural Conflict: The Third World against Global Liberalism*. Princeton: Princeton University Press.

Kronish, Rich. 1984. "Latin America and the World Motor Vehicle Industry Turn to Exports." In *The Political Economy of the Latin American Motor Vehicles Industry*, edited by Rich Kronish and Kenneth Mericle. Cambridge: MIT Press.

Kronish, Rich, and Kenneth Mericle, eds. 1984. *The Political Economy of the Latin American Motor Vehicles Industry*. Cambridge: MIT Press.

Kuhn, Thomas S. 1970. *The Structure of Scientific Revolutions*. 2d and enl. ed. Chicago: University of Chicago Press.

Ladas, Stephen P. 1975. *Patents, Trademarks, and Related Rights: National and International Protection*. 3 vols. Rev. ed. Cambridge: Harvard University Press.

Lall, Sanjaya. 1975. "Is 'Dependence' a Useful Concept in Analyzing Underdevelopment?" *World Development* 3 (11–12): 799–810.

———. 1977. "Private Foreign Investment and the Transfer of Technology in Food Processing." Manuscript prepared for Technology and Employment Branch, International Labour Office, Geneva.

LaPalombara, Joseph, and Stephen Blank. 1976. *Multinational Corporations and National Elites: A Study in Tensions*. New York: Conference Board.

Lerdo de Tejada, Francisco. 1977. *El Botín del Tigre*. Mexico City: Editorial Jus.

Levy, Dan. 1979. "University Autonomy in Mexico: Implications for Regime Autonomy." *Latin American Research Review* 14 (3).

Linz, Juan J. 1975. "Totalitarian and Authoritarian Regimes." In *Handbook of Political Science*, vol. 3, edited by F. Greenstein and N. Polsby. Reading, Mass.: Addison-Wesley.

Lipson, Charles H. 1976. "Corporate Preferences and Public Policies: Foreign Aid Sanctions and Investment Protection." *World Politics* 28 (April).

Los Angeles Times. "Survey of Mexico City Residents Conducted May 17–19, 1979."

Lowenthal, Abraham F. 1974. " 'Liberal,' 'Radical,' and 'Bureaucratic' Perspectives on U.S.-Latin American Policy: The Alliance for Progress in Retrospect." In *Latin America and the United States: The Changing Political Realities*, edited by Julio Cotler and Richard R. Fagen. Stanford: Stanford University Press.

Lukes, Steven. 1974. *Power: A Radical View*. London: Macmillan.

Malloy, James M. 1985. "Politics, Fiscal Crisis, and Social Security Reform in Brazil." *Latin American Issues* 2 (1).

———, ed. 1971. *Authoritarianism and Corporatism in Latin America*. Pittsburgh: University of Pittsburgh Press.

Marighela, Carlos. 1971. *For the Liberation of Brazil*. London: Penguin Books.

Martínez del Campo, Manuel. 1983. "Ventajas e inconvenientes de la actividad maquiladora en México: Algunos aspectos de la subcontractación international." *Comercio Exterior* 33 (2): 146–51.

May, Herbert K., and Jose Antonio Fernández-Arena. 1971. *Impact of Foreign Investment in Mexico*. Washington, D.C.: National Chamber Foundation published jointly with the Council of the Americas.

Meagher, Robert F. 1979. *An International Redistribution of Wealth and Power: A Study of the Charter of Economic Rights and Duties of States*. New York: Pergamon Press.

El Mercado de Valores. Mexico City.

Mexico Report.

Meyer, Lorenzo. 1972. *México y los Estados Unidos en el Conflicto Petrolero (1917–1942)*. Mexico: El Colegio de México.

———. 1977. "The Historical Roots of the Authoritarian State in Mexico." In *Authoritarianism in Mexico*, edited by José Luis Reyna and Richard S. Weinert. Philadelphia: Institute for the Study of Human Issues Press.

Meyer, Michael C., and William L. Sherman. 1979. *The Course of Mexican History*. New York: Oxford University Press.

Michalet, Charles-Albert. 1976. *The Multinational Companies and the New International Division of Labor*. Working Paper WEP2-28/WP 5. Geneva: International Labour Office.

Middlebrook, Kevin J. 1986. "Political Liberalization in an Authoritarian Regime: The Case of Mexico." In *Transitions from Authoritarian Rule*, edited by G. O'Donnell, P. C. Schmitter, and L. Whitehead. Baltimore: Johns Hopkins University Press.

Mintz, Sidney W. 1980. "Choice and Occasion: Sweet Moments." Paper prepared for the symposium "Psychobiology of Human Food Selection." Baylor University Medical Center, March 27–28.

Moran, Theodore H. 1974. *Multinational Corporations and the Politics of Dependence: Copper in Chile*. Princeton: Princeton University Press.

————. 1978. "Multinational Corporations and Dependency: A Dialogue for 'dependentistas' and non-'dependentistas.' " *International Organization* 32 (1): 79–100.

Morgan Guaranty Trust Company. 1988. "World Financial Markets."

Morrissy, J. David. 1974. *Agriculture Modernization through Production Contracting: The Role of the Fruit and Vegetable Processor in Mexico and Central America.* New York: Frederick A. Praeger.

Mytelka, Lynn. 1979. *Regional Development in a Global Economy.* New Haven: Yale University Press.

Nadal Egea, Alejandro. 1977. *Instrumentos de política científica y tecnológica en México.* Mexico City: El Colegio de México.

NAFINSA (Nacional Financiera, S.A.). 1977. *Statistics on the Mexican Economy 1977.* Mexico City: NAFINSA.

————. 1981. La economía Mexicana en cifras. Mexico City: NAFINSA.

NAFINSA (Nacional Financiera, S.A.) and CEPAL (Comisión Económica para América Latina). 1971. *La política industrial en el desarrollo económico de México.* Mexico City: NAFINSA.

National Academy of Sciences. 1978. *Technology, Trade, and the U.S. Economy.* Washington, D.C.

Navarrete, Jorge Eduardo. 1971. *México: La política económica del nuevo gobierno.* Mexico City: Banco Nacional del Comercio Exterior.

Nettl, J. P. 1968. "The State as a Conceptual Variable." *World Politics* 20 (July): 559–92.

Newfarmer, Richard, ed. 1985. *Profits, Progress and Poverty: Case Studies of International Industries in Latin America.* Notre Dame: University of Notre Dame Press.

Newfarmer, Richard, and Willard F. Mueller. 1975. *Multinational Corporations in Brazil and Mexico: Structural Sources of Economic and Non-economic Power.* Report to the Subcommittee on Multinational Corporations, Senate Committee on Foreign Relations. Washington, D.C.: U.S. Government Printing Office.

New York Times.

Nordlinger, Eric C. 1981. *On the Autonomy of the Democratic State.* Cambridge: Harvard University Press.

Nye, Joseph S., Jr. 1974. "Multinational Corporations in World Politics." *Foreign Affairs* 53 (4): 153–75.

O'Donnell, Guillermo A., and Delfina Linck. 1973. *Dependencia y Autonomía: Formas de Dependencia y Estrategias de Liberación.* Buenos Aires: Amorrutu Editores.

O'Donnell, Guillermo A., Philippe C. Schmitter, and Lawrence Whitehead, eds. 1986. *Transitions from Authoritarian Rule.* Baltimore: Johns Hopkins University Press.

OECD (Organization for Economic Cooperation and Development). 1979. *Impact of Multinational Enterprises on National Scientific and Technical Capacities: Food Industry.* DSTI/SRI/79.23-MNE. Paris: OECD, Directorate for Science, Technology, and Industry, Ad Hoc Policy Group on Multinational Enterprises.

Olson, Mancur. 1965. *The Logic of Collective Action: Public Goods and the Theory of Groups.* Cambridge: Harvard University Press.

Organization of American States, Permanent Council. 1976. *A Comparative Study of Latin American Legislation on the Regulation and Control of Private Foreign Investment.* Document OEA/Ser. G//CP/INF.680/75/3 November 1975. Washington, D.C.: OAS.

Packenham, Robert. 1976. "Trends in Brazilian National Dependency since 1964." In *Brazil in the Seventies,* edited by Riordan Roett. Washington, D.C.: American Enterprise Institute for Public Policy Research.

————. 1982. "Plus ça change . . .: The English Edition of Cardoso and Faletto's Dependencia y desarrollo en América Latina." *Latin American Research Review* 17 (1): 131–51.

Palloix, Christian. 1973. Les firmes multinationales et le proces d'internationalisation. Paris: François Maspero.

Parsons, Talcott. 1951. *The Social System.* Glencoe, Ill.: Free Press.

Pellicer de Brody, Olga. 1974. "Mexico in the 1970s and Its Relations with the United States." In *Latin America and the United States: The Changing Political Realities.* Stanford: Stanford University Press.

Polanyi, Karl. 1966. *The Great Transformation.* Boston: Beacon Press. First published 1944.

Purcell, Susan Kaufman. 1975. *The Mexican Profit-Sharing Decision: Politics in an Authoritarian Regime.* Berkeley and Los Angeles: University of California Press.

Purcell, Susan Kaufman, and John F. H. Purcell. 1980. "State and Society in Mexico: Must a Stable Policy Be Institutionalized?" *World Politics* 32 (2): 194–227.

Ramos Garza, Oscar. 1974. *México ante la inversión extranjera legislación, políticas, y prácticas.* 3d ed. Mexico City: Docal Editores.

Reynolds, Clark W. 1970. *The Mexican Economy: Twentieth Century Structure and Growth.* New Haven: Yale University Press.

Robinson, Harry J., and Timothy A. Smith. 1976. *The Impact of Foreign Private Investment on the Mexican Economy.* Menlo Park, Calif.: Stanford Research Institute (SRI).

Ronfeldt, David F. 1976. "The Mexican Army and Political Order since 1940." In *Armies and Politics in Latin America,* edited by Abraham F. Lowenthal. New York: Holmes and Meier.

————. 1985. "The Modern Mexican Military: Implications for Mexico's Stability and Security." Rand Note N-228-ff/rc.

Rosen, Steven J., and James R. Kurth, eds. 1974. *Testing Theories of Economic Imperialism.* Lexington, Mass.: D. C. Heath.

Rueschemeyer, Dietrich, and Peter Evans. 1985. "The State and Economic Transformation: Toward an Analysis of the Conditions Underlying Effective Intervention." In *Bringing the State Back In,* edited by Peter Evans, Theda Skocpol, and Dietrich Rueschemeyer. Cambridge: Cambridge University Press.

Sábato, Jorge A. 1971. *Ciencia, tecnología, desarrollo y dependencia.* Tucuman, Argentina: Universidad San Miguel de Tucuman.

———. 1976. "El cambio tecnológico necesario y posible en América Latina." *Comercio Exterior* 26 (5): 541–54.

———. 1978. *Transferencia de tecnología: Una selección bibliográfica.* Mexico City: CEESTEM.

Sanderson, Steven E. 1983. "Presidential Succession and Political Rationality in Mexico." *World Politics* 35 (3): 318.

Sauvant, Karl P., and Farid G. Lavipour, eds. 1976. *Controlling Multinational Enterprises: Problems, Strategies, Counterstrategies.* Boulder, Colo.: Westview Press.

Scherer, F. M. 1970. (Rev. ed., 1980.) *Industrial Market Structure and Economic Performance.* Chicago: Rand McNally.

Schmidt, Henry C. 1985. "The Mexican Foreign Debt and the Sexennial Transition from López Portillo to De la Madrid." *Mexican Studies/Estudios Mexicanos* 1 (2): 254.

Schmitter, Philippe C. 1974. "Still the Century of Corporatism?" *Review of Politics* 1 (36): 85–121. (Also published in *The New Corporatism: Sociopolitical Structures in the Iberian World,* edited by Frederick B. Pike and Thomas Stritch. Notre Dame: University of Notre Dame Press, 1974.)

———. 1977. "Modes of Interest Intermediation and Models of Societal Change in Western Europe." *Comparative Political Studies* 10:7–38.

Senghaas, Dieter. 1975. "Multinational Corporations and the Third World: On the Problem of the Further Integration of Peripheries into the Given Structure of the International Economic System." *Journal of Peace Research* 12 (4).

Sepúlveda, Bernardo, and Antonio Chumacero. 1973. *La inversión extranjera en México.* Mexico City: Fondo de Cultura Económica.

Servan-Schreiber, Jean Jacques. 1969. *The American Challenge.* New York: Atheneum, Avon Books.

Shafer, Michael. 1983. "Capturing the Mineral Multilaterals: Advantage or Disadvantage?" *International Organization* 37 (1): 93–120.

Shafer, Robert Jones. 1973. *Mexican Business Organizations: History and Analysis.* Syracuse: Syracuse University Press.

Shea, Donald R. 1955. *The Calvo Clause: A Problem of Inter-American and International Law and Diplomacy.* Minneapolis: University of Minnesota Press.

Simon, Herbert A. 1982. "Rationality." In *Models of Bounded Rationality: Behavioral Economics and Business Organization.* Cambridge: MIT Press.

Siqueiros, José Luis. 1975. *La regulación jurídica de las empresas transnacionales.* Mexico City: private printing.

Smith, Peter. 1977. "Does Mexico Have the Power Elite?" In *Authoritarianism in Mexico,* edited by José Luis Reyna and Richard Weinert. Philadelphia: Institute for the Study of Human Issues.

———. 1979. *Labyrinths of Power: Political Recruitment in Twentieth-Century Mexico.* Princeton: Princeton University Press.

Smith, Robert Freeman. 1972. *The United States and Revolutionary Nationalism in Mexico, 1916–1932.* Chicago: University of Chicago Press.

Smith, Tony. 1979. "The Underdevelopment of Development Literature: The Case of Dependency Theory." *World Politics* 31 (2): 2147–388.

Soberanis, Jaime Alvarez. 1979. *La regulación de las invenciones y marcas y de la transferencia de tecnología*. Mexico City: Editora Porrua.

El Sol de México. Mexico City.

Solis, Leopoldo. 1970. *La realidad económica mexicana: Retrovisión y perspectivas*. Mexico City: Siglo XXI Editores.

Spengler, Oswald. 1945. *The Decline of the West*. 2 vols. Translated with notes by Charles Francis Atkinson. New York: Alfred A. Knopf.

Stallings, Barbara. 1987. *Banker to the World: U.S Portfolio Investment in Latin America, 1900–1986*. Berkeley and Los Angeles: University of California Press.

Stavenhagen, Rodolfo. 1976. "Reflexiones sobre el proceso político actual." *Nueva Política* 1 (2).

Steinbruner, John. 1974. *The Cybernetic Theory of Decision: New Dimensions of Political Analysis*. Princeton: Princeton University Press.

Stepan, Alfred. 1978. *The State and Society: Peru in Comparative Perspective*. Princeton: Princeton University Press.

Stevens, Evelyn P. 1974. *Protest and Response in Mexico*. Cambridge: MIT Press.

Street, James H., and Dilmus D. James, eds. 1979. *Technological Progress in Latin America: The Prospects for Overcoming Dependency*. Boulder, Colo.: Westview Press.

Sunkel, Osvaldo. 1972. "Big Business and 'Dependencia': A Latin American View." *Foreign Affairs* 50 (3).

Survey of Current Business.

Tancer, Robert S. 1977. "Regulating Foreign Investment in the Seventies: The Mexican Approach." In *The Future of Mexico*, edited by Lawrence E. Loselow. Tempe: Arizona State University.

Tilly, Charles B. 1975. "Western State-Making and Theories of Political Transformation." In *The Formation of National States in Western Europe*, edited by Charles B. Tilly. Princeton: Princeton University Press.

Toulmin, Stephen Edelston. 1972. *Human Understanding*. Princeton: Princeton University Press.

Trejo Delarbre, Raul. 1979. "El movimiento obrero: Situación y perspectivas." In *México Hoy*, edited by P. González Casanova and Enrique Florescano. Mexico City: Siglo XXI Editores.

Truman, David B. 1951. *The Governmental Process: Political Interests and Public Opinion*. New York: Alfred A. Knopf.

Tugwell, Franklin. 1975. *The Politics of Oil in Venezuela*. Stanford: Stanford University Press.

UC-CTC. 1980. *Transnational Corporations in Food and Beverage Production*. New York: United Nations.

UNCTAD. 1975a. "Major Issues Arising from the Transfer of Technology to Developing Countries." New York: United Nations.

———. 1975b. "Report of the Intergovernmental Group of Experts on a Code of Conduct on Transfer of Technology." New York: United Nations.

———. 1975c. "The Role of the Patent System in the Transfer of Technology to Developing Countries." New York: United Nations.

———. 1979. "The Role of Trademarks in Developing Countries." New York: United Nations.

———. 1985. *The Capital Goods Sector in Developing Countries: Technology Issues and Policy Options.* Study by the UNCTAD Secretariat. New York: United Nations.

UNIDO (United Nations Industrial Development Organization). 1977. *Draft World-Wide Study on Agroindustries, 1975–2000.* UNIDO/ICIS.65. A sectoral study prepared by the International Center for Industrial Studies. Vienna: UNIDO.

United Nations. 1969. *Industrialization of Developing Countries: Problems and Prospects of the Food Processing Industry.* ST/CTC/19. New York: United Nations.

———. 1973. *Multinational Corporations in World Development.* United Nations Publications, Sales no. E.73.II.A.11. New York: United Nations.

United Nations Center on Transnational Corporations (UN-CTC). 1980. *Transnational Corporations in Food and Beverage Processing.* ST/CTC/19. New York: United Nations.

United Nations Department of Development and International Economic Cooperation. 1982. "Towards the New International Economic Order: Analytic Report on Developments in the Field of International Economic Cooperation since the Sixth Special Session of the General Assembly." New York: United Nations.

United Nations Department of Economic and Social Affairs. 1972. "Transfer of Operative Technology at the Enterprise Level." New York: United Nations.

United Nations, Economic and Social Council. Commission on Transnational Corporations. 1978. *Transnational Corporations in World Development: A Re-Examination.* E/C.10/38. New York: United Nations.

United Nations Statistical Office, Department of Economic and Social Affairs. 1971. *Statistical Yearbook.* New York: United Nations.

———. 1981. *Statistical Yearbook.* New York: United Nations.

Urquidi, Victor L. 1964. *The Challenge of Development in Latin America.* Translated by Marjorie M. Urquidi. New York: Frederick A. Praeger.

U.S. Congress. Senate. Committee on Finance. 1973. *Multinational Corporations: A Compendium of Papers.* Washington, D.C.: U.S. Government Printing Office.

Vaitsos, Constantine. 1974. *Intercountry Income Distribution and Transnational Enterprises.* Oxford: Clarendon Press.

———. 1975. "Power, Knowledge, and Development Policy." In *A World Divided,* edited by G. K. Helleiner. Cambridge University Press.

Vernon, Raymond. 1963. *The Dilemma of Mexico's Development: The Roles of the Private and Public Sectors.* Cambridge: Harvard University Press.

———. 1971. *Sovereignty at Bay: The Multinational Spread of U.S. Enterprises.* New York: Basic Books.

———. 1972. *The Economic and Political Consequences of Multinational Enterprise: An Anthology.* Boston: Harvard University Graduate School of Business Administration, Division of Research.

———. 1977. *Storm over the Multinationals: The Real Issues.* Cambridge: Harvard

University Press.

———. 1981. "Sovereignty at Bay: Ten Years After." *International Organization* 35 (3): 517–29.

———, ed. 1964. *Public Policy and Private Enterprise in Mexico.* Cambridge: Harvard University Press.

Villarreal, René. 1977. "The Policy of Import-Substituting Industrialization, 1929–1975." In *Authoritarianism in Mexico,* edited by José Luis Reyna and Richard S. Weinert. Philadelphia: Institute for the Study of Human Issues Press.

Von Bertalanfly, Ludwig. 1968. *General Systems Theory: Foundations, Development, Applications.* Rev. ed. New York: George Braziller.

von Bertrab, Herman. 1968. "The Transfer of Technology: A Case Study of European Private Enterprises Having Operations in Latin America, with Special Emphasis on Mexico." Ph.D. dissertation, University of Texas.

Von Wright, G. H. 1971. *Explanation and Understanding.* Ithaca: Cornell University Press.

Wall Street Journal, various issues.

Wallace, Don, Jr. 1976. *International Regulation of Multinational Corporations.* New York: Praeger.

Wallerstein, Immanuel. 1974. "The Rise and Future Demise of the World Capitalist System: Concepts for Comparative Analysis." *Comparative Studies in Society and History* 16 (4): 387–415.

Weber, Max. 1946. *From Max Weber: Essays in Sociology.* Translated and edited by H. H. Gerth and C. W. Mills. New York: Oxford University Press.

———. 1978. *Economy and Society.* 2 vols. Edited by Guenther Roth and Claus Wittich. Berkeley and Los Angeles: University of California Press. (First published in hardcover, New York, 1968.)

Weinert, Richard S. 1977. "The State and Foreign Capital." In *Authoritarianism in Mexico,* edited by José Luis Reyna and Richard S. Weinert. Philadelphia: Institute for the Study of Human Issues Press.

Weissberg, Miriam. 1980. "La cooperación científica y tecnológica internacional en México: Un intento de evaluación." *Ciencia y Desarrollo* 6 (33): 76–108.

Whiting, Van R., Jr. 1979. "Politics and the Regulation of Transnational Enterprises in Mexico." Paper presented at the World Congress of the International Political Science Association, Moscow.

———. 1981. "Transnational Enterprise and the State in Mexico." Ph.D. dissertation, Harvard University.

———. 1982. *Proceedings, Workshop on Mexico's Border Industrialization Program.* Berkeley: University of California Center for Latin American Studies.

———. 1983. "The Politics of Technology Transfer in Mexico." Program in U.S.-Mexican Studies, Research Report no. 37. La Jolla: University of California, San Diego.

———. 1985. "The International Food Processing Industry." In *Profits, Progress and Poverty: Case Studies of International Industries in Latin America,* edited by Richard N. Newfarmer. Notre Dame: University of Notre Dame Press.

Wilkins, Mira. 1970. *The Emergence of Multinational Enterprise: American Business*

Abroad from the Colonial Era to 1914. Cambridge: Harvard University Press.
————. 1974. *The Maturing of Multinational Enterprise: American Business Abroad from 1914 to 1970.* Cambridge: Harvard University Press.

Williams, Simon, and James A. Miller. 1973. *Credit Systems for Small-Scale Farmers: Case Histories from Mexico.* Austin: University of Texas at Austin.

Williamson, Robert B., William P. Glade, Jr., and Karl M. Schmitt, eds. 1974. *Latin American-U.S. Economic Interactions.* Washington: American Enterprise Institute for Public Policy Interactions.

Wionczek, Miguel S. 1964. "Electric Power: The Uneasy Partnership." In *Public Policy and Private Enterprise in Mexico,* edited by Raymond Vernon. Cambridge: Harvard University Press.

————. 1967. *El nacionalismo mexicano y la inversión extranjera.* Mexico: Siglo XXI Editores.

————. 1968. *Disposiciones para la transmisión de tecnología práctica a los paises en desarrollo: Estudio de México.* United Nations Economic and Social Council (ECOSOC) Doc. E/4452/Add.3. New York: United Nations.

————. 1971a. "Foreign-Owned Export-Oriented Enclaves in a Rapidly Industrializing Economy: Sulphur Mining in Mexico." *Foreign Investment in the Petroleum and Mineral Industries: Case Studies of Investor-Host Country Relations.* Project directed by Raymond Mikesell. Baltimore: Johns Hopkins Press.

————. 1971b. "Mexican Nationalism, Foreign Private Investment, and the Problems of Technology Transfer." In *Private Foreign Investment and the Developing World,* edited by Peter Ady. New York: Praeger.

————. 1986. "Industrialización, capital extranjero, y transferencia de tecnología: La experiencia mexicana, 1930–1985." *Foro Internacional* 104 (April–June).

————, ed. 1971c. *Crecimiento o desarrollo económico? Presente y futuro de la sociedad mexicana.* Mexico City: SepSetentas.

————, ed. 1973. *Comercio de tecnología y subdesarrollo económico.* Mexico City: National Autonomous University of Mexico, Coordinación de Ciencias.

————, ed. 1975. *Política tecnológica y desarrollo socioeconómico.* Cuestiones Internacionales Contemporaneas, no. 7. Mexico City: Secretaria de Relaciones Exteriores.

Wionczek, Miguel, Gerardo M. Bueno, and Jorge Eduardo Navarrete. 1974. *La transferencia internacional de tecnología: El caso de México.* Mexico City: Fondo de Cultura Económica.

Womack, John, Jr. 1978. "The Mexican Economy during the Revolution, 1910–1920: Historiography and Analysis." *Marxist Perspectives* 4 (Winter): 80–123.

World Bank. 1979. "Statistical Appendix to Report No. 2307-ME." Washington, D.C.: World Bank.

————. 1989. "Reviving Growth in Latin America," by S. Shahid Husain. *Finance and Development* (June).

World Intellectual Property Organization (WIPO). 1977. *World Intellectual Property Organization: General Information.* Geneva: WIPO.

Wright, Harry K. 1971. *Foreign Enterprise in Mexico: Laws and Policies.* Chapel Hill: University of North Carolina Press.

Index

Acquisitions, 273 n.3; in food industry, 180, 184; of Mexican manufacturing firms, 81–86
Administrative reform, 268 n.47
Aguilar, Enrique, 151
Akers, John, from IBM, 209
Alemán, Miguel, 272 n.34; industrial policy under, 72
Almond, Gabriel A., 263 n.37; on political systems, 13
American and Foreign Power Company, expropriation of, 74–75
Amparo (legal relief suits), 272 n.44; against Emergency Decree of 1944, 76
Apple Computer, in Mexico, 200
Apprenticeship strategy, 238
Apter, David, 263 n.37
Arteloitia, Eusebio, 131
Article 27, of the Mexican Constitution, 74, 243
Authoritarian regime: Linz's definition, 35; in Mexico, 36
Authority: institutionalization of, 39; of the state, 267 n.35
Automobile industry, 98; competition in, 214; dominance of U.S., 214; structure of, 211
Automobile industry in Mexico: "austere" cars, 222; balance of payments and trade, 215, 223; CKD kits, 212; decree of 1983, 221; economies of scale, 213, 231; export promotion, 215–17, 222; jobs in, 211; Manufacturing Decree of 1962, 75; merger plan, 215–16; "oligopolistic reaction," 213; policy proposals, 212–13, 224; sales, 220–21; structure, 212, 221, 224; trademarks in, 219
Autonomy, 280 n.16; Nordlinger's typology, 38
Avila Camacho, Manuel, regulations under, 71

Bain, Joe, on industrial organization, 169
Balance of payments, 274 nn.11, 17; in auto industry, 215; composition of outflows, 105; deficit in, 81, 87. *See also* Remittances
Banking and insurance, control of, 78
Bank of Mexico: and tax reform, 163; founded, 41
Bargaining, 21, 57; over food exports, 186; over "goodwill," 134; power, balance of, 18. *See also* Obsolescing bargain
Barriers to entry, in food industry, 179
Bastos Tigre, Paulo, 283 n.1
Bearer shares, elimination of, 159, 162
Becker, David, 262 n.26
Bennett, Douglas, 42, 144, 214; on "embedded orientations," 227
Beteta, Mario Ramón, 280 n.20
Bilateral Businessmen's Committee, 274 n.25; foreign investment, 92
Bolin, Richard, 279 n.12
Border Industrialization Program. *See* Maquiladora Program
Bracero program, termination of, 77, 139
Brazil, computer policy in, 198, 203–4
Bueno, Gerardo, in CONACYT, 120
Bunge, Mario, 10
Bureaucratic authoritarianism, 36; conflict in automobile policy, 214; politics, 280 n.26. *See also under individual ministries*
Burroughs, in India, 203
Business Coordinating Council. *See* CCE

Calles, Plutarco Elias, 270 n.18; and PRN, 40
Camp, Roderic, 49
Campillo Sáinz, José, 281 n.27; on linked trademarks, 128; role in fiscal

Designed by Nighthawk Design

Composed by JDL Composition Services
in Baskerville text and display
Printed by Thomson-Shore, Inc.,
on 50 lb. Glatfelter B-16